Strategic Integrated Marketing Communication

Theory and practice

Strategic Integrated Marketing Communication

Theory and practice

Larry Percy

Amsterdam • Boston • Heidelberg • London • New York • Oxford
Paris • San Diego • San Francisco • Singapore • Sydney • Tokyo
Butterworth-Heinemann is an imprint of Elsevier

Cover image courtesy Gregg LeFevre, www.gregglefevre.com

Butterworth-Heinemann is an imprint of Elsevier
Linacre House, Jordan Hill, Oxford OX2 8DP, UK
30 Corporate Drive, Suite 400, Burlington, MA 01803, USA

First edition 2008

British Library Cataloguing in Publication Data
A catalogue record for this book is available from the British Library

Library of Congress Cataloging-in-Publication Data
A catalog record for this book is available from the Library of Congress

ISBN: 978-0-7506-7980-0

For information on all Butterworth-Heinemann publications
visit our web site at http://books.elsevier.com

Typeset by Charon Tec Ltd (A Macmillan Company), Chennai, India
www.charontec.com

Printed in China

10 11   10 9 8 7 6 5 4 3 2

Contents

Preface

It has been some 25 years or so since the notion of IMC, integrated marketing communication, emerged, as it is now understood. And even though since its inception everyone in the world of marketing communication seemed to agree it was a good and even necessary thing, there is little evidence to suggest it is widely practiced today. There are many reasons for this, and a number of them are discussed in this book. Nevertheless, even though true IMC may prove difficult or impractical to effect, the *principles* of IMC can and should guide marketing communication planning and execution. It is the aim of this book to provide an understanding of those principles, and how they may be used for more effective marketing communication.

At its heart, IMC is really all about *planning*, and what it takes to deliver a consistent and effective message. This applies to all marketing communication, whether consumer, business-to-business, retail, or corporate. A consistent message, especially in terms of visual feel, is what helps build positive associations in memory that are quickly and easily linked to the brand. The importance of this to effective communication cannot be understated.

Ensuring this will happen follows from effective strategic planning. The strategic planning process for IMC begins with the selection of the appropriate target audience, and an understanding of how they go about making decisions in the market. This is critical, for it is this understanding that identifies where in that process marketing communication can have a positive impact. Based upon this, a positioning strategy must be developed and the appropriate communication objectives set. Finally, media that are consistent with the communication objectives, and that will reach the target audience at important touch points in the decision process, are selected.

As the media landscape changes, with new media and new uses of traditional media being introduced at an ever increasing pace, it is important to keep in mind that the strategic management of IMC remains constant. What is changing are the options available for delivering the message. This provides the manager with more ways of reaching a target audience, but they must still be considered in the same way. Which media offers the best fit with the communication objective, and the ability to reach the target at critical touch points in the decision process?

Using a disciplined strategic planning process is what ensures the right message reaches the right audience at the right time in order to maximize the likelihood it will be processed and lead to the desired communication effect. It is also what enables the manager to ensure every execution, regardless of how it is delivered, has a consistent look and feel. As will be discussed in the text, it is this consistency that is so important to effective IMC, and increases the likelihood of the message getting through, even in a world where people pay less and less attention to advertising. Marketing communication must be able to communicate under the most adverse conditions. A special case of this problem is brilliantly illustrated in the art of Gregg LeFevre, who has documented for many years what he describes as the 'transformations that product advertising undergoes when introduced into the flesh and blood of a living city'. His image of a graffiti marred poster shown nearby makes the point (and we would encourage a look at his web site at www.gregglefevre.com for many more examples).

When there is consistency in the look and feel of advertising and promotion over time and in all media, the merest glimpse will activate the appropriate memories for the brand. But without this IMC 'glue', every execution must be approached anew, with less and less likelihood of it being processed, because there are no existing links to the brand in memory.

One of the goals of this book is to provide the understanding and means for ensuring this consistency in execution, and how it follows from effective strategic planning.

We begin by taking a look at where IMC began, then move to a discussion of the important role it plays for both brands and companies. With this foundation, we proceed to a more detailed look at the various components of IMC: traditional advertising and promotion, as well as other options such as sponsorships, personal selling, public relations, and direct marketing. These are the ingredients of IMC. Next, we look at the message itself, how it is processed and what it takes to make that happen. Finally, we address how it all must come together.

Throughout the book we are conscious of the all too often conflict between academics and practitioners when it comes to marketing issues. It is essential to understand theory, but that will go for naught if it is not applied. We lay out the theory, but also show how it is used to plan and execute effective IMC campaigns. Along the way we offer many illustrations and cases, as well as examples of 'desk-top' tools that can help facilitate effective IMC strategic planning and implementation.

As with any undertaking as involved as writing and publishing a book, many more people than just the author are involved. I have had the good fortune to have been helped in this effort by so many people. To begin with, I am always in debt to my colleague and long-time friend John Rossiter, who in all things related to marketing communication has been my inspiration and intellectual mentor. For this text specifically I wish to thank Timothy Goodfellow at Elsevier for encouraging the undertaking, and Naomi Robertson who has helped in so many practical ways, especially in the thankless job of tracking down permissions for the adverts in the book. I am particularly indebted to Kristie Hutto who so remarkably managed the unenviable task of typing this manuscript from my not always legible, handwritten sheets. My thanks too to Gregg LeFevre for the cover image, and Carl Wåreus of OMD Sweden for so kindly providing the excellent cases you will find throughout the book. And of course, my thanks and appreciation for the encouragement and support throughout from my wife Mary Walton.

Larry Percy
March, 2008

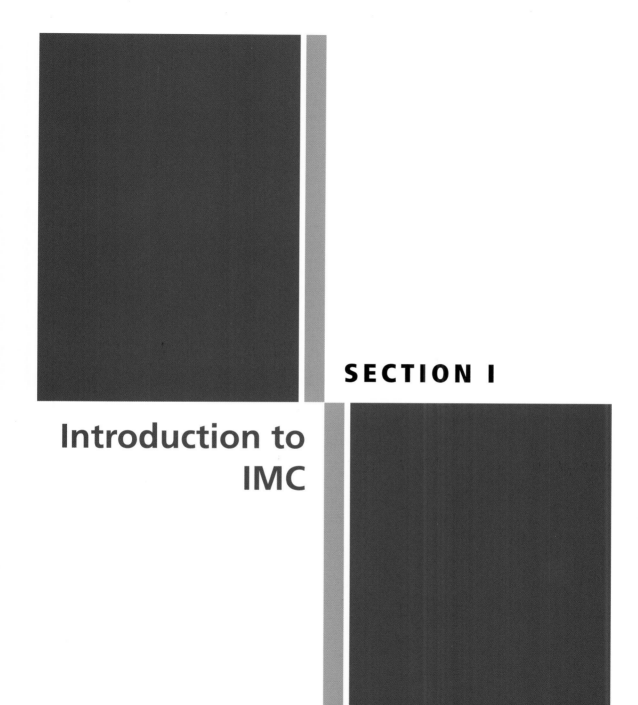

SECTION I

Introduction to IMC

In this first section of the book we shall be introducing the notion of Integrated Marketing Communication (IMC), and then looking at its overall role in building strong brands and strengthening companies. IMC as a marketing discipline is relatively recent, having emerged in the 1980s. This is not to say that marketers did not do many of the things implied by IMC prior to that time, only that it was not until then that the idea was formalized as it is understood today.

There were many definitions of IMC in those early days; and even today the term is used in a variety of ways in discussing marketing communication activities. To our mind, IMC is basically *planning* in a systematic way in order to determine the most effective and consistent message for appropriate target audiences.

Despite the fact that most marketers believe IMC is important, and should be practiced, the reality is that it is rarely successfully implemented. There are a number of reasons for this, largely concerned with the way companies are organized, their culture, and how those likely to be involved in a truly *integrated* marketing communication effort are compensated. If managers' salaries, promotions, and bonuses are linked to the size of their budgets, their primary concern will likely be to optimize their share of the IMC pie rather than consider what might be best for the brand overall.

To be effective, IMC must follow a thorough strategic planning process, and one will be briefly introduced in Chapter 1. It will outline what is involved in providing a firm foundation for gaining an understanding of the various aspects and elements of IMC that will be discussed in subsequent chapters, leading up to the final section of the book dealing with IMC strategic planning in depth. With this foundation in place, Chapter 2 will consider the role of IMC in building brands and Chapter 3 how IMC strengthens companies. The two are interrelated, as we shall see.

The keys to building effective brands are first finding the correct positioning, and then how to successfully create a strong, positive brand attitude. IMC is critical to ensure that all aspects of a brand's marketing communication is delivering a consistent message toward that end. It also plays an important role in managing the communication strategies associated with a company's branding strategy within its overall product and brand portfolio.

All of the marketing communication efforts for a company's brands will also contribute to its overall corporate identity, image, and reputation. While *marketing* communication is not the only communication effecting corporate identity, image, and reputation, it plays a significant role. IMC programs must therefore also be consistent with, and be a part of the management and delivery of all other aspects of a company's communication. Corporate meaning, which is comprised of all those elements, will inform a corporate brand; and this *corporate* brand must be compatible with all of the brands the company markets.

CHAPTER 1

Overview of IMC

In the world of marketing, there is no question that certain areas that have been practiced in one way or another over the years are suddenly dressed up in new clothes and touted as 'the' new thing. Relationship marketing comes quickly to mind. Marketers always understood (or certainly should have) the importance of sound relationships with their customers, but the mid-1990s saw an inundation of articles in the business press, 'airport books', and even academic work, in the area of 'relationship' marketing. Today, it seems to have morphed into customer relationship marketing, or CRM, and as we shall later see this idea is even informing definitions of IMC.

Why do we bring this up at the beginning of a book on integrated marketing communication? It is to make the point that unlike many fads in marketing, the idea of IMC really was something new in marketing; at least IMC correctly implemented. In fact, in the twenty or so years since the emergence of the idea of IMC in the mid- to late 1980s, few companies have yet been able to truly implement effective IMC. We shall touch on several of the key reasons why later in this chapter. First, however, we need to understand just what is meant by integrated marketing communication or IMC.

■ What is IMC?

We might briefly define IMC as the planning and execution of all types of advertising-like and promotion-like messages selected for a brand, service, or company, in order to meet a common set of communication objectives, or more particularly, to support a single 'positioning'. We believe strongly that the key to IMC is *planning*, and the ability is to deliver a consistent message.

Original definitions of IMC

In 1989, the American Association of Advertising Agencies (known as the Four A's) formed a task force on integration that was to define IMC from the viewpoint of the Four A's agencies. The task force came up with this definition of IMC: 'A concept of marketing communications planning that recognizes the added value of a comprehensive plan that evaluates the strategic roles of a variety of communication disciplines (e.g. general advertising, direct response, sales promotion, and public relations) and combines these disciplines to provide clarity, consistency, and maximum communication impact.'

In the same year, the investment firm Shearson-Lehman Hutton (1989) issued a detailed report on consumer advertising, with special emphasis on diversification into areas that would lead to integration. They concluded that a number of changes at work in the marketplace would force traditional packaged goods marketers to take a much more integrated approach to marketing. They noted that high-involvement non-service products (e.g. automobiles or cruise vacations) where the selling task is more complicated were at that time more apt to use integrated strategies. In general, the report concluded that the dynamics were in place for a surge in demand for integrated communications from all kinds of advertisers.

In their 1993 book *Integrated Marketing Communication* (perhaps the first book to really deal with the subject), Don Schultz and his colleagues talked about IMCs as a new way of looking at the whole where once we only saw parts such as advertising, public relations, sales promotions, purchasing, employee communications and so forth (Schultz et al., 1993). They saw IMC as realigning communications to look at it in the way the consumer sees it, as a flow of information from indistinguishable sources. They observed that professional communicators have always been condescendingly amused that consumers call everything advertising or public relations. Now they recognize with concern, if not chagrin, that that is exactly the point. It is all one 'thing' to the consumer who sees or hears it. They go on to say that IMC means talking to people who buy or don't buy based on what *they* see, hear, feel, and so on, and not just about a product or service. It also means delivering a return on investment, not just spending a budget. This definition 'looks back' at the goals of IMC. We will be looking at IMC largely from a strategic perspective for *planning and implementing* IMC.

At Northwestern University's Medill School in the USA (where Schultz was teaching) the curriculum was in fact changed to focus on this new idea of IMC rather than the more traditional programs in advertising. At the time, they offered their own working definition (Schultz, 1993): 'Integrated marketing communications is the process of developing and implementing various forms of persuasive communication programs with customers and prospects over time. The goal of IMC is to influence or directly affect the behaviour of the selected communications audience. IMC considers all sources of brand or company contacts that a customer or prospect has with the product or service as potential delivery channels for future messages. Further, IMC makes use of all forms of communication which are relevant to the customers and prospects, and to which they might be receptive. In sum the IMC process starts with the customer or prospect and then works back to determine and define the forms and methods through which persuasive communications programs should be developed.'

This definition, while more elaborate than ours, is still basically addressing the need for overall communication planning. It is critical to consider IMC as a *process*, not a 'thing'.

Early management perceptions of IMC

The 1989 Four A's definition was utilized in a study of large consumer packaged goods advertisers in 1991. The study was conducted among senior marketing executives of major packaged goods advertisers. Based upon the Four A's definition, two-thirds of the companies interviewed said that they were in fact now integrated. Generally the managers of these companies believed that IMC is a sound idea and that it has real value to their organizations. Most also believed that IMCs programs would increase the overall effect and impact of their marketing communications programs (Caywood et al., 1991).

Many of the questions in the study dealt with the reliance on or participation of advertising agencies in this integration process. While many of the managers believed that they would rely more heavily on outside marketing communications people in the future and that placing their business with one agency would make them a more important client, they were split on whether or not they would actually use the broader range of services which they expected advertising agencies to be offering. Part of this apparent inconsistency might be explained by the relatively strong disagreement these managers had with the proposition that most of the new ideas in marketing communications actually come from advertising agencies.

In fact, the study generally found that advertising agencies would probably *not* be a favorite supplier of IMCs. Many of the advantages that were seen by advertising agencies as reasons for them to be the integrating force for communications programs apparently were either not important to client companies or else they were not believed. Managers of these companies tended to feel that agencies that offered a variety of different communications alternatives beyond their traditional role would not necessarily have the highest level of talent across all areas of need. This study seems to indicate that advertisers in the early years of IMC were not convinced that advertising agencies were the best qualified to coordinate an IMC program, or that they could do it more cost effectively. Apparently advertising agencies had not demonstrated in the IMC programs they had been coordinating that using a single agency is the best way to implement an IMC program.

In a 1993 study where IMC was defined as 'the strategic coordination of all messages and media used by an organization to influence its perceived brand value', communication and marketing managers from companies (not advertising agencies or other marketing communication suppliers) were asked how valuable they thought IMC was or could be for their organizations (Duncan and Everett, 1993). The mean answer, based upon a 5-point bipolar scale in which 1 indicates 'very valuable' and 5 indicates 'not at all valuable', was a strong 1.76. A majority of these managers also felt their company would be making more use of IMC over the next 5 years, and they expected their agencies and vendors to work more closely together. There is no doubt that marketing and communications managers in the early 1990s felt that IMC was a valuable concept, and one that would play an increasingly more important role in their companies.

Yet after a few years, companies had not yet really begun to put in place the organizational structures needed to implement IMCs programs (Prensky et al., 1996). Marketing managers were in agreement about the need for, and the desirability of IMC, but it was proving difficult.

More recent definitions of IMC

The emphasis in those early days was certainly on *planning*, and to our mind this must remain at the heart of any definition of IMC. But today IMC is more likely to be talked about in terms of 'customer relationships'. In fact, Kotler (2003) has put it in just those terms. He now defines IMC as 'a way of looking at the whole marketing process from the viewpoint of the customer'. Yet only a few years earlier (Kotler et al., 1999) he was defining IMC as 'the concept under which a company carefully integrates and coordinates its many communications channels to deliver a clear, consistent and compelling message about the organization and its products'.

Others have taken this idea of IMC from a customer relationship view a great deal further. Tom Duncan, at the University of Colorado, who like Dan Schultz and his colleagues at Northwestern, was one of the early academics to restructure their advertising programs in terms of IMC, today sees it as *simply put* (our emphasis) a 'process for managing customer relationships that drive brand value' (Duncan, 2002). Nothing 'simple' at all we would argue. In fact, he goes on to say that what this means is that IMC is a 'cross-functional process for creating and nourishing profitable relationships with customers and other stakeholders by strategically controlling or influencing all messages sent to these groups and encouraging data-driven, purposeful dialogue with them'.

There is a lot here in this definition. Of course, marketing is (or should be) about satisfying consumer demand. But we would suggest that the real key here, in terms of IMC, is 'strategically controlling or influencing all messages sent', and to do that requires strategic planning. Duncan goes on to 'define' the major elements within his definition. The idea of a cross-functional process refers to a need for all parts of a company and vendors working on a particular brand to work together to 'plan and merge all messages a company sends to its target audiences'. We totally agree, but as we shall see, getting everyone involved in a brand's marketing communication to cooperate is very difficult. Creating and nourishing stakeholder relationships and profitable customer relationships refers to IMC identifying those target audiences most likely to contribute to long-term profit, including both consumers and others with links to a brand (e.g. Government regulatory agencies and investors). Strategically controlling or influencing all messages means that every contact with the market must be consistent, and encouraging purposeful dialogue implies that people want the ability to interact with a company.

As we said, there is a lot here in this definition. But in the end, IMC is really all about *planning* in order to deliver a *consistent message*. Effective IMC should certainly encourage strong customer relationships, but it does that through effective planning in order to develop an integrated communication program that will optimize specific communication objectives that lead to a desired behaviour on the part of a target audience. Actually, after Duncan explains his detailed definition of IMC (as we have reviewed), even he reminds us that *communication* is the foundation of brand relationships and the basic principle of IMC.

Strategies for building strong profitable relationships with customers and other stakeholders is part of the marketing plan, and effective marketing communication should support that plan. We shall leave it to others to discuss IMC in this broader marketing-oriented way. A *strategic* understanding of IMC must be based upon a rigorous planning process that will identify appropriate target audiences, set specific communication objectives for these target audiences, develop marketing communication that will accomplish those objectives in a consistent way, and find the best ways of delivering the message. That is what IMC, and this book, is all about.

■ Managing IMC

In the early years of IMC thinking, despite the feelings of many marketing managers that advertising agencies may not have been the best planning catalyst for IMC, they did play a major role in providing and managing these initial attempts at integrating marketing communications. A number of very large advertising agencies and agency groups were quite active in this new area of IMC. Such agencies as (then) Saatchi and Saatchi, Young and Rubicam, The Interpublic Group of Companies, WPP Group, Ogilvy and Mather, Leo Burnett Company, and DDB Needham, while all primarily advertising agencies, nevertheless delivered other marketing communication services either from specific divisions, subsidiaries of the groups, or through alliances or joint ventures. They were all selling themselves as able to provide all the services and disciplines a marketer could want for marketing communication.

But even at the time, what they were offering as IMC was not what their clients either wanted or for which they were willing to pay. While 85% of advertisers said they wanted IMC services, only a fraction felt their advertising agency would provide it. Major agencies tried to deal with this issue in different ways. Many agencies set up programs to educate their executives in IMCs. Prior to its break-up in 1995, Lintas Campbell-Ewald, a division of The Interpublic Group of Companies, had for several years offered an extensive training program in IMCs for their middle and upper level managers. Y&R launched a worldwide IMCs training program in the early 1990s aimed at educating top executives, with a goal to extend the training program to all agency managers. Leo Burnett, one of the early leaders in the IMCs arena, implemented a new integrated planning and communications program. Their goal was for all of the Burnett's then 2000 plus US employees to attend the 6-day seminars. Major advertising agencies may have gotten off to a slow or even wrong start, but there is no doubt that they seemed committed to delivering IMCs for their clients.

Even though the marketing communications industry has always been made up of a variety of specialty groups, almost by default traditional advertising agencies took the lead in the IMCs planning for their clients' brands. The reason was simple. The vast majority of a company's communication budget was usually with an advertising agency. But today, there has been a virtual explosion in the number of new agencies devoted to some aspect of marketing communication, fueled in a large part by the (unfortunate) trend toward an ever increasing emphasis on promotion, as well as alternative ways of delivering messages such as 'new media'. Unfortunately, this only complicates the ability to develop and manage sound strategies for IMC. Let us consider for a moment just some of the many groups that could play a role in the creation and delivery of marketing communications.

To begin with, there are all of the traditional sources of marketing communication messages such as advertising agencies (everything from full-service agencies to boutiques), sales promotion or collateral agencies, public relations firms, and specialty agencies (e.g. those that deal with trade shows or with event marketing). Add to them corporate identity groups, packaging specialists, branding companies, the increasing number of direct response agencies, and telemarketers. Then there are Internet agencies, new media, and media buying groups (who themselves are playing a greater role in overall communication strategy).

Distribution channels can also have an impact, and not only with trade communications. Retailers certainly play an influencing role via co-op programs or through channels marketing. All franchise organizations have participation from franchises in their marketing communications. Soft drink and beer companies have bottlers and distributor networks that frequently have a strong voice in the direction of their brand's marketing communication.

Then there is the company's organization itself, which could include any number of departments with some responsibility for marketing communication. And unfortunately, in most cases these departments have their own managers and operate independently of each other. Too many companies still practice vertical rather than horizontal management, and this means departments are often unlikely to even talk with one another let alone work together. Even in large companies where a single group has been created to oversee all marketing communication, and to coordinate the efforts of all outside agencies and suppliers (something essential for effective IMC, we would argue), it is often difficult to rest control from brand management. Also, there is a long history of tension between the sales force and marketing teams.

Now, multiply all of this by the number of countries where a company markets its brands. While it is not unusual for many marketing communication suppliers to have global networks, it is still a management nightmare. Global IMC must take into account local differences while still maintaining a consistent overall positioning for the brand. One way international marketers try to deal with this is by consolidating all their global marketing communication efforts in one agency with the capacity of handling most of its marketing communication needs, either within the agency itself or through its network of sister organizations.

But you begin to get the idea. All of this potential input into a company's marketing communication must be controlled and managed in order to ensure a consistent strategy and message. This is not easy, and even with the best of intentions it is difficult to implement effectively. But, if there is to be effective IMC, this problem must be solved. There must be a central source that has *real* responsibility for not only coordinating the efforts of all those involved in the process, but also the authority to make decisions. And perhaps the most important decision they must have the authority to make is how the marketing communication budget is to be allocated.

The role of advertising and promotion in IMC

We mentioned earlier that one of the main reasons traditional advertising agencies originally took the lead in managing IMC was because that was where most of the marketing communications money was to be found. But this is all changing. With the increasing short-term focus on the bottom line, promotion-oriented marketing communication is playing an ever larger role, and many companies are questioning the role of advertising today. They shouldn't.

What exactly is the role of advertising in IMC? As we have tried to make clear, IMC is a *planning* concept. So, the easy answer is that traditional advertising 'fits' when and where it makes sense in most effectively communicating with the target audience. But this easy answer will not be very satisfactory to many managers.

As Schultz (1995a) once put it, 'An integrated approach to communication planning and implementation does not necessarily reduce the role or value of traditional mass-media advertising'. We agree. In today's world, what is advertising? Television commercials include direct response 800 numbers or ask consumers to look for a coupon in the newspaper – and actually show the coupon. Is this advertising or is it promotion? In the past, advertising has been traditionally delivered via measured media: television, radio, newspaper, magazines, outdoor. But today advertising messages are also delivered through direct marketing and channels marketing (e.g., trade-oriented marketing such as co-op programs), areas where in the past one only found promotional messages.

Look at Figure 1.1. Is this an advertisement or a promotion for Olympus? It certainly looks like an advert, but the headline delivers a promotion-like message. This is a very good example of an advert-like promotion. It contains a well-executed brand-building advertising message, based upon key benefits of the brand, as well as a promotional offer of a free 2GB memory card, along with a 'praiseworthy new price', all designed to create an immediate intention to buy. Do you think this was paid for out of the advertising budget or the promotional budget? Would it make a difference? Not if it was part of an IMC campaign, because it would have been part of the IMC budget. It would have been created because it made good *strategic* sense for the brand as part of its IMCs program.

Figure 1.1
A very good example of an advert-like promotion. *Courtesy*: Olympus

The consumer certainly does not know (or, we suspect, care) what constitutes 'advertising', as we mentioned earlier. In an interesting study conducted in the US by the Leo Burnett agency, 1,000 consumers were called at random and asked what they would call a wide variety of marketing communication forms (Schultz, 1995b). They found that consumers answered 'advertising' to over 100 different forms of marketing communication. Many of the answers indeed would fit most advertising executives' definition of advertising. But what about such things as sweepstakes/contests/games, product catalogs, information brochures, window displays in stores, coupons, bill inserts, and such? Sounds more like traditional promotion, but well over 90% of the consumers interviewed called them 'advertising'. In fact, 92% said product packaging is advertising! Perhaps not surprisingly, consumers seem to see almost every form of marketing communication as advertising.

Rossiter and Percy (1997) make two interesting points about the role of traditional advertising versus promotion in today's marketing communication. Addressing the swing to promotion in marketing communication budgets, they point out that in spite of this swing (a) there has been an *increase*, not a decrease in the use of general advertising media in the last decade (from when they were writing in the mid-1990s), and (b) most of the growth in promotion, apart from all-but-required trade promotions, had been *additional* – and most of this in advert-like promotions.

Nevertheless, in traditional terms the rate of advertising growth has basically followed the pace of media inflation, while other areas of non-traditional advertising as well as promotion have experienced real growth. But this second point about advert-like promotions is very important. It is not traditional forms of promotion that are growing, but promotion-oriented messages that are very advertising-like. For example, as Rossiter and Percy point out, direct mail and telemarketing, by far the largest and fastest-growing forms of marketing communication, are generally thought of as promotion rather than advertising. Yet when properly used they are as much advertising, in the sense of building brand awareness and brand equity, as they are promotion in the sense of meeting some short-term sales objective. The same may be said of free standing inserts (FSIs), by far the most widely used way of delivering coupons. In the strictest sense these are promotion-oriented media, and we shall treat them as such in this book. But they are also very *advertising-like* in their ability to help build awareness and equity for a brand.

This blurring of the old distinctions between advertising and promotion is yet another reason for the importance of IMC, because what one might think of as traditional advertising skills now play such a critical role in every form of marketing communication. As we shall see, planning an effective IMC program requires the manager to address strategic creative and media questions that have always been addressed in traditional advertising. These principles are simply being applied to a wider range of options. In IMC, one is setting communication objectives and selecting media to maximize their ability to effectively reach the target market. But rather than only considering various ways of using advertising, or independently considering some form of promotion, the planning and execution of all marketing communication should be *integrated*. The point is that in the end one may consider any marketing communication that deals with brand building as delivering an advertising-like message, and marketing communication that is looking for short-term action on the part of the target audience as delivering a promotion-like message; and promotions should include advertising-like messages.

As we shall see in later chapters, the fact that marketing communication may be delivered via new media or old, as part of a direct marketing campaign or on the Internet, as an advert or promotion, the strategic foundation for the development and execution of the message remains the same. The brain will process the words and images the same way, regardless of how it is delivered. Sound is sound, words are words, and pictures are pictures to the brain, regardless of where the sense organs find them.

The role of advertising agencies in IMC

Because traditional advertising agencies have the experience with advertising-like, brand-building marketing communication, they should have a better sense for what is needed strategically in the planning of all IMC. Most of the new promotion-oriented agencies and media service groups specializing in particular areas will simply not have the advertising-like message skills or experience needed to fully integrate the advertising-like message component in their promotions, or IMC planning in general. For this reason, a strong argument could be made for an advertising agency, one with broad resources, to play the primary role in coordinating IMC; always under the client's management. Unfortunately, for many reasons, today's advertising agencies have fewer resources than they did 20 years ago. But, they are still in a better position for understanding *strategically* what is needed to deliver effective IMC, and to have the relevant creative talent.

■ Barriers to effective IMC

Despite the fact that most marketers seem to agree that IMC makes sense, after 20 years there is very little evidence that it is being practiced by many companies. To the extent that it is being used, it is probably most likely to be found among fast moving consumer goods (fmcg companies) operating globally as they look for ways to coordinate their international marketing communication needs.

It should not be assumed by marketing managers that if they are not practicing IMC they are simply not enjoying the potential benefits of it. Without IMC, a brand's marketing communication could actually be significantly *less* effective. And the more complex the market, the less effective it will be. The lack of IMC, the lack of coordinated communications planning and the delivery of a consistent message, could lead to multiple portrayals of a brand in the market. Even if the positioning is the same, if there is a lack of a consistent look and feel to all of a brand's marketing communication there will be no synergy or 'lift' from the overall program.

With a consistent look and feel (something we will be dealing with in Chapter 9), the overall impact of a campaign is much greater than the sum of its parts because the *processing* of each piece of marketing communication is facilitated by the prior processing of other messages in the campaign. When the individual messages being delivered lack this consistency, the processing of each different piece of marketing communication must begin from scratch. A promotion that contains the same general look and feel as the brand's advertising, which is carried over with the packaging and reflected in in-store merchandising, means that prior exposure to any of these pieces of marketing communication will aid in the processing of the others. If each of these pieces has its own unique look, there will be no prior learning or foundation available when someone sees it. They must process the message on its own. As we shall see in later chapters, getting someone to process marketing communication at all is difficult. Effective IMC helps.

In fact, research has shown that there is a link between IMC and increase in sales, market share, and profit (Marketing Week, 2002). So why hasn't IMC been more widely adopted? We like the reason offered by Pickton and Broderick (2005): it is 'partly due to ignorance, unwillingness and inertia, and partly due to the sheer difficulties of achieving the integration.' Indeed.

Perhaps the single biggest problem revolves around the decision-making structure of most marketing organizations. The structure or organizational make-up of a company or agency, and the way managers think about or approach marketing questions frequently pose problems in trying to implement IMC programs. We shall be looking at this in terms of specific organizational barriers to IMC and an organizations character. Additionally, the issue of compensation is often a serious roadblock to effectively implementing IMC.

Organizational barriers

While effective IMC requires coordination among all of a brand's 'voices', most organizations spend their time developing vertical communications programs. This results in a need for *horizontal* relationships struggling within *vertical* organizations. This leads to problems at the organizational level, where parallel structures, multiple departments, and functional specialties discourage the kind of communication *between* specialties required for IMC planning. This type of problem is epitomized by the brand management concept, and recent moves by some large packaged goods companies to category or channel management is only likely to make the problem worse. IMC requires a central planning expertise in marketing communication. With diffused resources, individual manager relationships with marketing communication agencies and vendors, and (critically) a lack of incentive to cooperate, it is no wonder there are problems when it comes to effectively developing and implementing IMC programs.

Organizational structure

Although there is a broad agreement among marketing managers over the need for IMC, the very organizational structure of many marketing companies stands in the way of it being effectively implemented. At the core of this problem is an organization's ability to manage the interrelationships of information and materials among the various agencies and vendors involved in supplying marketing communication services. There are a number of specific structural factors that can make this difficult.

The low standing of marketing communication in an organization

Unfortunately, for too many marketers, their marketing communication has a very low priority within the organization. For many in top management, spending money on marketing communication is a luxury that can be afforded only when all else is going well. One of the fastest ways for someone concerned with the financial statement to send large chunks of cash to the bottom line is to not spend budgeted marketing communication money.

With this sort of attitude, it is not surprising that those most responsible for marketing communication occupy lower-level positions within the organization. True, senior management does reserve the right to approve a campaign, and often does. But it would be rare indeed to find senior management involved in the *planning* of marketing communication. Rather, it is generally somewhat junior brand managers (or their equivalent) who do the actual strategic planning, and the results of their work are passed up the management ladder for approval. Even at companies where there are specific managers for advertising or promotion, these managers will have little power within the organization, and almost never final responsibility for the budget. Final decision on the budget will be with those managers doing the actual marketing.

We have always found this very shortsighted. As one brand manager put it (in a personal communication with the author), can you think of any other part of business where decisions involving millions are made with so little senior management involvement? If even half the average packaged goods brand marketing communication budget were going to bricks and mortar, no doubt everyone including the board of directors would be involved!

Adding to this problem is the trend toward decentralized decision making. With more and more people empowered to make decisions at lower and lower levels, it makes it very difficult, if not impossible, to ensure an IMC program. This is compounded by the tendency to look to specialists when confronted with large or complicated projects.

Specialization

To effectively manage IMC, those in charge ideally will be marketing communication generalists. Yet where do you find such a person in today's marketing organizations? In fact, what one is most likely to find in companies are people specializing in a particular area; and these specialists rarely talk with each other. They have their own budgets, their own suppliers, and jealously guard the areas they control. The problem becomes even more complex when one considers the marketing communication suppliers these specialists use. Each being a specialist in a particular area (e.g. advertising, direct mail, merchandising), they naturally advocate their own solutions for marketing communication. By their very nature, whether intraorganizational or between suppliers, these specialists will want to keep communications programs separate.

Given the narrow focus and understanding of these specialists, it is very difficult to bring them together in the first place, let alone expect them to have the broad understanding of many marketing communication options necessary for effective IMC planning. But even if they did have this understanding, getting them to give up control, especially when it is unlikely to be financially advantageous (which we shall discuss more specifically later), is a lot to ask. Yet this is precisely what is necessary for IMC to work within an organization.

Organizational character

In addition to the problems inherent in the way most marketing organizations are structured, there are more intangible aspects of an organization's thinking and behaviour that also pose problems for implementing IMC. We have just seen how traditional organizational structure can impede the flow of information and ideas within the organization. Because of this type of structural barrier, it is very difficult for an entire company to share a common understanding of that company's marketing communication.

Yet it is important for everyone working in a company to understand and communicate the appropriate 'image' in any marketing communication. Anyone who has contact with customers must reflect the image projected by the company's marketing communications. This means store clerks, sales force, telephone operators, receptionists; all are part of a company's marketing communication, and hence in many ways are IMC 'media'. Too often only those directly involved with the marketing communication program are familiar with it and this can be a serious problem.

Culture of the organization

How managers think is conditioned by both their own background and the culture of the company. This potential problem is then compounded in the IMC case when the culture of the marketer must interact with the culture of marketing communication agencies and vendors. Managers from different companies are likely to have different views of what makes effective marketing communication. This issue is also discussed later when we look at the potential problems inherent in how different managers perceive IMC. Here we are simply considering their general views of things and how that will be tempered by organizational culture. A great deal of literature on management addresses the idea that an organization will have its own defining culture, and that employees of the firm will absorb that culture. While that culture will not completely determine an individual manager's way of doing things, it will certainly have a significant impact upon its development (Prensky et al., 1996). This leads inevitably to such organizational feelings as 'This is the way we do it'; 'We've always done it this way'; 'It works for us.' Attitudes such as these can get in the way of integrated thinking and planning, both within an organization and working with outside agencies and vendors.

Management perceptions

How managers perceive IMC can often impede the implementation of effective IMC. When managers come from different backgrounds or different marketing communication specialties, either within the marketing organization or at marketing communications agencies or vendors, they are likely to have different perceptions of what constitutes IMCs and the roles various people should play in IMC planning and implementation. Additionally, there are strong proprietary feelings among managers toward the 'superiority' of their own specialty within the communication mix.

Because of this, it is not surprising to find that there are any number of notions about how best to go about implementing IMCs. The 1991 study among marketing managers discussed earlier in this chapter found a variety of opinions about how IMC should be achieved (Caywood et al., 1991). Among the managers who said they were familiar with the term 'integrated marketing communications' (a surprisingly low 59%), about 60% seem to look at the responsibility for IMC planning in roughly the same way as we do: 35% felt they would collectively set communication strategies with all of the appropriate agencies and vendors, and then specific assignments would be executed by the best qualified agency or vendor. Another 25% felt they alone were responsible for setting the IMC strategy, but would then make specific assignments to appropriate agencies or vendors, and expect them to coordinate the execution.

We, of course, argue that while the marketer must take the lead in IMC planning, strategy should be worked out among all relevant parties, who then execute creative work guided by the common creative brief(s), coordinated through the marketer. Among the remaining managers, 25% felt that they would work with one agency in setting strategy, and then leave it to the agency to execute everything (the notion of full-service agencies or 'one-stop shopping' encouraged by some advertising agencies); and

7% felt they would set the communication strategy and then have it executed by the individual agency or vendor most appropriate for each task (advertising, direct mail, merchandising, etc.). The remaining 8% held various other opinions.

Resistance to change

Different perceptions of IMC will certainly mediate effective implementation. But much more troubling is the natural resistance to change that the idea of IMC is likely to trigger, making it difficult to implement despite general acceptance of the benefits. The most serious concern is probably a fear that the manager responsible for IMC planning will not fully appreciate someone else's area of expertise. This is a problem that is especially compounded when advertising takes the lead (which it should in most cases, as we have seen) because of long-held feelings that advertising managers simply do not understand or even consider other means of marketing communications (which unfortunately, is too often the case). This is aggravated by the short-term tactical experience, for example, of those working in promotion versus the more long-term thinking of advertising managers. If employees feel the IMC manager does not fully appreciate their worth, they are certain to worry about where their specialties will fit in department budgeting, and fear their jobs will become less important or even redundant. Such feelings could easily cause resistance to the implementation of IMC planning.

Another way of looking at some of these issues of resistance to change is in terms of both intraorganizational and interorganizational politics. It doesn't matter if the motivation is individual self-interest or actual belief in the superiority of one's way of doing things, the result is the same. People, departments, and organizations want power and the rewards that go with it. Too often managers and their staff believe they will be giving up too much if they implement effective IMCs planning. Compensation is only one aspect of this problem. There are feelings of prestige and position that have in many cases been hard-won, that the combining of responsibilities required by IMC seem to threaten. This can be a very difficult problem.

Financial emphasis

Another important aspect of the character of an organization that bears upon IMC implementation is the misguided emphasis upon financial rather than consumer considerations in the development of marketing strategy. The attitude of many managers is to let financial considerations drive their thinking when setting marketing objectives, rather than consumer wants or needs. But the consumer should be at the center of IMC planning. IMC requires an understanding of how consumers make decisions and behave, as we shall discuss later in the book. When a marketer's attention is more financially focused than consumer focused, the planning environment will be less likely to successfully nurture IMC.

Compensation

Compensation issues are less of a direct problem within a marketing organization than with agencies and vendors. Still, even there it is a problem. We have already referred to several circumstances where marketing communication specialists within a company are likely to be concerned about the importance of their position in a realigned IMC-oriented marketing communication group. Such concerns lead quite naturally to worries about salaries and promotion, and dampen enthusiasm for IMC.

But the real concern over compensation lies with those agencies and vendors that serve the marketing communication needs of the marketer. This has certainly proved to be a stumbling block to many large advertising agencies that have tried to offer their clients a full range of marketing communication services. Group managers at these agencies are traditionally rewarded based upon their total billings and income. That being the case, how likely is it that the management of the advertising group will suggest to their client that perhaps they would be better off spending more of their money on direct marketing, even if there is a direct marketing group at the agency, let alone if the work would need to be done elsewhere?

Somehow these managers (at least within an agency or vendor offering multiple communication services) must be compensated without regard to how much is spent on their particular specialty, but in terms of the overall business. Without such a scheme, IMC is impossible because those in charge of a particular type of marketing communication will be more concerned with 'selling' their specialty, not with how their specialty will best contribute to an overall IMC program.

This problem is aggravated when a number of competing agencies or vendors are asked to work together. In fact, this is the primary reason many agencies and vendors have sought to provide a number of different types of marketing communications in order to maximize their chances of retaining business. Such firms have either tried to create groups within their organization to provide a variety of marketing communication services or have merged with other suppliers. While such moves offer the potential for higher profit or greater financial stability overall for the agency or vendor, as discussed above it is not easy to manage the compensation between the competing specialties.

It should not be surprising that any company will want to maintain its profitability in a changing world. In doing this, it should likewise not be surprising that they will be more interested in their own financial well being than in providing the best overall IMC program for their clients. This underscores the need for tight control of planning by the marketer.

Overcoming the barriers

Although the need for IMCs is widely understood and accepted, as the foregoing discussion makes clear, the path to implementation is hampered by many potential barriers. We have summarized these potential barriers in Figure 1.2. Yet these barriers are not insurmountable, and the rewards from effective IMC make the effort worthwhile. By becoming aware of these potential problems, and identifying them within their own organization, managers are on the way toward overcoming them.

Organizational barriers
- Vertical organizational structures where cooperation is needed between functions
- Structure makes it difficult to manage information from various agencies and vendors
- Low standing of marketing communication function

Organizational character
- Rigid organizational culture
- No common understanding of what constitutes IMC
- Resistance to change and fear over who will be in charge
- Financial considerations placed ahead of consumer considerations

Compensation issues
- Without budget control, communication specialists fear they will lose position and financial reward
- Rewards are linked to budget size or billings, not the overall program

Figure 1.2
Barriers to effective IMC

We do not pretend that dealing with these problems is easy. After all, they go to the heart of how companies function day-to-day. The way decisions are made, the way an organization is structured, are all part of the operational lifeblood of a company. Change requires trust, and this trust comes from a total understanding of what is involved and the long-term potential.

■ Identifying IMC opportunities

It could be said that every opportunity to use marketing communication is an IMC opportunity because all marketing communication should be based upon careful strategic planning in order to ensure a consistent message; and in almost any case more than one way will be required to deliver that message. Remember that *any* communication between a brand and its market is part of its marketing communication. So even if all that is used is a direct mail program, there must be correspondence between the content of the mailing and the envelope it is mailed in; and if there is a package involved, that package should reflect the benefit and imagery contained in the direct mail piece.

If you own a small business in a small town, say a dress shop, and you want to place an advert in the local newspaper announcing a sale, the imagery presented in that advert should be consistent with the image of the shop itself: the type of merchandise, the signage, and the general 'feeling' the customer will experience when visiting the shop.

But more often when one is thinking about IMC one is concerned with larger marketing communication programs. Perhaps the single best key to identifying a need for an IMC program is the complexity of the market with which one is dealing. The more complex, the more likely it will be that multiple or novel solutions will be required. Many things can contribute to the complexity of a communication problem. The most obvious is multiple communication objectives, but there are others that involve the target audience, the product or service itself, and the distribution of the product or service, as outlined in Figure 1.3.

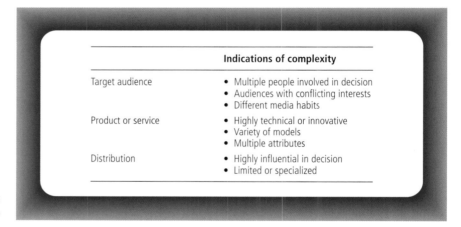

	Indications of complexity
Target audience	• Multiple people involved in decision • Audiences with conflicting interests • Different media habits
Product or service	• Highly technical or innovative • Variety of models • Multiple attributes
Distribution	• Highly influential in decision • Limited or specialized

Figure 1.3
Market complexity

Target Audience Complexity There are a number of target audience considerations that lead to complexity in planning and delivering marketing communications. To begin with, the more people involved in the decision process, the more difficult the communication task. In the simple case, where one person plays all of the roles in a decision, such as someone looking for a snack in the afternoon for an energy boost, a straightforward message to a single individual is all that is needed. But as more people become involved in the decision, the potential need for multiple messages through a variety of media or delivery systems increases. This can happen in situations as varied as a family where children are lobbying parents for a special treat to a large company planning to update its word processing systems in all of its departments.

Product or Service Complexity If the product or service is highly technical or innovative, the communication task can be more complex. For example, when a new consumer electronics product is introduced, people need to be made aware of it, and interest stimulated. But they also will want a high level of information to complete what is usually a high-involvement decision. If a number of models are available, again the information requirements will be greater. Even with seemingly less complex consumer needs, this opens up opportunities for IMC. For example, dehydrated soups can be marketed as soup or as cooking ingredients, as great for lunch or good to take on a camping trip.

Distribution Complexity An often-overlooked opportunity for IMC can be found in the distribution for a product or service. This goes beyond simple trade promotions. Many delivery systems have a great deal of influence on a brand being chosen. A good example would be travel agents, who almost always will have a significant influence on everything from minor considerations such as what hotel to stay at or what car to rent, to a major decision such as what cruise line to select for a Caribbean cruise.

Understanding consumer decision-making

The more complex the market, as we have just seen, the more likely it is that an IMC program will be needed. But even in seemingly uncomplicated situations a more extensive IMC program may be needed than is apparent at first glance. In Chapter 11 we will be talking about consumer decision-making, and will introduce something called a behavioural sequence model (BSM), which helps a manager better understand how his or her target audience makes purchase decisions in the brand's product category. It provides a detailed and dynamic picture of the target audience in terms of the overall decision process and enables a manager to recognize potential IMC opportunities.

A BSM utilizes a flow chart format to identify where a target audience is taking action or making decisions that will ultimately affect purchase. It identifies the major behavioural stages preceding, including, and following purchase or use. Then for each stage in the decision process it summarizes roles involved, where it occurs, when, and how. As a manager reviews all of this information, he or she is in a perfect position to organize their objectives and identify those touch points at which marketing communication may be most effectively employed.

Suppose you are the brand manager for a new product entry into a frequently purchased packaged goods product category; something like a new laundry detergent or fabric softener. How would understanding the way consumers make decisions in the category help you recognize IMC opportunities? If you find that a single person is likely to play all the roles involved in the purchase decision (which would make sense for something like a laundry detergent or fabric softener), then you would only have that person to worry about in you communication's planning. However, you still must be concerned with whether that person requires a single message to stimulate purchase, or whether several messages, perhaps delivered in different ways, would be necessary. Since we are talking about a new product, you will probably need more than one delivery medium. For example, broadcast advertising does a great job of raising people's awareness and awakening latent interest in a product. Unfortunately, most packaged goods categories do not excite the consumer, so it is quite easy for people to forget about a new product. For that reason, it would make sense to perhaps provide an incentive for trial with a coupon, and some sort of in-store display or shelf-talker to arrest the shopper's attention and remind them of any interest in the product that the advertising generated.

If all one did was advertise, there would be no guarantee that shoppers would spot the item at the point of purchase because their behaviour in the store is so routinized (Howard, 1997). In this example, broad-cast advertising would be great for driving up awareness and interest, but additional help may be needed when the actual purchase decision is made; help traditional advertising would not provide. This would be made clear from an understanding of the decision process, as it reminds you that even though only one person is involved in the decision, the decision is not finalized all in a moment. Initial interest is aroused, but will likely lie latent until re-aroused in the store.

A good understanding of how a target audience makes decisions will alert a manager to the many possible marketing communications options that might be required, and help pinpoint:

- Complexity of the target audience
- Complexity of the distribution
- Complexity of the purchase decision
- Short- versus long-term communication objectives
- Need to isolate segments
- Need for multiple messages
- Opportunities for unique message delivery
- Opportunities for trade incentives
- Likely importance of retail messages

We have seen how complexity in the market in-and-of itself implies a need for IMC. Understanding consumer decision making helps alert the manager to more subtle complexities that are more a function of how consumers make decisions than of actual market conditions. For example, the roles played by various members of the target audience may add a complexity not otherwise easily noticed; and the ways in which inform-ation is gathered may signal *consumer-perceived* complexity within distri-bution that might otherwise be overlooked.

But the most important insight into the need for IMC and the guidance for strategic IMC planning provided by an understanding of consumer decision making is related to message needs. As one looks at how people go about making decisions in a category, the more complex the process, the greater the need for multiple options to deal with that complexity. If the decision is one that builds over time, such as the decision to buy a new automobile, it will help identify short versus long-term commu-nication objectives. Continuing with the automotive example, over the long-term one must nurture an image for a vehicle that will help bring it into the consumers' considered set when they begin to think about a new car, but also provide detailed information and incentives for the short-term when the final choice is being made. The need for an IMC program under these circumstances would be obvious from an understanding of how decisions are made for a new automobile.

The roles people play, and the number of people involved in the decision, may suggest a need to isolate particular segments or a need for multiple messages. When, where, and how various stages of the decision process occur may suggest opportunities for unique message delivery. How important is the trade in affecting the decision? How much of the decision takes place in the store? Answers to such questions may suggest an opportunity for trade incentives or the likely importance of retail messages. Where and how understanding the brand decision-making process fits within the overall strategic planning process is briefly addressed below, and in more detail in Chapter 11.

■ IMC strategic planning

In the last three chapters of this book we will be taking a close look at the strategic planning process and how it leads to effective IMC. At this point, however, a brief introduction to the steps involved in IMC strategic planning is in order. This will provide a framework for better understanding the importance of the material in the chapters leading up to the specific discussion of IMC strategic planning in the development of effective IMC.

The strategic planning process itself begins with consideration of the marketing plan. Although the ultimate consumer is at the heart of any communications program, with IMC there is much more. The marketing plan will identify generally whom we wish to reach as ultimate purchaser or user. For example, it will indicate whether a trial or repeat purchase strategy is to be pursued. Is the brand looking primarily to attract new users (a trial action objective) or to increase business from existing customers (a repeat-purchase action objective)? But the marketing plan does not deal with others who may play an important role in the decision process. The manager needs to know as much as possible about all of the influences in the market that are likely to contribute to a positive response to the brand. The ultimate purchasers or users, along with anyone who may influence their decisions, are potential targets for communication. This could include other people who may have an influence upon the ultimate consumer, the trade, or even the image and reputation of the company (as we shall see in Chapter 3). Gaining this additional insight will be part of strategic planning process.

Additionally, the marketing plan will provide a *general* positioning for the brand. It will identify the brand's major competition and such things as whether it will be marketed as a 'value' brand or 'luxury' brand, etc. While this will set the overall parameter for the brand's positioning in the market, how the brand will be positioned within its marketing communication is part of the strategic planning process.

In order to develop effective marketing communication for a brand, it is important for managers to organize their thinking in terms of how an IMC program will help meet the brand's marketing objectives.

Reviewing the marketing plan proves the necessary background on how the brand is to be marketed, and identifies the target market and overall positioning for the brand. With this background the manager is ready to begin the strategic planning process that will lead to an IMC plan that will support the marketing objectives for the brand.

The five-step strategic planning process

Strategic planning for IMC involves a five-step process. First, one must identify and select the appropriate target audience; next, determine how they make brand decisions; establish how the brand will be positioned within its marketing communication, and select a benefit to support that positioning; then set the communication strategy; and finally match the appropriate media options to that strategy to optimize delivery and processing of the message. Figure 1.4 provides an overview of the IMC strategic planning process, which will be discussed in detail in Chapter 11.

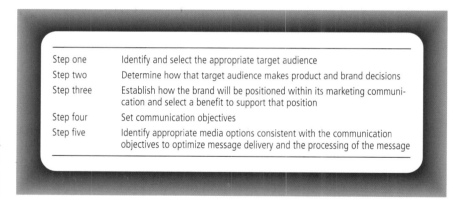

Figure 1.4
The five-step IMC strategic planning process

Step one	Identify and select the appropriate target audience
Step two	Determine how that target audience makes product and brand decisions
Step three	Establish how the brand will be positioned within its marketing communication and select a benefit to support that position
Step four	Set communication objectives
Step five	Identify appropriate media options consistent with the communication objectives to optimize message delivery and the processing of the message

During this process, the manager must begin to weigh the advantages and disadvantages of various advertising and promotion options for satisfying the communication objectives. Advertising and specific promotions have particular strengths, and these must be matched to the communication tasks. It will not be at all unusual at this stage to consider many more potential communication options than the brand has the resources to execute. But this is part of the strategic planning process, and one of the real strengths of IMC. *Everything* is considered, then the best choices are made within strategic and budget parameters.

Consider this example. Suppose a company is introducing a new snack product. If we want mothers to purchase the new snack for their children, we will probably need to make both mother and children *aware of the brand* and to form a positive *brand attitude*, and we will certainly want the mother to form a positive *brand purchase intention.* One can advertise to both children and mothers to make them aware of the brand, but probably in different media. For example, one might use television advertising in children's programming and print adverts in women's magazines. These same vehicles could also be used for messages aimed at creating a positive brand attitude. In fact, the same adverts would no doubt do both jobs. But would this be enough? Perhaps a premium could be offered to children to stimulate heightened interest, especially if there is heavy and popular competition. Where is a mother actually likely to make up her mind to buy the snack? Probably at home, at the insistence of the child. But if the child is not with the mother when she is shopping, will she remember? To help, some in-store merchandising might work.

You can see that even with this rather simple example, a number of alternative communication tasks are suggested, using both advertising and promotion, and delivered in various ways. It may be that in the end only a single commercial is produced and run in early evening family programming. That would still constitute IMC even though only television advertising was used. IMC is the strategic planning *process*, not whether multiple marketing communication voices are used. Strategic IMC planning is used to arrive at the optimum solution within strategic and budget constraints, whatever the eventual execution. While this would be highly unusual, this underscores the important point that IMC is the result of a planning process that leads to the optimum communication program for a brand, what ever that might be.

This strategic planning process may seem simple enough, and managers may think, 'We do this already, or near enough.' We agree that the logic is rather straightforward, but the implementation requires a great deal of attention and understanding. That is what this book is all about.

Summary

In this chapter a number of IMC definitions were introduced. From the beginning, definitions of IMC have built around two key elements: the role of multiple communication vehicles and the need for consistency in message delivery. At the heart of these definitions is the idea of *planning*. Even though more recent definitions have considered IMC in terms on of 'customer relationships' (reflecting the late 1990s marketing interest in the subject), we have argued that at its core IMC is about *planning* in order to deliver a *consistent message*.

There is no really settled way in which IMC is managed and delivered. Early on, large advertising agencies and their holding companies began to offer a variety of marketing communication services to clients, drawing upon their wide base of operations. But in the end, this did not work out well, even though it tends to remain the best option for ensuring central planning (especially for global marketers).

To effectively implement IMC, it is critical to understand the roles of traditional advertising and promotion in the marketing communication mix. In today's world it is often difficult to decide whether something is an advert or promotion offer. From a strategic standpoint, the only important consideration is how the message fits within the overall IMC program. As we shall see in later chapters, advertising-like messages are used for longer-term strategic efforts to build brand awareness and attitude while promotion-like messages are designed for shorter-term tactical needs to stimulate an immediate sales response.

While most marketers believe IMC is important for their brands, there are a number of barriers that stand in the way of effective implementation. In fact, true IMC is the exception, not the rule. The difficulty comes from the ways in which most companies are structured, the character of most organizations that militate against change, and compensation issues. Overcoming such deeply rooted organizational practices is very difficult, and requires the commitment of top management to succeed.

Almost any marketing communication task is an opportunity for IMC, and identifying the important touch-points for communication comes from an understanding of how consumers make brand decisions in the category. This is a key part of the strategic planning process. It begins with a review of the marketing plan, leading to target audience selection, modeling the brand decision process, identifying the optimum positioning for the brand, establishing the communications strategy, and then selecting media consistent with that strategy to effectively deliver the message.

■ Review questions

1 How would you define IMC?
2 Discuss why you feel recent definitions of IMC are or are not an improvement upon earlier definitions?
3 What is required for effective management of IMC?
4 How is the trade involved in a brand's IMC?
5 What are the unique roles of advertising and promotion in IMC strategy?
6 Why is it so difficult to implement effective IMC?
7 How can the barriers to IMC be overcome?
8 Identify companies you believe practice IMC, based upon their marketing communication, and discuss what it is about their marketing communication that makes you say that.
9 What are the important keys to identifying IMC opportunities for a brand?
10 Is IMC appropriate for all brands?

References

Caywood, C., Schultz, D.E., and Wang, P. (1991) *Integrated Marketing Communications: A Survey of National Consumer Goods.* Evanston, IL: Department of Integrated Advertising/Marketing Communicators, Northwestern University.

Duncan, T.R. (2002) *Principles of Advertising and IMC*. New York: McGraw-Hill.

Duncan, T.R. and Everett, S.E. (1993) Client perceptions of integrated marketing communications. *Journal on Advertising Research*, 33, May/June, 30–39.

Howard, J.A. (1977) *Consumer Behavior: Application of Theory*. New York: McGraw-Hill.

Kotler, P. (2003) *Marketing Management: Analysis, Planning, Implementation and Control*, 11th edition, New York: Prentice-Hall. p. 563.

Kotler, P., Armstrong, G., Saunders, J., and Wong, V. (1999) *Principles of Marketing*, 2nd European edition, Europe: Prentice-Hall.

Marketing Week (2002) Everyone wins integration game, 18 April.

Pickton, D. and Broderick, A. (2005) *Integrated Marketing Communication*, 2nd edition, Harlow, England: Prentice-Hall. p. 25.

Prensky, D., McCarty, J.A., and Lucas, J. (1996) Integrated marketing communication: Examining planning and executional considerations. In E. Thorson and J. Moore (eds.), *Integrated Communication*. Mahwah, N.J.: Lawrence Erlbaum Associates, pp. 67–184.

Rossiter, J.R. and Percy, L. (1997) *Advertising Communications and Promotion Management*. NewYork: McGraw-Hill.

Schultz, D.E. (1993) Integrated marketing communications: Maybe definition is in the point of view. *Marketing News*, January 18, 17.

Schultz, D.E. (1995a) Traditional advertising has a role to play in IMC. *Marketing New*, August 28, 18.

Schultz, D.E. (1995b) What is direct marketing. *Journal of Direct Marketing*, 9(2), 5–9.

Schultz, D.E., Tannebaum, S.I., and Lauterbuin, R.F. (1993) *Integrated Marketing Communications*. Lincolnwood, IL: NTC Business Books.

Shearson-Lehman Hutton (1989) Report titled *Diversification Begets Integration*.

CHAPTER 2

Brands and IMC

The key to building a brand, beyond the obvious marketing considerations such as a viable product, effective pricing strategy, and distribution, is to correctly position the brand, and build positive brand attitude that will lead to a strong brand equity. This is what gives a brand meaning, and it is marketing communication that *drives* the meaning of a brand. One could argue (and we do) that without marketing communication, and especially advertising, it would be difficult, if not impossible, to have what we generally understand as a brand.

Effective IMC assumes a consistent positioning and communication strategy across every contact with the market, building a strong positive brand attitude. Without it, different messages and images can lead to confusion in the minds of the consumer as to exactly what is the meaning of a brand. In this chapter we will be introducing how one goes about positioning a brand generally (we will go into more detail in Chapter 11), how building a strong brand attitude leads to brand equity, and what all of this means for brand portfolio decisions.

■ The role of IMC in building brands

Interestingly, the original meaning of the word brand is thought to have come from an old Norse word meaning 'to burn', *brandr*. We recognize this meaning, which is in fact, the second meaning offered in the Oxford English Dictionary (OED). What then is the first? If you look up the word brand in the OED you will find the following definition: 'goods of particular name or trade mark'. While this may be literally what is meant by a brand, something that identifies a particular product or service, it is a long way from what we understand a brand to be. That 'particular name or trademark' does a lot more than simply distinguish one good from another. Brands have specific *meanings* to consumers, and these meanings derive in part from experience, but in the main from how a brand has been positioned and presented to people via marketing communication; ideally, through IMC.

Before going further, let us pause to be certain of just what we mean when we are talking about marketing communication. Marketing communication is *every* contact between the brand and the market. This means much more than simply advertising and promotion. It means everything: packaging, the outside of the truck that transports the company's products, sales kits for the trade, business cards, sponsorships, store signs, collateral, retail store layout (if the brand is sold at retail, or is in fact a retail store), newsletters – you get the point. This is why IMC is so critical in building successful brands. Management of a brand must coordinate all these aspects of the brand's communication, ensuring a consistent message.

Returning to what is meant by a brand, we see it in terms of a *label*, again following the OED: something that is 'attached to an object to give information about it'. The concept of a brand transcends its 'particular name or trademark', providing information about itself, *meaning*. And this meaning develops over time, as a result of the brand's marketing communication. Effective IMC ensures control over this meaning.

Even if we take the idea of a brand and extend it to politicians or celebrities (a frequent metaphor), the point remains. A politician or celebrity becomes a 'brand' when people learn things about them through various forms of mass communication; and it is communication in one form or another that sustains them as a 'brand' in their market. Without it, that person is merely someone working in government (or wanting to), or an unknown. Just as with a product or service, successful politicians and celebrities want their name to mean something very specific to their market. They want their 'brand' to carry with it a very particular meaning. Just like other brands, they accomplish this through effective positioning and building a strong favourable attitude.

Social meaning

The meaning of brands goes well beyond the traditional ideas of providing information and understanding. Brands can often represent, or can be used to create, social meaning (Elliott and Percy, 2007). The role of IMC in building social meaning parallels what we have just been discussing. Within a social context, among other things, brands can be a catalyst for social differentiation or integration, and for brand communities. This follows from the personal meaning brands can have.

People often think about brands in terms of human characteristics. This can occur as a direct result of how they perceive users of a particular brand, or perhaps owing to a celebrity endorser. It may also follow indirectly from marketing communication, everything from advertising or symbols associated with a brand to the brand name itself (Aaker, 1997). Another key factor in personalizing brand meaning comes from the emotional associations people have with brands (Percy et al., 2004).

There is a great deal of evidence that men and women understand the same advertising execution in very different ways (Elliott et al., 1995). While much of this no doubt follows from a difference in the motivation that often drives male versus female decisions to use a particular product, there is no question that marketing communication can inform social differentiation. This offers the potential for the effective use of IMC to reflect gender identity in creating a social differentiation brand strategy; or on the other hand, to implement different creative strategies to minimize differentiation. An effective IMC program is essential to a social differentiation strategy for a brand, because such a strategy requires even more coordination and control.

The idea of social integration and brands, on the other hand, reflects the notion that in the everyday use of brands their meaning can help create and maintain social relationships (Douglas and Isherwood, 1979). Kates (2000) has even suggested that brand meaning can be used as a social integration strategy for non-heterosexuals. This follows from the idea that brands are involved in the building and nurturing of groups as a result of a common or shared brand meaning, leading to 'brand communities'. Brand communities were defined in a well-regarded study by Muniz and O'Guinn (2001) as 'non-geographic' communities based on a clearly structured set of relationships among brand admirers. A part of this idea of brand community results from a shared feeling that competitive brands simply do not measure up. It is taking the idea of brand loyalty beyond the individual brand user, suggesting there is a certain communal sense that they are different, more legitimate uses of the brand, than others who merely purchase it.

IMC can certainly play a key role in the development of brand communities. It is the coordinated effectiveness of IMC that ensures a correct, consistent message. But beyond that, as part of an IMC program a brand can encourage brand communities through such activities as 'brandfests'. Dahmler-Chrysler's Jeep brand, for example, hosted events for owners, and found that it significantly increased the likelihood of repurchase among those who attended (McAlexander et al., 2002).

It is the same two pillars of marketing communication that also drives social meaning for a brand: positioning and brand attitude. Of course, for both product and social brand meaning there is a lot more involved. If one is not aware of a brand, they will not know how it is positioned; if one does not correctly process messages about a brand, it is unlikely that they will come to the desired meaning or build positive brand attitude. But positioning and brand attitude provide the foundation for building a strong brand equity, and are at the heart of brand building with strategic IMC.

■ Positioning

Positioning is the first step in laying the foundation for building a strong brand with IMC. When thinking about positioning a brand with marketing communications one talks about something different from what is generally seen as 'positioning' in a marketing sense. A marketing plan will have established a general positioning for a brand in terms of such things as pricing strategy and product features, and in relation to specific segments of a market.

Positioning in marketing communication involves how a brand is to be positioned within message executions to the target audience. There are two fundamental questions that must be answered in order to ensure an effective positioning. To what need, from the consumer perspective, should the brand be linked? The answer to this question helps position the brand to optimize brand awareness. The second question is what benefits should be emphasized in order to best communicate what the brand offers? The answer to this question will help position the brand to build a strong, positive brand attitude.

But before these questions are addressed, it is necessary to understand the difference between two basic types of brand positioning: central versus differentiated. A brand that is *centrally* positioned must be seen as delivering all of the basic benefits generally associated with the product category. The market regards centrally positioned brands as among the best brands, if not the best, in a category. Because of this, their marketing communication does not need to continually remind people of their benefits. They are assumed. It is enough to remind people that the brand is 'the best'. The ultimate central positioning is when the brand name becomes a generic term for the category. This would include such brands as Xerox, Kleenex, and Hoover.

With all other brands, a *differentiated* positioning should be used. As the term implies, a differentiated positioning looks for a way to differentiate the brand from its competitors. This is accomplished by looking for a specific benefit (or a small set of benefits in some cases where there is a high-involvement purchase decision) that is important to the target audience, and that they believe, or can be persuaded to believe, the brand will deliver better than any of its competitors. The only exception to this is when a brand is believed to be just as good as the category leader, especially if it is lower priced. In that case, the manager could choose to use a central positioning because the brand, like the centrally positioned category leader, will be seen as delivering on all the main category benefits.

Once the basic positioning structure is established, whether the brand should be centrally or differentially positioned, it is time to deal with the questions introduced earlier. The first step in answering those fundamental questions is to gain an understanding of just how *consumers* look at a category.

Understanding how markets are defined

In the beginning of this section we pointed out that how the term 'positioning' is used in marketing differs from how it is used in marketing communications. Nevertheless, the *marketing* positioning will inform the positioning strategy for a brand's marketing communication. The bridge between the two is how the market is understood and defined by the consumer.

Among other things, a brand manager will look at how competitors are positioned within the market, and along what benefit dimensions. Decisions must be made as whether to position a brand in 'gaps' (if they exist), or to attack the position of a specific competitor. Earlier we suggested that two of the criteria often used in market positioning are pricing strategy and product features. If there are no lower priced high-quality brands in a market, and a brand's margins can sustain it, a manager might decide to reposition the brand at a lower price point.

This would have a direct effect upon how that brand would need to be positioned in its marketing communication. But, it need not suggest that the communication positioning must be based specifically upon the lower price. In fact, it would probably make more sense to reinforce the quality image in light of the lower pricing strategy to reassure users that the product quality was not being sacrificed for the lower price. The key is how the consumer sees the market. Do they believe, or can they be persuaded to believe, that a high-quality product in this category can be sold at a lower price?

Let us consider another example. In mid-2005, the UK soft drink marketer Britvic decided to reposition its Tango brand after a five-year slide in sales, and increasing competition from leading brands like Coca-Cola (AdAge, 2005). With the introduction of Coke's 'Z' range of zero-added-sugar soft drinks, they decided to reposition Tango, in marketing terms, by introducing a clear, low-sugar product as Tango Clear. This obviously required a change in how the brand was positioned within its marketing communications, leading to a variation of the brand's long-running campaign that featured some unlucky person being violently attacked, followed by the tagline 'You know when you've been Tango'd'. The new positioning within its advertising followed the product change, focussing upon the benefit of a 'clear' soft drink, and with a new tagline, changed slightly from the original, 'It's clear when you've been Tango'd'. This consistency with earlier advertising reflects good IMC, as we discussed in the first chapter, and will deal with at length later on in this book.

In this case, the brand was following a shift in consumer demand from heavily sugared fizzy soft drinks to more healthy alternatives. But, it still begs an important question for positioning. What exactly is the market in which Tango competes? The obvious answer is the soft drink market, but there is much more to it than that. Of course Tango is a soft drink; and the new Tango Clear has no colour, and it is low in calories. So, should Tango be positioned in the fizzy drink market? Should it be positioned in the fruit drink market, or the clear drink market, or the low-calorie market? As you can see, the answer is really not that obvious.

Positioning and brand awareness

From an IMC positioning standpoint, getting the right answer here is critical to effective positioning. If we do not fully understand how Tango's customers define the market, we will not be able to optimize the positioning for brand awareness. It is essential to understand what Tango is associated with in its target market's memory so that when they think about Tango it is linked to the correct category need.

One of the ways to look at how consumers 'see' a market is with something called hierarchical partitioning. The thinking behind this approach is that there is a particular set of product attributes that a consumer will consider when defining a market, and that they use that set of attributes to sub-divide the market into successively smaller segments. The smaller the segment, the more alike the products and brands in that set will be seen by the consumer and it will be from that hierarchically defined set that an actual choice will be made.

As we have just seen, Tango might be seen as competing in any of a number of markets. Figure 2.1 illustrates one way the market might be defined by the consumer. If this was indeed the case, Tango's marketing communication must seek to link the brand in the consumer's mind with fizzy fruit soft drinks so that when the 'need' for a fizzy fruit soft drink occurs, Tango will come to mind. Notice that this partitioning of the market ignores the fact that Tango is colourless and low in calories. But if this is how consumers see the market, those attributes are unnecessary for building brand awareness.

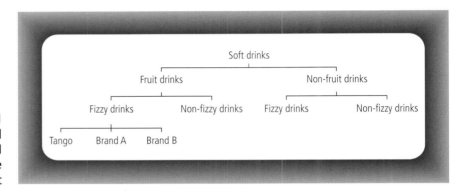

Figure 2.1
Hypothetical hierarchical partitioning of the soft drink market

But, this does *not* mean that either 'colourless' or 'low in calories' should not be used as benefits in the brand's marketing communication. It only means that they do not figure in how the consumer *defines* the market. It could be very effective to select the 'colourless' attribute to focus upon in the IMC campaign (as the brand did) in order to help build positive brand attitude.

On the other hand, perhaps the soft drink market is defined by consumers as shown in Figure 2.2a or 2.2b. If Figure 2.2a was correct, it would mean that Tango was seen by consumers as a clear fizzy drink, competing with other clear carbonated soft drinks like Pepsi Clear. If Figure 2.2b reflected how consumers see the market, they would see Tango as a low-calorie fruit drink, competing with both fizzy and non-fizzy products. The way consumers define a market identifies a brand's competitors.

What we have been discussing is the most common way most markets are defined by consumers – in terms of product attributes. But it is also possible for markets to be partitioned by consumers in terms of such things as end-benefits or usage situations. Continuing with our Tango example, the soft drink market might be seen in terms of end-benefit such as 'healthy' or 'refreshing'. If this were the case, the essential positioning link would seek to associate Tango in the consumers' minds as either a 'healthy' or 'refreshing' drink so that when they wanted either a

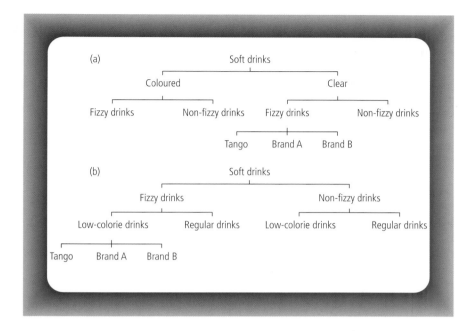

Figure 2.2
Hypothetical
alternative
hierarchical
partitioning of the
soft drink market

healthy or refreshing drink they would think of Tango. Similarly, the soft drink market might be seen in terms of usage situations like 'after exercise' or 'watching weight'.

It should now be clear why it is so important to get this correct. The first job of positioning is to establish the link between the brand and the category need in the mind of the consumer, so that when the need occurs, the brand comes to mind. This is what brand awareness is all about.

Positioning and brand attitude

The second issue that must be considered in positioning a brand in marketing communications is how it will be presented within the message and execution. One is looking for the best way to communicate what the brand offers, and that it will be seen to be not only different from competitive brands, but better. This reflects the positioning decision for optimizing brand attitude. Later, in Chapter 11, we will look more closely at how to go about selecting the benefit to talk about, and how to best focus upon the benefit in the execution to reflect the underlying motivation driving behaviour in the category.

What we want to focus upon at this point is the initial positioning decision a manager must make about how to position what the brand offers, the decision as to whether the message should be about specific characteristics of the brand or product, or about the user of the brand. In addressing the question of what a brand offers, there are two basic options for positioning. The brand may be positioned towards the user or towards a specific benefit of the brand (or in some cases a set of benefits). These are generally referred to as user-oriented versus product-oriented positioning.

It is not often that a user-oriented positioning should be used in IMC, but it can be an option when a brand is being marketed to a particular segment, and the strategy is to specifically address them in the message. This might be the case, for example, if one were advertising a high-end music system and wanted to target a small segment of 'knowledgeable' buyers. A user-oriented position here might use a message that talked about the brand as being for 'sophisticated' or discerning buyers.

Another case where a user-oriented positioning might be considered is where social approval is the primary motivation driving the behaviour of a brand's target audience. Social approval is one of the two positive motivations that can drive purchase behaviour (the other positive motive is sensory gratification). Motivation is one of the foundations of brand attitude strategy, along with involvement, and will be covered in depth in Chapter 4. When social approval is motivating the target audience, it means they are buying the product in search of an opportunity for social reward through personal recognition. An example here would be when a man buys the woman in his life an expensive piece of jewellery. It is unlikely that he is buying it for personal enjoyment, but rather for a positive response from the lady. Advertising messages here might talk about the brand as ensuring the man will be rewarded by the lady when he buys it.

These are the two principle situations where the manager has the option of utilizing a user-oriented positioning. In the one case the brand is positioned to 'flatter' a specific segment of the market being targeted, and in the other it offers the personal recognition the target audience is seeking in buying the product. One may also use a product-oriented positioning in these cases, but in all other cases, a product-oriented positioning is required.

With a product-oriented positioning, the benefits of a product are the message. While the execution may feature users, the focus of the message will be upon the benefit and the brand's performance. Utilizing benefits that are important to the target audience and that the brand is seen as delivering (or can be persuaded it delivers), a product-oriented positioning will seek to present what the brand offers in a way that it will be seen as not only different from the competitive brands, but better.

Positioning is the first pillar in the foundation for building strong brands. In this brief overview we have seen how positioning in marketing communications is not necessarily the same as the positioning of the brand in a marketing plan; but it will always be in support of the brand's overall positioning in the market. A brand will be either centrally or differentially positioned, and assume either a user- or product-oriented positioning as appropriate. There is more to it of course, as we shall see in later chapters. Establishing the correct positioning is critical to building a strong brand attitude. In the next section we take an initial look at brand attitude, and we will continue to re-visit it throughout the book.

■ Brand attitude

Brand attitude is the second pillar in the foundation for building strong brands with IMC. What exactly is brand attitude? Everyone has brands that they like and brands that they don't like. That preference *reflects* their brand attitude. But where does it come from? People who study consumer behaviour like to use something called an Expectancy-Value model to explain how people form attitudes (Fishbein and Ajzen, 1975).

In its simple form, the Expectancy-Value model of attitude suggests that someone's attitude towards an object (A_o), a brand in our case, is a function of everything they know or believe about that object (b_i) weighted by how important each of those beliefs is to them (a_i):

$$A_o = \sum_{i=1}^{n} a_i b_i$$

where A_o = attitudes towards the object
a_i = importance of belief, and
b_i = belief about the object.

Let us consider an example. Think about a product like toothpaste. What are some of the things you 'know' or believe about toothpaste? Perhaps, that it has fluoride, helps whiten the teeth, freshens breath, helps prevent tooth decay, etc. How important is it to you that toothpaste has fluoride, helps whiten teeth, etc.? Now consider a brand of toothpaste like Crest. Do you believe Crest has fluoride, helps whiten teeth, etc.? Does it have a lot of fluoride; does it really whiten teeth or only do an average job?

In the end, your attitude towards Crest will be the result of how many of the things that are important to you in toothpaste are delivered by Crest. The more benefits, important to you, that you feel Crest offers, the more positive your brand attitude for Crest will be. If it offers a lot of benefits important to you, you will probably really like it. If it doesn't, or perhaps more importantly if you do not think that it does, or know it doesn't, you will not have as favourable an opinion or attitude towards it. And if you feel it does a really bad job on a very important benefit, you may not like it at all.

Of course, you have probably never really thought about toothpaste in quite this much detail before. Nevertheless, perceptions of benefits like these have made their way into your memory, and associations of brands with these benefits have gone into forming your overall summary judgements about them. You do not need to 'think through' why you hold the attitude you do for different brands, you need only to recall the summary judgement. You simply 'like' Crest better than Colgate. In effect, the brand name and its meaning frees you from making extensive evaluations of brand alternatives every time you make a purchase decision.

Where does most of the brand knowledge come from that informs brand attitude? Marketing communication, and how the brand is positioned in the message. Experience, to be sure, plays a role, but for most people, for most brands, they simply 'know' something about them. Think about two very different product categories, like beer and computers. You probably are aware of many more brands in each category than those with which you have had personal experience, but you probably have 'attitudes' about all of them. You think some brands are better than others; this is a strong lager, that is a faster computer. Each brand in the category with which you are aware has taken on a meaning that reflects your experience, knowledge, beliefs, and feelings about it: brand attitude. The primary source of that information comes from the positioning of the brand and what is said about it in marketing communication. Effective IMC ensures strong and consistent support for building and nurturing a positive brand attitude.

How IMC is used to effectively build a positive brand attitude will be dealt with in Chapter 4 when we look at the role of traditional advertising in IMC. What we want to talk about here is how positive brand attitude leads to strong brand equity.

Building brand equity

We have mentioned several times that positive brand attitude leads to a strong brand equity. But what exactly is brand equity? While there are almost as many definitions of brand equity as there are people talking about it, almost all will have in common the idea that brand equity represents an *added value* to a product, a value that goes well beyond the objective characteristics of the product itself (Elliott and Percy, 2007). This added value quite literally makes the brand name itself a strong financial asset to the company marketing it. It does this because a strong brand equity means that a brand is well known, is positively associated in the mind's of consumers, is seen as 'better' than other brands, and is likely to have a strong core of loyal users (Aaker, 1991). This in turn ensures better distributors and strong demand.

Think of some of the products you buy, especially fast moving consumer goods or other low-involvement products. Is there really that much of a difference between brands of washing powder, brios, mouth rinse, toilet tissue, underwear, or tinned tomatoes? Why do most people prefer to buy a branded aspirin rather than generic when both are nothing but aspirin? Why do some people not only prefer Coke to Pepsi (or Pepsi to Coke), but *passionately* prefer it to the point of not even wanting to drink the other? And this in spite of the fact that these passionately loyal drinkers cannot tell the difference between the two in blind taste tests? Obviously, something is going on here that goes well beyond the sensory characteristics of the product.

So what is it about certain brands that lead people to feel they are better than others, even when they may use the same basic ingredients, get the job done equally well, or even taste the same? The answer is brand equity. For these people, there is just something 'better' about it, and there is no arguing with them. Ask the people at Coke who tried to introduce New Coke in the mid-1990s. Managers at Coke felt they were losing share to Pepsi among the younger demographic, and thought the reason was that Pepsi's formulation was somewhat sweeter. They decided to introduce a re-formulated product that people, Coke drinkers and Pepsi drinkers, preferred to both their current products. When they developed a product that was indeed preferred by everyone, it was introduced as New Coke, with the intention of replacing the original product.

But there was an almost violent reaction in the market among loyal Coke drinkers. They were incensed that the company was considering phasing out their beloved product! The company quickly backtracked, and it was New Coke that was retired. How could they have made such a mistake? They completely ignored the strong brand equity Coke had built with over 100 years of advertising reminding drinkers that 'all the world loves a Coke' and 'Coke is it'. All the many taste tests conducted to find the perfect formulation were conducted 'blind'. No one knew what product they were drinking. You can bet that had they tested the 'preferred' formulation with original Coke when Coke drinkers knew what they were drinking, original Coke would have been preferred.

This entrenched power of brand equity was illustrated in a very interesting neuroimaging study. As we shall see later in Chapter 8, emotional associations with brands are an important part of how people process information about them, and these emotional memories (stored in the amygdala) interact with knowledge and assumptions about brands that come from the hippocampus when we make judgements. A group of neurobiologists used functional magnetic resources imagery (fMRI), a process that measures brain activity, to determine what parts of the brain are energized when taste preferences are made (McClure et al., 2004). The test was conducted in both labeled and blind conditions, and among loyal and non-loyal drinkers of the brands: and the brands were Coke and Pepsi.

What they found was that when people did not know what they were drinking, only that part of the brain dealing with sensory evaluations (the ventromedial prefrontal cortex) was active, and preference was basically random. Regular drinkers were no more likely to pick their 'favourite' than the one they did not drink. But when there was brand knowledge, for loyal Coke drinkers the hippocampus, dorsolateral prefrontal cortex and midbrain were also active. These are the areas of the brain known to be involved in influencing behaviour based on emotion and affect (i.e. 'liking'). And no surprise, they preferred Coke. In effect, they were showing the influence of brand equity. The positive feelings associated with the brand were activated by the knowledge that they were drinking their favourite brand.

In a very real sense, a brand only exists in the mind of the consumer, in the meaning that has been built over time through marketing communication. To the extent that this marketing communication, in all its aspects, has been consistent in well positioning the brand and building positive brand attitude, a strong brand equity will evolve leading to loyalty that goes well beyond any rational consideration of the product. This is what results from truly effective IMC. Of course, even the best IMC programs will not lead to complete loyalty to a brand among everyone. But, it will encourage a positive brand attitude that does energize positive brand equity, and this will help maximize brand loyalty.

Again, think of your own feelings for different brands. You may be fiercely loyal to a particular brand in a category, but still feel that one or two other brands in that category are also quite good. You may in fact feel that some brands have strong brand equity, indeed stronger and more positive than the brand you buy, yet you do not buy them. Examples here might include brands such as Roles Royce or Lear Jet. You just 'know' they are good brands; and not because of your experience with them. You know they are good brands because over time the marketing communication for those brands has built a positive brand attitude in your mind, leading to strong brand equity.

In these examples, you may not even be aware of much exposure to their marketing communication. After all, you are unlikely to be in their target audience. But you will have been exposed to them indirectly through such things as product placement in movies, and through general word of mouth. All of this is an important part of effective IMC in building a brand.

■ Brand portfolio considerations

Most marketers, even relatively small ones, offer more than one product or brand. This may take the form of something as simple as a line of items under a single brand name to multiple products and brands offered by large multinational companies. For any marketer offering more than a single product, it is important that the marketing strategies for their brands be coordinated in order to optimize the overall profitability of the company. This coordination is generally thought of as product portfolio management, and within it, brand portfolio management.

One might think about this in terms of a grid, as illustrated in Figure 2.3. Here, all of the products a company markets would be shown along the top, with the brands offered beneath each product. While we are not going to discuss this in depth because it is more properly covered in a

	Product portfolio			
Brand portfolio	**Product Type A**	**Product Type B**	**Product Type C**	**Etc.**
	Brand 1 Brand 2	Brand 1 Brand 2 Brand 3 Brand 4	Brand 1	

Figure 2.3
Product and brand
portfolio grid

strategic brand management text (e.g. Elliott and Percy, 2007), it is none-theless important to have a general idea of what is involved in product and brand portfolio management because it informs IMC strategy.

Product and brand portfolio management looks at everything a company now markets, as well as future plans for acquisitions, product line extensions, and brand extensions, in order to optimize the contribution of each product and brand for the overall health of the company. Issues such as the core competencies and equity of the parent company and individual brands must be considered; the market segments to be served; and competitive positioning within those markets. The implementation of such planning relies fundamentally upon branding strategy, and the implementation of branding strategy is the job of IMC.

Branding strategy

Branding strategy involves something Kapferer (1997) has called 'brand hierarchy', which reflects the level at which a brand name is used. The basic question is: should a product be uniquely branded or encompass some combination of an existing brand name (or the parent brand) with a new one, generally known as sub-branding? Sub-branding has many permutations, but comes down to adding a new brand name to an existing brand name in order to borrow the already existing strength and equity of that brand, while at the same time creating a specific brand identity for the new brand. The advantage of sub-branding is that it permits the creation of brand-specific beliefs, but without the necessity of starting from scratch.

In Kaferer's discussion of branding strategy, he introduces a useful distinction. He looks at alternative branding strategies in terms of the extent to which a brand will function as an indicator of product origin versus differention of the product. A stand-alone or uniquely branded product seeks to differentiate the brand. It implies that the company behind the brand is unknown. This provides greater latitude for brand extensions, but requires a heavy initial investment in marketing, especially marketing communication.

Sub-branding strategies seek to provide an indicator of the product's origin. The two most commonly understood types of sub-branding are known as *source* branding and *endorser* branding. With a source branding strategy, the parent company or brand is supporting the quality of the product, and the brand must be positioned to reflect the equity of the parent. If a source branding strategy is used, either the company or an appropriate brand name from the company's brand portfolio is used to *introduce* the new brand. Examples here would be IBM ThinkPad, and Nestle's Crunch.

An endorser branding strategy implies that the parent brand has given its 'approval' and support to the product, while assuming a secondary position, encouraging the brand to develop its own image with the cross-potential of nurturing the parent. With an endorser branding strategy, the brand name comes first, with the parent brand second, and often with a significantly reduced presence. Examples here would be Philadelphia Cream Cheese from Kraft and Kira St Johns Wart from Lichtner Pharma.

Stand-alone brands

The advantage of a unique, or stand-alone, brand is that it enables a brand to create its own identity independent of a parent brand. As mentioned, this usually requires more of an investment, but it permits the brand to develop more in directions that may not be compatible with a parent brand's core competency or equity. It also avoids the possibility of negative associations with the parent informing the image of the brand, or even the possibility of a negative response to the brand reflecting upon the parent.

Just such a possibility influenced Anheuser-Busch branding strategy when they first introduced a lower calorie beer. They were not willing to risk the equity of their existing brands, especially their flagship brand Budweiser, by initially introducing a sub-brand like Bud Light. They were concerned that potentially negative associations with 'light' beers among their core market could reflect badly upon their brands. As a result, they created a new brand that, while it used the parent company as a source, avoided the use of existing brand names: Anheuser-Busch Natural Light.

This case provides a good example of how IMC is involved in brand portfolio strategy. The marketing communication for the new brand needed to link Natural Light to Anheuser-Busch, but without associating it in memory with existing Anheuser-Busch brands. It required its own, distinct, identity. The initial advertising and other marketing communication treated the new brand specifically as a source brand, always prefacing Natural Light with Anheuser-Busch. Unfortunately, research discovered that when people ordered it they asked for a Bud Light or Busch Light (what the industry refers to as the 'bar call'). They quickly changed the advertising, dropping the reference to Anheuser-Busch and focusing attention on 'Natural', spending much of each execution establishing the beer call as 'give me a Natural'.

Over time as the market for lower calorie beers established itself, Natural Light eventually became a price brand without marketing support, and the brewery introduced a lower calorie version of each of their key brands: Bud Light, Busch Light, and Michelob Light. In branding strategy terms, this represents a brand extension where the Anheuser-Busch Natural Light branding strategy was a 'corporate source' strategy, with the corporation endorsing the quality of the beer and acting as a seal of approval. The product was not meant to seem autonomous.

A good example of a stand-alone brand being created specifically to avoid negative carry over from the parent company is the case of O_2. In 2002 BT Cellnet was a brand in real trouble, loosing share to competitors like Orange and Vodafone in the UK. A decision was made to de-merge parent BT Wireless from BT, and reintroduce the brand as O_2 distancing itself completely from its antecedent. While this required a significant marketing investment, coupled with the need to supply an ongoing revenue stream to support what was in many ways an existing brand, the new brand enjoyed strong initial support, quickly reaching and surpassing the old levels of its predecessor brand BT Cellnet. The company attributed much of this success to the benefits of an IMC campaign addressing consumers, trade, and staff.

Sub-brands

As discussed earlier, sub-branding generally follows either a source or endorser branding strategy. These sub-branding strategies may operate at either a corporate or brand level. Nestle's Crunch is an example of a *corporate* source branding strategy, with the parent company supporting the quality of the product. Nescafe Gold Blend is an example of a *brand* source strategy, where the brand Nescafe supports the quality of the product. Nescafe, of course, is a Nestle brand, but it is a stand-alone brand. While there is an obvious alliterative reference to the parent company, it is not explicitly a part of the branding strategy. This same corporate or brand level distinction operates with endorser branding strategies as well (for example, Norwich Union an AVIVA company).

Product and brand portfolio strategies informs a company's branding strategy, and how IMC will be used to establish the brands in their markets. To illustrate, let us consider Interbrew. Interbrew is one of the world's largest brewers, yet there is no 'Interbrew' beer brand. Do you know what brands they market? They market over 15 brands in Western Europe alone. Looking at their product portfolio strategy, they have chosen to market a few global stand-alone premium lager and speciality beers, but their core strategy is the marketing of 'local' brands. According to their 2001 Annual Report, Interbrew's strategy as the 'world's local brewer'© is to 'build strong local platforms in the major beer markets of the world'. This is the positioning of the *parent* company, but it will certainly inform the branding strategy for individual brands. The 'brand' Interbrew in reality only exists for the *financial* community, but bear in mind that this too must be considered as a part of their overall IMC campaign.

Let us look more closely at this. Figure 2.4 presents a partial product and brand portfolio grid for Interbrew. Are you surprised at the brands in their portfolio? It is part of Interbrew's branding strategy to *not* link their individual brands with the parent company. With the exception of the international premium and specialty brands, whose channel costs are already paid and thus return a higher profit, the heart of their portfolio

	Product portfolio		
	International premium brands	**International speciality brands**	**Local brands**
Brand portfolio	Stella Artois Beck's	Hoegaarden Leffe Bass	Tennet's Klinskoye Chernigirski Labatt Blue Jupiler

Figure 2.4
Partial Interbrew product and brand portfolio grid

strategy is local brands representing in most markets either the number one or number two selling brands in that market.

IMC strategic planning for Interbrew, among other things, would need to take into account the fact that the overall corporate positioning is to look at most of their brands as 'local'. This means that a brand like Tennent's or Diekirch should *not* be positioned in their marketing communications along brand lines suggesting they are, say, 'one of Europe's best beers'. Rather, they should adopt a position reflecting an easily identified local association: for example, Tennent's 'the original lager brewed in Scotland'. However, Interbrew's global brands such as Becks and Stella Artois should be positioned more broadly in their IMC campaign, perhaps along the lines of something like 'one of the world's favourite beers'. This is, of course, a very simplistic look at positioning, meant only to illustrate the link between product and brand portfolio strategy and IMC. Later in Chapter 11 we will be looking at how to optimize brand positioning.

At another level of branding strategy within the brand portfolio, consider Interbrew's Labatt brand. Labatt markets three products under this name: Labatt Blue, Blue Light, and Ice. In a sense, Labatt acts as a source for the 'brands' Blue and Blue Light, but Ice is a stand-alone brand. From a branding strategy standpoint, each of the three products will have its own specific communication. But from an IMC strategy standpoint, there must be a 'sense' that these are all Labatt beers. Beyond this, the link between Labatt Blue and Blue Light should be stronger than the link between them and Labatt's Ice. This does *not* mean that the advertising must create unique brand identities, but at the same time something must communicate the brand equity associated with Labbat. We will be dealing with this sometimes-difficult issue of a consistent 'look and feel' later in the book.

Interbrew offers an example of where the parent company itself is not a brand, or a part of the branding strategy. Volkswagen offers a much different example of product and brand portfolio strategy. Everyone knows that Volkswagen is a 'brand', with a number of sub-brands such as Polo and Passat. Many people may also know that they are the parent company for other automotive 'brands' such as Audi. But not many people know that they are also the parent company of Lamborghini, Buggatti, and Bentley.

Think about this in terms of IMC strategy. If you are marketing Bentley, would you want people to know that you are a Volkswagen company? VW's brand equity may be positive in many respects, but it is unlikely to favourably transfer to Bentley. On the other hand, while it might seem that the perceived high quality and luxury associated with Bentley could help boost the perception of the VW brand, the problem is that the two brands are simply not compatible. They satisfy different category needs and market segments.

People would be unlikely to believe that a Volkswagen, priced at €20,000, could deliver the same high quality as a Bentley, priced at €200,000. In positioning, this reflects the need to correctly link the appropriate need with a brand. Effective IMC will help ensure that when a need for a particular type of motor car occurs, the advertised brand comes to mind. This requires building the appropriate links in memory, as discussed earlier.

Volkswagen itself basically uses a source branding strategy. Recall that a source branding strategy is where the parent company is supporting the quality of its sub-brands, and the sub-brands reflect the equity of the parent brand. In terms of IMC strategy, an umbrella family spirit should be present, even though the sub-brands have their own individual names and specific communications strategy. In the early 2000s, for example, regardless of whether it was advertising for a Golf, Passat, or other VW sub-brand, while each sub-brand's advertising was unique, it was all tied together with the tagline 'Drivers Wanted' under the VW logo.

In this section we have taken only a brief look at how product and brand portfolio strategy informs branding strategy, which in turn establishes the foundation for IMC strategy. The point is that a manager cannot approach the development of an IMC program for a brand without an understanding the company's overall branding strategy within its portfolio management. The hard work of developing an effective IMC strategy for a brand is of course specifically brand centered, but it must be consistent with the overall marketing strategy for a firm's portfolio of brands, as reflected by its branding strategy.

Summary

In this chapter we have looked at how IMC helps build brands. Brands have meaning, and that meaning builds over time largely as a function of marketing communication. An important part of a brand's meaning will also include social meaning, and this to is informed by marketing communication. It might even be argued that one could not have a brand without marketing communication. This is because marketing communication should be seen as literally *every* contact between a brand and its market. This means everything from advertising and promotion in its traditional sense to such things as store presentation, packaging, events, product placement in movies. In other words any representation of the brand. It is IMC that offers the manager the ability to ensure consistency of meaning over all contact with the market.

This begins with establishing the optimum positioning for the brand. While the general positioning will have been provided by the marketing plan, a specific positioning must be established for marketing communication. This requires correctly identifying the link between the brand and category need in order to effectively build awareness for the brand, and selecting the correct benefit for increasing positive brand attitude. Brand attitude is critical in building strong brands because it is positive brand attitude that leads to a strong brand equity.

IMC must also take into account brand portfolio considerations, especially branding strategies. To the extent that a company offers different brands within a category or brand extensions, the branding strategies will inform how the communications strategy for those brands or extensions will be developed. Stand-alone brands provide an opportunity for unique identification, independent of a parent brand (where one exists). Sub-brands will reflect the identity of the parent brand, either as a source or endorser. With a source branding strategy, the parent is supporting the quality of the product. Any endorser branding strategy implies that the parent brand approves and supports the brand, while assuming a secondary position.

■ Review questions

1 How does IMC help build brands?
2 How is IMC involved in creating social meaning for a brand?
3 Identify brands you feel that have created social meaning, and discuss how IMC is likely to have contributed.
4 Why is positioning so critical to effective IMC in building brands?
5 Identify competing brands that are clearly positioned differently, and discuss which position is likely to be more effective.
6 Is there likely to be a centrally positioned brand in the beer category? What about household cleaners, computers, and designer fashions?
7 Identify brands that use a user-oriented positioning and discuss its appropriateness.
8 What is the relationship between positioning and brand awareness and brand attitude?
9 How would you define brand attitude?
10 What is the role of IMC in establishing and building brand attitude?
11 How does a brand's portfolio management impact upon IMC strategy?
12 Identify examples of stand-alone, source, and endorser brands, and discuss how IMC should be used to support their brand strategy.

References

Aaker, D.A. (1991) *Managing Brand Equity*. New York: Free Press.

Aaker, J. (1997) Dimensions of brand personality. *Journal of Marketing Research*, XXXIV, 347–356.

AdAge (2005) 13 June, 18.

Douglas, M. and Isherwood, B. (1979) *The World of Goods: Towards an Anthropology of Consumption*. London: Alter Lane.

Elliott, R., Jones, A., Benefield, A. and Barlow, M. (1995) Overt sexuality in advertising: A discourse analysis of gendered responses. *Journal of Consumer Policy*, 18(2), 71–92.

Elliott, R. and Percy, L. (2007) *Strategic Brand Management*. Oxford: Oxford University Press.

Fishbein, M. and Ajzen, I. (1975) *Belief, Attitude, Intention, and Behaviour: An Introduction to Theory and Research*. Reading, Massachusetts: Addison-Wesley Publishing Company.

Kapferer, J.N. (1997) *Strategic Brand Management*, 2nd edition. London: Kogan Page.

Kates, S. (2000) Out of the closet and into the streets: Gay men and their brand relationships. *Psychology and Marketing*, 17(6), 493–504.

McAlexander, J., Schouten, J. and Koenig, H. (2002) Building brand community. *Journal of Marketing*, 66, 38–54.

McClure, S.M., Li, J., Tomlin, D., Cypert, K.S., Mantague, L.M. and Montague, P.R. (2004) Neural correlates of behavioural preference for culturally familiar drinks. *Neuron*, 44, 379–387.

Muniz, A. and O'Guinn, T. (2001) Brand communities. *Journal of Consumer Research*, 27, 412–432. March

Percy, L., Hansen, F. and Randrup, R. (2004) *Emotional response to brands and product categories*, Proceedings from ESOMAR, Lisben.

CHAPTER 3

Companies and IMC

In the last chapter we saw how a company's name may be used as a brand, or as a source or endorser within its branding strategy. In this chapter we will be looking at the *company itself* as a 'brand', not as the name of a product. There is a vast literature on corporate and organizational identity and imagery, and we will be looking into this area along with reputation. However, our primary concern is with the role integrated marketing communication (IMC) plays in these areas and the development and nurturing of a company as a brand, just as we were concerned with the role of IMC in building and sustaining product brands in the last chapter.

What we shall see is that there is a great deal of similarity, at least on the surface. Companies are positioned, usually talked about as a 'vision', and they work to establish positive attitudes toward the company among their various publics and stakeholders in order to build a strong corporate brand equity.

■ The role of IMC in strengthening companies

People who work in the area of company imagery and identity are generally concerned with the idea of the company as either an organization or corporate entity, and how it is represented and communicated to its various audiences (Hatch and Schultz, 2000). Corporate identity is usually thought of as being different from organizational identity, although there is some overlap (Hatch and Schultz, 2000). The principle distinction between these two views of a company reflects an internal versus external perspective.

When considering *organizational* identity and imagery, one is looking *within* the company at employees or other internal stakeholders. When considering *corporate* identity and imagery, one is usually concerned with looking outside the company to external audiences (Figure 3.1). IMC should and must play a role in the establishment and maintenance of a company's identity, but generally within the area of corporate, not organizational, imagery and identity.

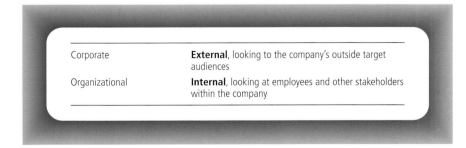

| Corporate | **External**, looking to the company's outside target audiences |
| Organizational | **Internal**, looking at employees and other stakeholders within the company |

Figure 3.1
Corporate versus organizational identity and imagery

This is a broad statement, of course. The image of a company that is projected to the outside world must find consonance within the organization. This is especially true of service industries, and to a lesser degree business-to-business firms, where employee contact with the consumer plays a significant role in building both corporate and brand attitude. But researchers in organizational identity like to think about it in terms of (among other things) the perspective from which identity is defined.

As Hatch and Schultz (2000) have described it, corporate identity will reflect the thinking and direction of top management, even if they take into account the opinions of other members of the organization. Organizational identity, however, will reflect the many ways everyone within an organization thinks about themselves as an organization. As they put it 'corporate identity requires taking a managerial perspective, while appreciation of organizational identity requires an organizational perspective' (Hatch and Schultz, 2000). While acknowledging a potential overlap between corporate and organizational identity, and the fact that IMC's direct role in building corporate identity will inform organizational identity, we shall be looking at IMC's role in strengthening a company in terms of corporate identity.

It should be obvious that corporate communication in all of its forms (press releases, annual reports, sponsorships, etc.), but especially corporate advertising, must be consistent with its general marketing communication. The arguments for consistency in the delivery of a brands message (as outlined in Chapter 1) holds for corporate communication. Such consistency creates a recognizable picture of a company, regardless of the channel of communication (van Riel, 2000).

Consider this example. If a company presented itself as modern and innovative, yet marketed 'traditional' products, would that make any sense? In terms of our discussion in the last chapter on branding strategy, what if they were using a source or endorser branding strategy? Even though the corporate message would be separate from the brand messages, the corporate brand equity that is being relied upon to 'guarantee' the brand would be at odds with the image the brand has established. The two images would simply not be compatible.

Even if our hypothetical company used only a stand-alone branding strategy for the products they market, this would still not be a good idea. While the brand images would not be connected with the parent, the parent would be connected to the brands. It would be hard to imagine a company like Proctor & Gamble, which does not incorporate the corporate name as part of their branding strategy, not including their brands in some fashion within their corporate communication. Recall our discussion of Interbrew. Their corporate communication is all about their brands, but Interbrew does not appear as a part of their brand marketing communication. Not only must brand messages be consistent across all channels of communication, and corporate messages be consistent in all their media, but brand and corporate messages must be consistent.

Christensen and Cheney (2000) have made the interesting observation that corporate existence can no longer be separate from the question of communication. In their view, companies have convinced themselves that success will depend very much upon their ability to not only differentiate their products or services from competitors, but to actually justify their existence through the corporate image they project. To quote them: '… identity is the issue, and communication seems to be the answer.'

This is reminiscent of how back in the 1970s Mobil Corporation (now Exxon-Mobil) was perhaps the first company to integrate advertising, public relations, and policy statements from the company into an explicit 'corporate advocacy' campaign (Crable and Vibbert, 1983). They became proactive in the face of public and government concern over oil prices and supply. One of their efforts in trying to better manage their overall image was to publish a series of 'advertorials' on a number of socio-political issues. What this did was move the overall positioning of Mobil as a company beyond the image of their products. But as we have discussed, that still must be consistent with the image of their products.

With increased scrutiny of companies from a wide range of sources ranging from advocacy groups to government, to say nothing of the '24-7' media news cycle, companies today are more and more concerned with their general image and identity. Many are following what Dahler-Larsen (1997) has called 'moralized discourses', using corporate communication to gain what the company sees as 'responsibility'. IMC must play a central role in coordinating the image of the corporation with that of its products. BP (British Petroleum) offers a good example of what we have been talking about. For several years their corporate communication has been helping change its image and identity from petroleum to a more broadly based Energy Company paying attention to environmental concerns.

■ Corporate identity, image, and reputation

The terms corporate identity, corporate image, and corporate reputation are often used interchangeably, but there are important differences between them that a manager should understand because they inform strategy. These differences are often painfully detailed by academics, but this should not deter us from appraising the strategic implications associated with each of the concepts.

Grahame Dowling (2001) has offered a set of rather clear and helpful definitions for each of these concepts that identify the principle differences between them. He describes *corporate identity* as: 'the symbols and nomenclature an organization uses to identify itself to people (such as the corporate name, logo, advertising, slogan, livery, etc.)'. Following this definition, examples of corporate identity would include such things as IBM, the Nike 'swoosh', and the MacIntosh Apple.

Corporate image is regarded as 'the global evaluation (comprised of a set of beliefs and feelings) a person has about an organization'. The important point here is that an 'image' is in the eye of the beholder. To the extent that a company has succeeded in creating a consistent image over time, there should be a general consensus within its target markets as to what that image is. Volvo is concerned with making 'safe' automobiles; Rolls Royce with making high quality, luxurious automobiles. Regardless of the nameplate (the word the automobile industry likes to use for brand), if you know it was made by Volvo, because of the company's image, you would expect it to be 'safe'.

But as Dowling (2001) points out, not everyone is likely to hold the same beliefs and feelings about a company. This means it is unlikely that any company has a *single* image. The job of IMC is to build and nurture as consistent an image as possible among the largest number of a company's various audiences. The fact that a company has many different audiences to address (e.g. government regulators, shareholders, employees, consumers) complicates the job, and underscores the need for effective IMC; a centrally managed communication effort in order to project a consistent image.

Dowling (2001) defines *corporate reputation* as: 'the attributed values (such as authenticity, honesty, responsibility, and integrity) evoked from the person's corporate image.' Again, this means there is the potential for a wide-ranging understanding of a company's reputation owing to the potential differences in value assessment among different people, and among various target audiences. What is important to one person or group may not be to another; and certain values may carry different weight among different people and groups. This potential problem increases for multinational companies because of the ways in values can be culturally driven.

With this introduction to corporate identity, image, and reputation as a foundation, let us now take a closer look at each concept.

Corporate identity

The idea of corporate identity as defined by Dowling (2001) is rather straightforward: the words and symbols a company uses to set itself apart from other companies so people will recognize it. Originally, the study of corporate identity tended to be centred around a rather narrow, graphic design perspective. There is no doubt that visual imagery via graphic design can play a significant part in corporate identity (just think of the 'golden arches'). Yet there is much more to it, as we shall see. In fact, there is a good deal more to it, but the field of identity studies is well beyond the scope of this book. Nevertheless, some appreciation for the scope of corporate identity studies is in order if we are to understand the role of IMC in the development and sustaining of corporate identity.

In introducing a collection of articles on corporate identity in their book, John Balmer and Stephen Greyser (2003) offer a useful way of looking at the field of identity studies. They suggest regarding it as inhabiting three different 'worlds', a *triquadri orbis* in their words. It begins with the narrow world of graphic design, and what they call *visual identification*. Graphic presentation is an important consideration in developing an IMC program. As an example, from its earliest years IBM has been informally known as 'Big Blue'. In the early 2000s, IBM's advertising reflected this visually by framing graphically all of their adverts, even television commercials, with horizontal blue bars on the top and bottom of the page and screen. With consistent use of this graphic devise, soon one immediately identified these messages with IBM, even before exposure to the corporate tag.

The second 'world' of identity is what Balmer and Greyser (2003) called *organizational identity*. As they put it, this reflects the use of corporate identity in answering the question 'who are we.' This aspect of corporate identity addresses the internal audience of the organization, and is of less interest to us given our focus on a company's external audiences. But we cannot ignore it. How employees see the company for which they work is critical to overall communication efforts in service industries, and in any business where employees have significant contact with customers (e.g. banks and retail stores). Here is where such things as company newsletters and other internal corporate communication must be consistent with the overall image being projected to the population at large, and as a result, part of IMC.

The third 'world' of identity studies is *corporate identity*. It seeks to answer the questions 'what are we?' as well as 'who are we?' This is the world of identity studies with which we are most concerned, and the one generally addressed by the marketing literature. But it is important to keep in mind that both the visual identification and organizational identification worlds will play their part in the overall perception of a company's identity. The role of corporate identity is critical to any discussion of corporate strategy, and this includes image, reputation, and importantly, communication.

As Dowling (2001) has suggested, while managers generally have a pretty good understanding of corporate image and reputation, they often confuse corporate image with corporate identity. This can, and often does, result in wasting a great deal of a company's communication budget. Part of the responsibility of IMC is to ensure there is no confusion between identity and image in a company's corporate communication. It is also the job of IMC to ensure that there is no confusion *within* corporate identity.

Corporate identity types

According to Balmer and Greyser (2003), corporate identity should not be viewed as a monolithic phenomenon, but one comprised of multiple types of identity. They argue that companies have more than one identity, and that they can coexist together without problems when well managed. Five identity types are proposed: actual identity, communicated identity, conceived identity, ideal identity, and desired identity (Figure 3.2).

The *actual identity* of a corporation reflects its various realities, everything from management style to market performance, structure to performance. *Communicated identity* is driven by corporate communication,

Figure 3.2
Multiple corporate
identities. *Source*:
Adapted from
Balmer and Greyser
(2003)

Identity	Description
Actual	Reflects reality
Communicated	Driven by corporate communication
Conceived	Perception held by target audiences
Ideal	Optimum positioning for corporation
Desired	Top management vision

as well as more informal and non-controlled communication such as word-of-mouth and media commentary. The *conceived identity* of a company is the perception of it held by their various audiences. The *ideal identity* reflects what would be the optimum positioning for a company, and is subject to change over time in relation to the correct environment. *Desired identity* is what top management sees as their vision for the company. It differs from the ideal identity in being more likely to reflect the CEO's ego than the strategic realities of the day.

As you can see, these various identities devolve from both internal and external sources. Beyond the obvious, this will also include such things as the internal response to company culture and values, as well as the external influence of industry culture and socio-cultural influences generally. Corporate communication, as part of an IMC program, is likely to drive communicated identity and inform conceived and actual identity. A company's ideal identity should be a goal of corporate communication; and to the extent that a corporation's vision is strategically based, will be reflected in its corporate communication.

IMC should serve as a mediating factor for all aspects of corporate identity. One of the concerns voiced by Balmer and Greyser (2003) in discussing multiple corporate identities is that all too often there is a 'misalignment' of the identities, which leads to identity problems. They suggest that it is the responsibility of corporate leadership groups to manage identities to ensure broad consensus; and we see IMC as the key to implementing their effort.

Corporate image

In concept, corporate image parallels brand image. Both are in the 'eye of the beholder', the result of an overall evaluation of the brand or company in terms of a 'set of beliefs and feelings' as Dowling (2001) put it in his definition. This has been the traditional way of looking at image, and from a consumer behavioural or psychological perspective has been studied within the context of information processing. Compounded with corporate identity, this is an important point that reflects a critical difference between the two concepts. Corporate identity is usually studied from a management perspective, looking at how a company wishes to be seen by its various publics. Corporate image, on the other hand, is the result of how those various publics have processed the information they have about a company (Figure 3.3).

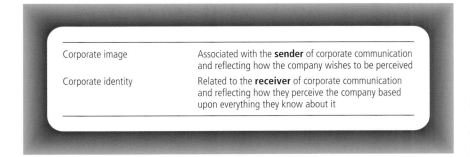

| Corporate image | Associated with the **sender** of corporate communication and reflecting how the company wishes to be perceived |
| Corporate identity | Related to the **receiver** of corporate communication and reflecting how they perceive the company based upon everything they know about it |

Figure 3.3
Corporate image versus corporate identity

Corporate image will inform how people make decisions and form attitudes about companies. There is discussion among scholars in the area as to how all this occurs (Christensen and Askegaard, 2001), but we need not get into that discussion here. The important point about an 'image' (whether a company, brand, or anything else) is that it is the result of processing information. This information is then consolidated in memory. Image in the sense with which we are concerned is not 'imagination'. It is the result of associations in memory that are reviewed and updated when new information about a company is received. This means that corporate image is always subject to change.

One of the key differences between corporate identity and image is the *source.* Christensen and Askegaard (2001) consider this a very important point. In reviewing the literature on corporate identity and image, they found that generally speaking the idea of corporate identity is associated with the *sender* of communication messages (i.e. internal, the source is the company). A company chooses how to 'identify' itself, as we saw in the last section.

On the other hand, corporate image is more commonly related to the *receiver* of communication messages (i.e. external, the audience is the source). In a very real sense a company's image is 'created' in the minds of its various audiences as they process communications about the company. The resulting image will of course be significantly mediated by the content of the message sent, but that message will always be filtered through each individual's existing knowledge and assumption about the company, and what is said about it.

Perhaps it is because corporate image is constructed externally, by individuals rather than organizationally driven, that it seems to attract less attention from those involved in the study of corporate identity, image, and reputation. A suggestion of this might be found in the 'problems' with corporate image identified by Balmer (1998): multiple meanings; negative associations; the difficulty or impossibility of control; its multiplicity; and the different effects on various audiences.

Looking at these difficulties, they simply seem to imply that a company does not have *direct* control over its image, and this is seen as a problem. But we would argue that where corporate image communication is an integral part of a company's IMC program, they will be exercising a significant level of control over the resulting image. When all of a company's communication about itself and its brands are coordinated and addressing a consistent, viable strategy, the perception of the company, it's corporate image, will reflect that communication. People will be processing a consistent message, one projecting a specific image. Successful processing of that message will result in the desired corporate image. How to accomplish this is what this book is all about, at both the brand and corporate level.

According to Balmer and Greyser (2003), when considering corporate image academics look at image from one of four perspectives: the transmitter of images, receiver-end image categories, the focus of images, and construed images. Within each perspective there are a number of ways of looking at image. Each reflects various ways corporate image might be treated strategically within an overall communication plan.

The first category focuses upon the company as the transmitter of images. This is similar to the general perspective taken of corporate identity, but here refers to image management. Corporate image is being looked at in terms of its communication strategy and objectives. Here we find such things as the creation and delivery of a single image to all of a company's audiences and the notion that corporate image is principally a function of the company's overall visual identity (which you will remember is a key element of how corporate identity is defined).

The remaining three perspectives are from the perspective of the market, not the company. With receiver-end image, one is looking at corporate image in terms of the *immediate* processing of a message from the corporation (transient image). This reflects everything from adverts to packaging to logos. It also is concerned with the congruence of the projected image of the company and how customers see themselves. The key is that the focus is on the receiver of the message, not the sender. What Balmer and Greyser (2003) called focus-of-image looks at corporate image in terms of the various brand and category images. Finally, corporate image may be looked at in terms of what one group, such as the company's employees, *think* another group, such as their customers, believes about the company.

This gives some idea of the complexity involved in dealing with corporate image. There are many ways of looking at it, with a corresponding potential for multiple interpretations. One of the tasks for IMC is minimize the chance of multiple interpretations. From a communication standpoint, in the end a manager is concerned with creating a corporate image that is understood by the target audiences in the way in which it was intended. IMC ensures that all of a company's communication, both corporate and brand, consistently reinforce the desired image.

Corporate reputation

Dowling's (2001) definition of corporate reputation is based upon the values a person associates with their understanding of a company's image. As he puts it, it is a *value-based* construct. When looking at corporate reputation this way, it is important to understand it is enduring values that are being considered (or at least values that are likely to be held over the long-term by most people, and unlikely to change in the short-term). These values would include such things as integrity, honesty, and responsibility. When a company is seen as holding values important to its target audiences, it will enjoy a positive corporate reputation. This in turn, *because* of the perception of shared values, will lead to feelings of trust and confidence in that company.

Many people look at corporate image and corporate reputation as overlapping constructs, but as Dowling reminds us, it is important to keep them separate. In fact, he suggests that the way to a strong corporate reputation is via a strong corporate image. Companies seek a strong corporate image built upon positive beliefs and feelings about the company, consistent with an overall corporate positioning strategy. And as we have seen, it is one of the tasks of IMC to build and nurture that image.

Once a corporate image is established, it should be linked to values important to its target audiences. This is because values do not change, at least not in the short-term. But it is possible to change or alter perceptions about a company. The role of IMC here is critical. Everything communicated about a company and its brands must be consistent with the establishment of the desired corporate image, and with the association in memory to the appropriate values. In this case values operate very much like emotions in framing an understanding of brands and companies. Companies, like brands, are linked in memory with specific emotional associations. These emotions are present in working memory any time someone is thinking about that company or processing new information about it. We will be dealing with the role of emotion in processing messages in much more detail in Chapter 8.

In the same way, the effective linking of a company in memory with positive values should ensure the presence of the resulting reputation in working memory when a person is thinking about that company, and there when processing communications about it. This is the result of something neuropsychologists call top-down processing, where one's knowledge and assumptions about a thing (the company here) will be present in working memory whenever one is consciously processing information about it.

Because corporate reputation is value-based, it enjoys a strategic advantage over corporate image. While both are dependent upon individual perceptions, the strength of a positive reputation will be greater than a positive image. Part of the reason is that an image is less permanent and more variable because it is based upon beliefs and feelings while reputation, based upon values, is less subject to short-term change. Another is that a company's reputation will be more stable in the presence of negative publicity. Because it is value-based and not belief-based, negative information about the company will have a much more difficult time altering the association in memory.

Imagine a pharmaceutical company that enjoys a corporate image for high-quality products, but no well-formed reputation. Imagine another with a corporate reputation for trustworthiness. Now suppose that a question is raised in the press about the efficacy of a drug they both market. Each company launches a campaign affirming the quality of their product, but which one is most likely to be believed by more people? It is more likely to be the company with a reputation for trustworthiness. Why? An image for quality products could have been built upon many things; for example a long history in the business. But the beliefs upon which that image was built are unlikely to include 'truthfulness'. It simply is not likely to come into most people's minds when building an image of a company's products. On the other hand, a reputation for trustworthiness reflects an association with individual values. If a person believes a company is trustworthy, they will believe they tell the truth.

■ Building corporate identity, image, and reputation

Now that we have an overview of what constitutes corporate identity, image, and reputation, it is time to examine what is involved in successfully developing and communicating each. Before beginning, however, it will be important to look at the interrelationships among them. As should already be clear, there is a certain overlap between these constructs, and each is somewhat dependent upon the others.

In fact, you may be thinking that a great deal is being made of very little in crafting such specific differences in these constructs. In many ways this is true, but for academics these differences are important. They permit looking at aspects of corporate strategy and how both the internal and external audiences and stakeholders of a company 'see' that company. From a manager's perspective, understanding that their company may be seen in different lights by different people, and for different reasons, should help in developing an effective overall communications program to position the company in the minds of its audiences. Each of these three ways of 'seeing' a company must be accounted for in a firm's IMC.

The study of corporate meaning that lead to the constructs we have been talking about began in the 1950s with a focus on corporate image. This was joined in the 1970s by the idea of corporate identity. Then in the late 1980s, the study of corporate reputation was added to the mix. With the addition of each new perspective, offering a different way of looking at companies, more was understood about corporate meaning. Now, there is a new focus on corporate meaning, *corporate brands* (which we shall address in due cause).

Balmer and Greyser (2003) have suggested that there are six critical questions that characterize the study of corporate meaning, and five of the six bear directly upon our discussions. Three of these questions relate directly to the constructs we have been talking about, and two others indirectly. Each of these questions and their related construct are detailed in Figure 3.4. Taken together, they provide insight into the areas that must be addressed in effectively building a positive corporate identity, image, and reputation.

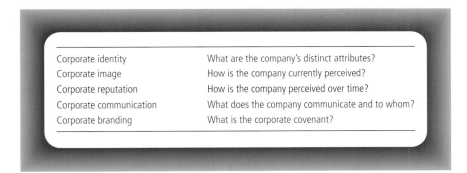

Corporate identity	What are the company's distinct attributes?
Corporate image	How is the company currently perceived?
Corporate reputation	How is the company perceived over time?
Corporate communication	What does the company communicate and to whom?
Corporate branding	What is the corporate covenant?

Figure 3.4
Keys to corporate meaning. *Source*: Adapted from Balmer and Greyser (2003)

The first question, 'What are the corporation's distinctive attributes?' relates to corporate identity. The second, 'How are we perceived now?' relates to corporate image, and the third, 'How are we perceived over time?' to corporate reputation. In answering these questions, the manager will have addressed the fundamental issues driving corporate communication strategy. They also outline the underlying relationship between the constructs. Corporate identity sets out the character of the company that set it apart from competitors, which when successfully communicated to the appropriate target audience will inform how it is perceived at any one time; the corporate image. How it is perceived over time will result in its corporate reputation.

Dowling (2001) addresses this issue of corporate meaning directly. He suggests that a good corporate identity (especially in terms of corporate symbols) will enable people to more easily recognize a company. Symbols and other features of corporate identity act as triggers in memory for helping to recall and elaborate its image. When you see Apple's trademark logo or McDonalds' 'Golden Arches' it will quickly activate the beliefs and emotions in memory associated with the brand, but also the company, its corporate image. When these are positive and consistent with someone's values in terms of corporate behaviour, it will lead to a positive corporate reputation.

Perhaps the most important question this raises is: To whom and what do we communicate? This, of course, defines communication, and in terms of IMC we would add: and how? Getting this correct is what will ensure the desired corporate meaning among a company's target audiences and key stakeholders. Of the remaining questions raised by Balmer and Geyser, we shall briefly look at the idea of corporate branding next. The issue of organizational identity, because of its internal company orientation, is generally unrelated to the fundamental development of IMC strategy, which looks primarily at external consistencies. As a result, that aspect of corporate meaning is of less interest to us in this book (although it will not be totally ignored).

■ Corporate brand

In a sense, a corporate brand is the reflection of corporate meaning as we have been discussing it. As shown in Figure 3.5, the key concepts of corporate identity, image, and reputation are related as suggested by Dowling (2001), and as each is communicated to the company's target audience they contribute to building a corporate brand. It is a summary image that acts as an umbrella over all of the firm's marketing activity, as well as its communication with all of its stakeholders. There are all types of associations outside of product or brand considerations that may become linked to corporate brands, as Brown (1998) and his colleagues remind us. In effect, the dimensions of corporate meaning reflect this, and their fusion provides the foundation for corporate brand equity.

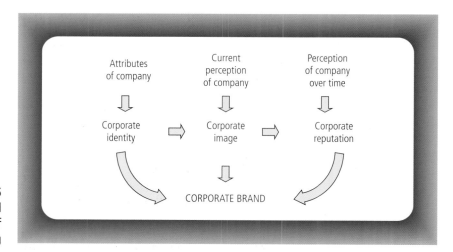

Figure 3.5
Corporate brand
as a function of
corporate meaning

Much of the effort in creating a corporate brand is in response to a realization that among consumers such things as how a company treats its employees, addresses environmental concerns, and other issues related to its role in society is being factored into their brand purchase decisions. This has led to more and more companies building corporate brands as a strategic marketing tool in order to improve overall financial performance (Roberts and Dowling, 1998; Hatch and Schultz, 2001).

There is much more to a corporate brand than a single unifying tag line or logo. According to Hatch and Schultz (2001), there are three critical interdependent elements that go into making an effective corporate brand: vision, culture, and image. The job is difficult because different groups drive each element. Vision will come from top management, usually the CEO. Culture reflects the internal organization's values and behaviour and how employees feel about the company. Image (used here in its broad meaning) is how the rest of the world sees the company.

It is critical to a successful corporate brand that a consensual image (again in its broadest sense) be built among its various target audiences, one that is both an accurate representation of the company as well as being consistent with overall corporate strategy. This requires the consistency in communication that results from an effective IMC program, one that is informed by corporate communication strategy. In addition to effectively communicating with it's external audiences, the corporate brand must be internalized by the organization, and communicated through all of its personal contacts with those outside the organization; everyone from vendors to the trade to consumers to stakeholders.

Corporate brand equity

In the last chapter we introduced the idea of brand equity. In much the same way, corporate brands acquire an equity. According to Keller (2000), it 'occurs when relevant constituents hold strong, favorable, and unique associations about the corporate brand in memory.' With a strong corporate brand equity, just as with product brand equity, relevant target audiences will feel more favourably toward the company, leading to a more favourable response to all of its corporate communication, beyond any purely objective reading of the message.

Just as with marketing communication for brands, in building corporate brand equity there are several possible objectives for corporate communication (Biehal and Shenin, 1998). But also just as for brands, awareness and attitude will *always* be objectives. Keller has also suggested that it is important to link beliefs to the company that can be leveraged by marketing communications for brands. Strong corporate brand equity results from achieving awareness and salience for the company, and the establishment of attitudes toward the company that reflect a positive corporate reputation.

This means ensuring that beliefs about the company, learned and nurtured through its communication, must be linked in memory to appropriate values held by target audiences. This is a step beyond what is necessary for building positive brand attitude, but it is the beliefs associated with the company's brands through marketing communication that will help reinforce the corporate image, and hence corporate brand equity. The role of IMC in assuring consistency and continuity between marketing communication and corporate communication in driving both product brand equity and corporate brand equity is critical.

One remaining point should be considered here. Corporate brand equity is not the same as the equity for its products, even when the brand name for the product is the company name, or is the company name used as a source or endorser. The equity associated with a company through its branding strategy will of course help inform the corporate image and corporate brand equity. But, as we have seen, corporate meaning extends well beyond product or brand perception. A good example of this would be Benetton. Benetton as a clothing retailer has one image, as a corporation taking strong stands on social issues, another. One may like the products found at Benetton, while not agreeing with the positions the company takes; or for that matter, even know about them. On the other hand, one may disagree so strongly with the company's social positions that even though you find their merchandise stylish and attractive, you will not buy them. Or, you may shop there simply to show your support for their social positions, even though you find their clothing rather like that found at other stores.

■ Corporate communication

Now that we have an idea of what is involved with corporate meaning and corporate brands, it is time to look at corporate communication. As we saw in comparing brand equity with product brand equity, the essence of corporate communication versus marketing communication is that corporate communication is much broader. Where marketing communication is focused upon the consumer or potential consumer and relies (primarily) upon specific paid media for delivering the message, corporate communication must deal with a wide range of different audiences, including an important emphasis upon communicating with employees, and is not limited to paid media. Public relations, for example, can play a significant role here.

van Riel (2003) has characterized corporate communication as a fusion of marketing, management, and organizational communication. But Balmer and Gray (2003) take a much broader view, something they call 'total corporate communication', consisting of primary, secondary, and tertiary communication. What they define as primary communication is really indirect communication, the result of such things as product or service performance, company policy, and employee behaviour. These do 'communicate' something about that company and effect corporate image, but we would not include it directly within strategic IMC planning.

The secondary communication, on the other hand, is directly related to IMC. They see it as 'planned, "formal" communication policies of organizations' including such things as advertising and other forms of marketing communication, including public relations. They define tertiary communication in terms of the *effect* of third-party communication. This would include communication about the company from such sources as word-of-mouth, and even what competitors have to say about them. While this type of communication about a company is not directly controlled by the company, it must still be carefully nurtured as a part of any effective IMC plan. Together, all of this may indeed account for 'total corporate communication', and it will all be important in defining corporate meaning. But from a managerial and not academic standpoint, our concern must be with strategically planned and controlled corporate communication.

One way of appreciating the complexity of corporate communication is to consider Berstein's (1984) idea of a corporate communication wheel, or more particularly Balmer and Greyser's (2003) adaptation of it (Figure 3.6). Basically it begins by asking corporate management to identify all of the important audiences with whom they need to communicate. These groups form the outer ring of the wheel. Then it requires a list of all the available channels of communication for delivering the message. These become a circle within the circle of potential target audiences. In the Balmer and Greyser modification, they include eleven potential target audience groups and eleven possible communication channels. As they explain, that alone results in 121 considerations!

But that is not all. A number of other considerations are contained within the two outer circles of the wheel. These include such things as country of origin, business partnerships, and category or industry image, among others. All of these must be considered for each target audience group – communications channel combination. And within each target group, there could be segments; and various channels of communication themselves are comprised of multiple delivery vehicles (think of just the alternatives available with mass media alone, which is only a single communication channel).

In reality, management must set priorities; but that in itself requires careful planning. Then in addition to optimizing with whom you wish to communicate and to most effectively deliver the message, there is the task of developing a *consistent* message. A recent suggestion has been something called the *sustainable corporate story.*

Corporate story

Many people have written about the sustainable corporate story, basically describing it as a comprehensive narrative about the entire company, including things like its history and mission statement (van Riel, 2000). Because it is unique to each company, and goes beyond corporate image to include more descriptive elements, it offers an opportunity for creating a consistent, believable impression. van Riel (2003) has identified four criteria that he feels are necessary to the development of an effective corporate story. It should be *relevant* with regard to the company's various target audiences; *responsive* in that it allows for an interaction

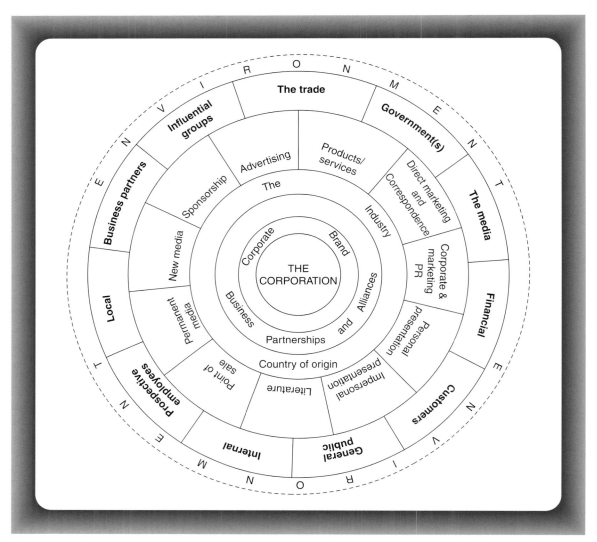

Figure 3.6
The new corporate communications wheel. *Source*: Adapted from Balmer and Greyser (2003)

between the audience members and the company; *realistic* in focusing upon the company's unique and enduring characteristics; and it should be *sustainable*, satisfying the needs and desires of relevant audiences while meeting its own objectives (Figure 3.7).

The story itself should only be a few pages in length (Larsen, 2000), and use rich narrative to deliver the message (Shaw, 2000). The key is that the corporate story must inform *all* of a company's corporate communication, including spontaneous day-to-day interactions among employees and between any company representative and its external

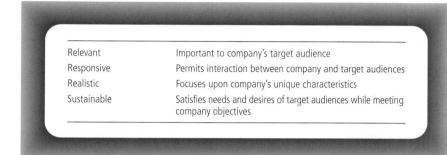

Relevant	Important to company's target audience
Responsive	Permits interaction between company and target audiences
Realistic	Focuses upon company's unique characteristics
Sustainable	Satisfies needs and desires of target audiences while meeting company objectives

Figure 3.7
Keys to an effective corporate story.
Source: Adapted from van Riel (2003)

audiences. It is the sustainable corporate story that helps align all of a company's messages, regardless of the audience. Larsen (2000) has argued that a corporate story can be a powerful tool for differentiating a company and its products from competitors, and even suggests that it may become the primary vehicle for differentiation.

The sustainable corporate story provides a way of ensuring consistency in everything the company communicates, planned and unplanned. When there is a corporate story in place, it will set the parameters for the strategic development of all corporate and brand communications. The corporate story acts as a starting point (in the words of van Riel, 2000), and provides the umbrella under which all of the company's communication falls. IMC provides a way of *managing* the strategic development and delivery of all of a company's *planned* communication.

Corporate advertising

We have spent most of this chapter looking at corporate communication from the perspective of academics who study organizational or corporate communication. This provides important insight into the complexity of the issue, and the various ways in which a company may communicate with its internal and external audiences, whether planned or not. Dowling (2001), although a respected academic in the field, offers a more traditional view of corporate communication, at least from the manager's perspective, focusing upon corporate advertising. He uses the term advertising in its broadest sense to include all forms of corporate communication. This is consistent with our definition, following from the Latin root of the word *advertere* roughly translated as 'to turn toward'.

The job of advertising in this sense is to build positive attitudes toward the company, leading to a strong corporate brand equity; and this regardless of the communication channel involved. An advertising-like message can be delivered through channels well outside traditional media: communication channels such as the annual report, employee newsletters, the chairman's speech to a financial group, web sites, etc.

Figure 3.8
A good example of corporate advertising. *Courtesy*: Credit Suisse

An important issue for managers is the role corporate advertising should play in the overall communication mix. This, of course, will depend upon the overall strategic corporate and marketing objectives. But corporate advertising should play a role, and be consistent with the brand message. Dowling (2001) sees corporate advertising as either 'image' or 'issue' oriented. In this traditional view of things, corporate 'image' advertising deals with such issues as communicating with financial markets, employees, creating goodwill, and addressing special interest groups. Corporate 'issue' advertising deals with positioning the company on social or industry issues, and countering adverse publicity. In effect, these traditional views of corporate advertising cover the areas addressed by the academic views of corporate communication, only more generally.

In Dowling's discussion of corporate advertising, he makes a point about its quality, with which we agree (and imagine you may also). He feels that too often corporate advertising is simply 'awful', and invites the reader to have a look through world-wide business magazines like *Review 200, Business Week, The Economist, Forbes*, and *Future* as proof. As he puts it, much corporate advertising is self-important, and both long-winded and dull or short, and vague about what the company does; basically uninteresting and uninspiring. As a result, many managers (especially top management) feel that corporate advertising is always ineffective, whether for companies or brands. There are exceptions, of course, and the Credit Suisse advert shown in Figure 3.8 is a good example. Here the benefit of well-invested money is clearly communicated with the visual, and linked to the brand with copy underscoring the company's expertise (since 1856) and way of approaching business. Strategically well planned and creatively executed advertising can and will be effective. One of the goals of this book is to provide the insight and tools necessary to ensure that happens.

Summary

In this chapter we have looked at the role of IMC in strengthening companies, and specifically *companies as brands*. We saw that this primarily involves a company's identity and image, along with reputation. A distinction was made between companies as organizations versus corporations, where organizational identity and imagery is concerned with internal audiences and corporate identity and imagery with external target audiences. IMC's role is primarily with companies as corporations, not organizations.

Corporate identity has been described as those symbols and words used to identify a company to its target audience, and corporate image as how that target audience 'sees' the company, the beliefs and feelings they have about the company. While on the surface this seems a rather straightforward distinction, much more is involved. Corporate identity includes graphic associations with the company, and also includes how employees see the company (especially important when those employees interact with customers). But from an IMC standpoint, it is a broad range of identities projected by the company that is of interest: active identity, communicated identity, conceived identity, ideal identity, and desired identity. IMC helps mediate all of these various aspects of corporate identity.

Corporate image reflects how a company's target audiences evaluate it in terms of their collective beliefs and feelings (i.e. their attitudes toward the company). As a result, corporate image informs the decisions people make about that company, and is subject to change as new information is processed about the company (from IMC sources as well as other external communications, e.g. press accounts). While a company does not have direct control over its image, in the sense that it cannot literally dictate what people should think about it, clearly effective IMC will mediate that image.

Corporate reputation reflects the values its various target audiences associate with their understanding of its image. In this sense, reputation and image are related, but it is important to consider them separately. One of the jobs of IMC is to ensure that the image of a company is positively associated in people's minds with appropriate values. These values that people hold will act very much like emotions in 'framing' how new information about the company will be received and processed. Corporate identity helps drive corporate image, which in its turn informs corporate reputation.

All of this is part of corporate meaning, and corporate meaning is now drawn together into something thought of as a corporate brand. This idea of creating a corporate brand has been a response to heightened awareness on the part of senior corporate management that such things as how the company is perceived on important social issues can have a direct bearing on brand decisions. This means building a corporate brand equity as well as individual brand equities. It is the job of corporate communication to accomplish all of this, and one way of dealing with it is with what is now known as a sustainable corporate story. IMC provides a way of managing both the strategic development and delivery of all of the company's planned communication: corporate and brand.

■ Review questions

1 What is the role of IMC in strengthening companies as opposed to brands?

2 Discuss the difference between a company's image and its identity. How does this differ from a company's reputation?

3 Identify examples of corporate identity.

4 Find examples of corporate communication that address the company's identity.

5 Discuss the problems associated with establishing corporate image.

6 Identify companies that you feel share your values, and companies that do not.

7 In what ways does a company's reputation have a strategic advantage over its image?

8 What is corporate meaning, and what role does IMC play in it?

9 How is a corporate brand different from a product brand, and in what ways are they alike?

10 Discuss the interrelationships between a company's corporate brand equity and the brand equity of its products.

11 How does corporate communication differ from brand communication?
12 What is the role of IMC in corporate communication?
13 Create a corporate story for a company with which you are familiar.
14 Find examples of good corporate advertising.

References

Balmer, J.M.T. (1998) Corporate identity and the advent of corporate marketing. *Journal of Marketing Management*, 14(8), 963–996.

Balmer, J.M.T. and Gray, E.R. (2003) Corporate identity and corporate communications: creating a competitive advantage. In J.M.T. Balmer and S.A. Greyser (eds.), *Revealing the Corporation*. London: Routledge, pp. 124–136.

Balmer, J.M.T. and Greyser, S.A. (2003) *Revealing the Corporation*. London: Routledge.

Berstein, D. (1984) *Company Image and Reality: A Critique of Corporate Communications*. Eastbourne, UK: Holt, Reinhart and Winston.

Biehal, G.J. and Shenin, D.A. (1998) Managing the brand in a corporate advertising environment. *Journal of Advertising*, 28(2), 99–110.

Brown, T.J. (1998) Corporate associations in marketing: Anecdotes and consequences. *Corporate Reputation Review*, 1(3), 215–233.

Christensen, L.T. and Askegaard, S. (2001) Corporate identity and corporate image revisited: A semiotic perspective. *European Journal of Marketing*, 35(3/4), 292–315.

Christensen, L.T. and Cheney, G. (2000) Self-absorption and self-seduction in the corporate identity game. In M. Schultz, M.J. Hatch, and M.H. Larsen (eds.), *The Expressive Organization*. Oxford: Oxford University Press, pp. 246–270.

Crable, R.E. and Vibbert, S.L. (1983) Mobil's epideictic advocacy: Observations of prometheus-bound. *Communicator Monographs*, 50, 380–394.

Dahler-Larsen, P. (1997) Moral functionality and organizational identity: A perspective on the new 'moralized discourses' in organizations. In M.A. Rahim and R.T. Golembiewsky (eds.), *Current Topics in Management*, Vol. 2. Greenwich, CN: JAI Press, pp. 305–326.

Dowling, G. (2001) *Creating Corporate Reputations*. Oxford: Oxford University Press.

Hatch, M.J. and Schultz, M. (2000) Scaling the tower of babel: Relational differences between identity, image, and culture in organizations. In M. Schultz, M.J. Hatch, and M.H. Larsen (eds.), *The Expressive Organization*. Oxford: Oxford University Press, pp. 11–31.

Hatch, M.J. and Schultz, M. (2001) Are the strategic stars aligned for your corporate brand? *Harvard Business Review*, 1, 129–134.

Keller, K.L. (2000) Building and managing corporate brand equity. In M. Schultz, M.J. Hatch, and M.H. Larsen (eds.), *The Expressive Organization*. Oxford: Oxford University Press, pp. 115–137.

Larsen, M.H. (2000) Managing the corporate story. In M. Schultz, M.J. Hatch, and M.H. Larsen (eds.), *The Expressive Organization*. Oxford: Oxford University Press, pp. 196–207.

Roberts, P.W. and Dowling, G. (1998) The value of enhancing the firm's corporate reputation: How corporate reputation helps attain and sustain superior profitability, working paper, Australian Graduate School of Management, University of New South Wales.

Shaw, G.G. (2000) Planning and communicating using stories. In M. Schultz, M.J. Hatch, and M.H. Larsen (eds.), *The Expressive Organization*. Oxford: Oxford University Press, pp. 182–195.

van Riel, C.B.M. (2000) Corporate communication orchestrated by a sustainable corporate story. In M. Schultz, M.J. Hatch, and M.H. Larsen (eds.), *The Expressive Organization*. Oxford: Oxford University Press, pp. 157–181.

van Riel, C.B.M. (2003) The management of corporate communication. In J.M.T. Balmer and S.A. Greyser (eds.), *Revealing the Corporation*. London: Routledge, pp. 161–170.

Components of IMC

In the first section of this book we look generally at integrated marketing communication (IMC), its definition and a broad introduction. IMC's role in building brands and strengthening companies was discussed. In this section we begin to examine the fundamental building blocks of IMC, the elements that go into building brands and strengthening companies. In Chapters 4 and 5 we shall look at what is meant by traditional advertising and promotion, noting that they represent a fundamental *strategic* difference in communication objective. Marketing communication that is primarily directed towards building brand equity through a strong brand attitude over time is what is trad-itionally understood as advertising. When the primary objective of marketing communication is to generate an immediate brand purchase intention, that is what is traditionally understood as promotion. *All* marketing communication, regardless of how the message is delivered, will be either advertising or promotion, depending upon its primary communication objective.

Advertising tends to be associated in most people's minds with mass media like television, newspapers, and magazines and promotion with print media and direct mail. But there are many, many other ways of delivering an advertising or promotion message. In fact, any contact between a brand and its target audience occurs via media of some kind. In addition to mass media, this would include such things as the so-called 'new media' (vehicles like the Internet and even cell phones), sponsorships, product placement in entertainment programs or movies, even the package itself. Strategic IMC planning must look at every available option for delivering both advertising and promotion messages: and for reaching both a brand's and company's target audience.

While certain media tends to be associated with advertising or promotion, there is no reason to exclude any option that makes sense given the IMC plan; and critically, is compatible with the processing requirements associated with the communication objective (something that will be covered in Chapter 11). In Chapter 6 we shall be looking at a number of alternative ways of delivering an IMC message beyond mass media. Chapter 7 will be looking at direct marketing, because it too is an IMC option for delivering a message (under certain conditions). What makes it different from other alternatives is that it uses a database in identifying and refining target audience selection.

CHAPTER 4

Traditional advertising

With this chapter we begin a section that looks at the various options that are available for delivering a message in an integrated marketing communication (IMC) campaign. But before we discuss the roles these various options may play, and how they might best be utilized within an IMC campaign, it is important to understand a fundamental strategic difference in the messages delivered. This difference involves what is meant by traditional ideas of advertising versus traditional ideas of promotion.

One of the more troublesome issues associated with IMC is the 'role' of advertising and promotion. This has become a problem because of the blurring of the traditional distinction between them, as we saw in Chapter 1. In the past, advertising has been delivered via what was known as 'measured media', so-called because independent services 'measured' the size of the audience for such things as television, radio, newspapers, magazines, and outdoor. But today, advertising messages are delivered through direct marketing and channels marketing (for example through trade-oriented marketing such as co-op programs), areas where in the past one only found promotional messages. And what about the Internet? There you find adverts as well as coupons to print.

The point here is that whether or not something is an advert or a promotion is not a factor of how the message is delivered, but the strategic intent of the message. With advertising, the primary intent is to build brand awareness and brand attitude; with promotion, it is to drive short-term sales or product usage. These are strategic concerns that reflect the desired communication objective for a particular message in an IMC campaign. How that message is delivered will be a factor in terms of an appropriate fit with the communication objective (as we shall see in Chapter 11), and then optimizing a media strategy within an overall IMC plan.

The old way of looking at advertising versus promotion in terms of how they are delivered no longer holds. In fact, what generally has been thought of as advertising skills now play a critical role in all forms of marketing communication, including promotion-like messages (again as pointed out in the first chapter). In the remainder of this chapter we shall begin to look at advertising issues. But as they are discussed, we must remember that these same principles will apply to direct marketing, sponsorship, event marketing, and even with traditional ways of dealing with promotion if an advertising-like message is also being used. In other words, if the primary communication objective is to build brand attitude, this is advertising.

■ The role of advertising in IMC

A good way to understand the role of advertising in IMC is to go back to the Latin root of the word. Daniel Starch (1926), one of the pioneers in advertising theory and measurement, was perhaps the first to use the Latin root of advertising in defining it, back in the 1920s. Advertising's Latin root is *advertere*, which translates roughly as 'to turn towards', and this is the job of advertising. Advertising-like messages in IMC are meant to 'turn' the consumer's mind towards the advertised brand. It does this by raising awareness for the brand among the target audience, and by building positive attitudes towards the brand.

All marketing communication should help build brand awareness and contribute to a positive feeling for the brand. But when this is the primary communication objective, it is specifically advertising. Because brand awareness and brand attitude take time to build, advertising plays a more long-term strategic role in IMC. Over time, effective advertising will successfully seed the brand in memory as satisfying an appropriate need, and will associate the brand with positive attitudes that are linked to positive motivations to buy and use it when that needs occur.

As we discussed in Chapter 2, both brand awareness and brand attitude are important in positioning a brand, so it follows that a critical role for advertising in IMC is to effectively position a brand relative to its competition. We talked generally about how this is done, and will look more specifically at positioning in Chapter 11. We also saw in Chapter 2 that brand attitude is arguably the key component in building and sustaining brand equity. Within an IMC program, it is the advertising-like messages that are critical to the process of building and maintaining a brand's equity.

In summary, advertising's role in IMC is to raise awareness for a brand, linking it to an appropriate category need. At the same time, advertising-like messages will build positive brand associations in memory that lead to a positive attitude towards the brand. As a part of this, advertising will be optimally positioning the brand within its category, uniquely differentiating it from competitors on benefits important to the consumer, and what they believe (or can be persuaded to believe) the brand delivers. This, in its turn, will lead to strong brand equity.

■ Types of advertising

Different authors discuss 'types' of advertising in different ways. Pickton and Broderick (2005), for example, take a narrow, detailed view of what constitutes different types of advertising. For print advertising alone they talk about such things as: full-display advertising, ROP (or run-of-paper), double-page spreads, specially positioned with no other adverts around it, prime positioning, semi-display adverts, classified advertising, and advertorials.

The majority of these distinctions are in terms of the creative freedom involved in the execution, or where the advertising is placed within a newspaper or magazine. Classified adverts and advertorials are distinguished by their content. They also make distinctions as a function of media: for example infomercials being the television equivalent to advertorials in the press, or intermercials being the Internet equivalent to television commercials. In effect, they are illustrating the great variety of ways advertising may be created and delivered. This notion is echoed by many others writing about IMC who talk about different types of advertising in terms of creative tactics: humor, hard sell, testimonial corrective, advocacy, fear appeal, etc.

Rossiter and Bellman (2005), on the other hand, take a much broader view of what constitutes different types of advertising. For them, the main types of advertising are: brand advertising, by which they mean advertising placed in mass media; direct-response advertising; and corporate image advertising and other company-oriented advertising (e.g. sponsorships) that is not advertising specific brands. They are making a primary distinction between a brand focus versus company focus, as well as singling out direct-response advertising, which has as its goal creating immediate positive brand attitude in order to elicit an immediate response to the message.

Our own view is more along the lines of Rossiter and Bellman, looking at a broader classification of advertising. From our perspective, in considering different types of advertising within an IMC framework, it makes sense to look at the task objective for the advertising, the contribution the advertising is making to overall IMC strategy. Fundamentally, we see this as directly related to the type of message and its target audience because the creative approach will be different depending upon the general target audience.

Even though all advertising within an IMC campaign must have a consistent 'look and feel', brand advertising to consumers will generally be different from retail advertising to consumers; adverts for one business advertising to another will look different from corporate image advertising. The approaches are different even when the same people are part of the target audience. Looked at in this way the main types of advertising would include: consumer-oriented brand advertising (COBA), retail advertising, corporate image advertising, and business-to-business (B2B) advertising.

A brand, store, or company will be positioned differently within each of these types of advertising, and the creative executions are likely to differ. In fact, one can usually easily recognize each of these different types of advertising by simply looking at them. These differences are evident in the examples of each type illustrated below. In each case, because it is delivering an advertising-like message, the primary communication objectives are brand awareness and brand attitude. And when different types of advertising are part of an IMC campaign, even though the approach may be different, effective executions will nonetheless have a consistent 'look and feel'. Anyone looking at them will understand them to be advertising from the same company.

In summary, then, we can think of advertising in terms of the following four types (Figure 4.1):

- *COBA*: This is what most people think of when they are thinking about advertising. It is brand focused, seeking to make consumers more aware of a brand, and to form positive attitudes about it, 'turning' the mind of the consumer towards a positive consideration of the

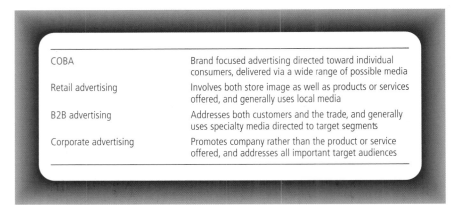

COBA	Brand focused advertising directed toward individual consumers, delivered via a wide range of possible media
Retail advertising	Involves both store image as well as products or services offered, and generally uses local media
B2B advertising	Addresses both customers and the trade, and generally uses specialty media directed to target segments
Corporate advertising	Promotes company rather than the product or service offered, and addresses all important target audiences

Figure 4.1
Four basic types of advertising

brand. The advert for Finn Crisp in Figure 4.2 offers a good example of a typical COBA. It is clearly targeted to a consumer, and provides strong brand identity (the clear package presentation illustrating the correct recognition brand awareness strategy that we shall be discussing later).

- *Retail advertising*: The unique aspect of retail advertising is that it generally involves two brands: the store itself and the products or services it offers. Retail advertising may be 'image' oriented, raising awareness of the store and creating a positive attitude towards the store; or it may be used to raise awareness of the products it sells, nurturing a positive brand attitude for those brands, in order to indirectly enhance awareness and favourable attitudes for the store itself.
- *B2B advertising*: The difference here is that B2B advertising need not specifically address the end-user. B2B advertising may seek to build awareness and positive brand attitudes not only among their customer base, but also among the trade and other aspects of the distribution system with which they deal.
- *Corporate image advertising*: Traditionally, this is advertising that promotes a company itself rather than the products or services it markets. It seeks to positively raise the salience of the company, and create a favourable attitude towards it, among particular target audiences that can range from consumer markets to the financial community to government regulatory agencies (as we discussed in the last chapter).

We shall now take a closer look at these four different types of advertising.

Consumer-oriented brand advertising

The job of COBA is the building and nurturing of brands. In Chapter 2 we discussed the idea of brands and their relationship with IMC in some detail, and pointed out that in many ways, without marketing communication, and especially advertising, there would not be brands. Roderick White (1999) suggests that because advertising is the most intense and

Figure 4.2
A good example of COBA with a clear package presentation for recognition brand awareness. *Courtesy*: FinnCrisp

visible form of marketing communication, it has a key role to play in the successful marketing of a brand. As he puts it 'Advertising cannot turn a sow's ear into a silk purse, but, given a good or – ideally – superior product, it can help to build it into a strong brand'. Or as John Phillip Jones (1999) has put it 'Advertising's greatest single contribution to business is its ability to build brands'.

White (1999) has also suggested that the role of advertising has traditionally been seen as aiding sales, and does it by creating awareness for a brand, providing essential information about the brand, helping to build a relevant brand image, and once the brand is established by reminding the consumer to try, buy, or use the brand. Or as we have put it, the primary communication objective for advertising is to build brand awareness and positive brand attitude.

COBA media

How does COBA reach its target audience? Generally speaking, COBA is placed in mass media, because it can do the best job of creating awareness for a brand. This is especially true for national or international advertisers. Mass media includes such things as television, radio, newspapers, magazines, and outdoor. Of these, the best medium for driving brand awareness will usually be television. And in fact, because of the intrusive nature of television and its ability to sustain attention, as well as the dynamic nature of the medium (e.g. pictures, movement, seen and spoken words, music), it is also the strongest medium for building brand attitude. Only when a complex message is involved, requiring more information to be presented and processed, will television not be the primary medium (e.g. with high-involvement informational advertising, as we shall see later in the chapter). Other mass media, especially print, will of course be part of the IMC plan, but for most COBA, television should be the primary medium. We shall be dealing with all of this in much more detail when we discuss media in Chapters 11 and 12, as well as brand awareness and brand attitude strategies later in this chapter.

Actual media expenditure data supports the fact that television is indeed the dominant medium for COBA (Figure 4.3). In 2004, total expenditures in the US market on television advertising was over US $60 billion, more than the next two largest expenditures combined (radio and newspaper, each about US $20 billion). While print media, especially newspaper and outdoor, play a more significant role in markets outside the US, television is still likely to be the most significant single media. In the UK in 2000, about a third of all COBA spending was in television. The dominant position of television is underscored by a study done in Australia (reported in Rossiter and Bellman, 2005). When asked what media they used, advertisers almost all say they use television, and most say they use radio and print. And when asked which medium they use most, over two-thirds said television, compared with less than a quarter replying newspapers, and only a few magazines, radio, or outdoor (see Figure 4.4).

Medium	Expenditure in US$ (billions)
Broadcast television	43.1
Cable television	18.5
Radio	20.9
Newspaper	20.0
Magazines	11.7
Internet	8.4
Outdoor	4.8

Figure 4.3
Advertising expenditures: USA, 2004. *Source*: Marketing News (2005)

Media	Use (%)	Use most (%)
Broadcast television	92	61
Cable television	38	2
Newspaper	84	21
Magazine	84	5
Radio	79	3
Internet	77	0
Outdoor	61	1

Figure 4.4
Advertisers' use of media: Austria, 2002. *Source*: Adapted from Starcom Worldwide, Media Future Report 2003 as reported in Rossiter and Bellman (2005)

COBA should be the dominant form of marketing communication in any IMC campaign for a *brand*. The primary means of delivering the advertising message in almost all cases should be television because of its unique ability to reach large audiences and sustain attention. Other mass media, as well as other non-traditional means, may also be used where appropriate.

Retail advertising

Retail advertising, as already pointed out, may focus on either the image of the store itself, or on the products or services it offers. But even when the advertising features products or services, it will influence the image of the store. Anything connected with a retail store will be part of how that store is perceived, because those things will be part of the associations in memory linked to it. So, while retail image advertising has a direct effect on building brand attitude for a store, adverts for products it sells will have an indirect effect on attitudes towards the store.

If you were to see advertising for a new women's clothing store and it was featuring very expensive designer labels in the adverts, this will certainly inform your initial attitudes, and your perception of the store's image. You have knowledge and assumptions about such clothing in memory, and this will be associated with this new store as you form initial attitudes about it. On the other hand, if the new store featured mass-market brands of women's sportswear, your initial attitudes will be much different. A retail store's image will clearly be affected by the products it sells.

In every sense, retail advertising is *brand* advertising, whether featuring brands on offer or the store itself as a brand. But it should be pointed out that most retail 'advertising' is not traditional advertising as we are defining it. Most is promotion. In other words, for most of the 'advertising' run by retailers the primary communication objective is immediate brand purchase intention, not building brand attitude for the store. The retailer wants you to come and visit the store. Even though most people, even marketing managers, call this 'advertising', it is important to understand that strategically unless the primary communication objective is brand awareness and brand attitude, it is not advertising. Building positive awareness and attitude is the role traditional advertising performs in IMC.

Some retail advertising may be partially or wholly paid for by the manufacturers of the products advertised. This is called co-op advertising, and it will be covered in Chapter 7.

Retail advertising media

Most retail advertising is local in nature because the target audience for any particular retail store will be drawn from its immediate geographic area. This means media selection will be oriented to local media. However, retailers with stores in many cities or even multinationally (e.g. large franchise operations like Benetton or McDonalds, or large retailers such as H&M) will, of course, utilize media with broader reach. Regardless, the appropriate media device must reflect the advertising's strategic and communication objectives.

At the strategic level, when advertising is dealing with products or services offered by the retailer, newspaper will generally be the primary medium. An important aspect of the appropriateness of newspapers for retail product advertising is that it relies upon the fact that the products advertised also have COBA support. Thus retail adverts are basically reinforcing brand awareness, and alerting the consumer to where the brand may be purchased. Remember that we are talking about retail *advertising* here, not retail promotion where the emphasis will be on price.

When a retailer is advertising their own product or service, the same media appropriate for COBA should be used. This means primarily local television, with print in support. This should also be the choice for store image advertising, again for the same reasons discussed for COBA. In all cases, the media chosen must be appropriate for the specific brand awareness and brand attitude strategies (which are discussed later in the chapter).

B2B advertising

B2B advertising is advertising targeted to those who are part of the decision-making process for purchasing products or services for a company, which may or may not be the end-user. This is especially true for advertising targeted to the trade (e.g. wholesalers or distributors). In such cases, B2B advertising is concerned with maintaining awareness and positive brand attitude for a company's products so that the trade will stock and sell them.

Given the nature of the market for B2B products, the target audience for advertising tends to be much smaller than the target audience for most COBA. Yet while the target audience is likely to be small (relatively), the composition of that target audience tends to be more complex. IMC programs with B2B advertising will be targeted not only in terms of the decision-makers involved, but also targeted to the type of product or service being offered. The first step is to identify target companies, then the right people in those companies involved in the decision process.

For most B2B purchase decisions, there will be more than one person involved in the process. But while many people may be involved, it is important to remember that advertising must be directed to *individuals*; individuals in their role within the decision process. This is the case, of course, for all advertising. But the likelihood of a number of different people playing important yet different roles in the purchase decision process is much greater in B2B marketing.

Consider Rolls Royce jet engines. Their target market is obviously quite small, comprised of only a handful of jet aircraft manufacturers. But within that select market, they must maintain a high-brand salience (when the need for jet aircraft engines arises, they want Rolls Royce to come to mind), and they need to build and nurture a positive brand attitude among all of those in the target companies likely to be involved in the selection of a jet engine supplier. This is likely to be a group decision at the target companies, but the advertising must be strategically targeted to each individual within the role they play in the decision process. There will be technical experts and engineers who help influence the selection; there will be senior management involved; and there may also be outside consultants advising the company. The message to each group must reflect their role, yet be consistent in terms of the overall approach.

IMC plays a key role in keeping images consistent over different messages to different target audiences. While it may make strategic sense to focus upon different benefit sets for each target, requiring different executions, overall the 'look and feel' must be the same, projecting a consistent overall image for the company and brand. This is especially important for something that has been called *dual channel marketing*, where a company sells virtually the same product or service to both consumers and business (Bremans, 1998).

B2B media

Depending upon the size of the target market, the appropriate media for B2B advertising will vary. With very small target markets, traditional media advertising as such may not make much sense, beyond advertising-like messages in brochures or other aids for the sales force. With larger target markets, direct mail targeted to appropriate decision-makers may be used, and depending upon their specific reach, certain trade publications or business magazines will be appropriate.

As with most things, there are exceptions. If a company's target market is potentially very large, mass media would make sense. International carriers such as DHL or UPS, for example, use television advertising because of its broad reach. Their target would include anyone responsible for shipping at any company with shipping needs. Think of advertising you have seen for them. It is addressing individuals in their role as someone responsible for deciding how things are to be shipped.

The influence of the Internet on B2B marketing has been dramatic. Advert-like messages on a company's home page are also an option, as well as other Internet advertising at appropriate sites. There was a significant movement by B2B marketers to Internet advertising in the 1990s, and away from more traditional print media. But now there is a notable return to traditional print media, as well as the use of television (especially on business-oriented programming). This follows a realization that while business decision-makers do go to the Internet for specific, targeted information, there is a need to raise the salience of a company's products *before* they are looking for more targeted information. More traditional media provides this opportunity.

Corporate image advertising

Corporate image advertising is traditionally defined as advertising that promotes a company rather than a specific product or service. The decision to include corporate image advertising as a part of an IMC program in addition to other brand-oriented advertising is an important strategic decision. It is important because it helps in building and sustaining corporate image, identity, and reputation (as discussed in Chapter 3). Overall, it tends to be used more by larger companies than smaller companies.

Many managers feel that corporate image advertising sends an important message to other businesses, reinforcing its reputation within its market. Studies have suggested, for example, that the more a company uses corporate image advertising, the more it is 'admired' among B2B marketers (Clow and Baack, 2004). In the early 1990s, in the US 65% of service companies, 61% of business goods manufacturers, and 41% of consumer goods companies included corporate image advertising as part of their marketing communication program (Schumann et al., 1991).

Because corporate image advertising does not promote any one product or service, some consider it an extension of public relations (PR). But

PR relies upon a company's message being delivered by various media without cost to the company; and with PR a company does not have control over the final message that is delivered. For those reasons, we feel corporate image advertising should be considered as wholly a part of the advertising-like component of IMC, and not as an extension of PR.

In addition to direct corporate image messages, there are two *indirect* ways in which corporate image advertising may be used to help enhance the image and reputation of a company: advocacy advertising and cause-related advertising (Myer, 1999). Corporate advertising that deals with important social, business, or environmental issues is known as *advocacy advertising*. To the extent that the issues addressed are salient and important to a company's target market, and the message succeeds in positively associating the company with that issue, it will help build positive attitudes towards the company. When a company is linked with a charity as part of cause-related marketing, and that link is advertised, it is referred to as *cause-related advertising*. This too can help build positive attitudes towards the company. Research has in fact shown that 80% of consumers report a more favourable attitude towards a company that is seen as supporting a worthy cause (Harvey, 1999).

Corporate image advertising and brand strategy

In Chapter 2 we discussed branding strategy, and talked about stand alone, source, and endorser brands. Rossiter and Percy (1997) have identified four cases that follow from branding strategy, and which will inform the decision to use corporate image advertising. The four cases they discuss are (1) when the corporate name is not apparent on the product or service offered; (2) when the corporate name is used with some brands but not others, such as Nestle's Crunch and Taster's Choice (which is a Nestle brand); (3) where the company always uses the corporate name along with its brand names; and (4) when the corporate name is the brand name.

In the first and last case, a company would be using a stand-alone branding strategy for all of all of its products or services. When the company name is completely separate from its brands, it will be important to include corporate image advertising in an IMC program because it will be the only way advertising can help build awareness and positive attitudes towards the company. When such a company has brands with strong brand equity, corporate image advertising that ties the company to the brands can be a useful tactic. When the company name and brand name are the same, in effect brand advertising is serving as corporate image advertising as well. The stronger a brand's equity, the less necessary it may seem to run separate, specific corporate image advertising. But corporate image advertising goes beyond brand advertising. In order to help build a company's image and reputation beyond an association with well-regarded products, specific corporate image advertising will be necessary. This is a situation when advocacy advertising or cause-related advertising could make sense.

In the two mixed-cases, where either a source or endorser branding strategy is used, corporate image advertising can be used in a number of ways. However, it is important *strategically* to separate the effects of corporate image on branding strategy versus the need to establish a strong corporate image, identity, and reputation. Of course, a strong identity and reputation will carry over to a company's brands; this is a major reason for considering a source or endorser branding strategy. The positive equity in the corporate name, acting as a parent brand, helps to enhance brand awareness and brand attitude. But this positive brand association is *product* based, and does not necessarily work in the other direction, enhancing corporate identity and reputation in the broader sense discussed in Chapter 3.

This means that within an IMC program, the role of corporate image advertising must be seen as separate from that of brand advertising, even when the corporate name is acting as a parent brand.

Corporate image media

We saw with B2B advertising that the choice of media depended upon the size of the target market. In the case of corporate image advertising, the choice of media will vary as a factor of both the size of the company and the size of the target market. With small companies, it is often the case that corporate image advertising, at least on a broader scale, is not affordable. If that is the case, the company's consumer-oriented advertising or B2B advertising should include some component that addresses corporate image. This could be as simple as a tag line in association with the company's logo that reinforces the desired corporate image and identity. But even when broad-reach media is unaffordable, *local* media, especially sponsorships, should be considered. Advertising in local school athletic programs, at community activities, or at cultural events can be an effective way of raising awareness for the company, and linking it positively to community support, which will have a positive effect on corporate image and reputation.

With medium or large companies, appropriate local and mass media should be used. When the target market is small, just as with B2B advertising, direct mail and adverts in business and trade publications should be considered. Companies with larger target markets should consider television, newspaper, and mass circulation magazines. The specific media, as with all market selection, must be consistent with the awareness and attitude communication strategy.

■ Brand awareness and brand attitude strategy

Regardless of the type of advertising, in any marketing communication brand awareness and brand attitude will *always* be a communication objective. A brand will need to stimulate awareness, and to positively contribute to its equity, with every piece of its marketing communication. As a result, brand awareness and brand attitude will always be an important part of IMC planning. We shall briefly introduce these effects now, and will return to them in almost every chapter because of their significance in effective marketing communication.

Brand awareness strategy

If asked, marketing managers are certain to say that awareness of their brand is critical. But how often do you see an advert or promotion, and not noticed who the sponsor was? In fact, it is not unusual to talk about a funny or unique commercial in some detail, yet not be able to identify the advertiser! You are probably thinking of an example or two now. How can this happen?

One of the biggest dangers in creating advertising-like messages is the assumption that the target audience is going to 'get' the message. It is an easy and understandable trap to fall into. When it is your brand and you have spent a great deal of time and energy on an advertising execution, *you* certainly know what the brand is and what you are trying to communicate. Unfortunately, the target audience has not been involved in the creation of the advert; and they do not spend most of their waking hours thinking about the brand.

As a result, simply mentioning the brand name will not guarantee brand awareness. One must carefully think about where and how awareness of the brand will feature in the decision to purchase or use the brand by the target audience. What one is after is to provide the target audience with sufficient detail to identify the brand within the category at the time the decision to purchase or use is made. It may even be that sufficient detail does not require the identification of the brand name as such. Often it is no more than a visual image of the package that a consumer uses to identify a brand.

If one does not 'think aloud' about a specific brand, and simply waits until they see and recognize it at the point-of-purchase, then brand awareness does not require the recall of the brand prior to purchase. Of course, there are many cases when you do need to recall a brand prior to purchase. Understanding these differences in brand awareness is extremely important to IMC planning. Brand *recognition* and brand *recall* are two distinct types of brand awareness, and which one to use depends upon which communication effect occurs first in the mind of the target audience (Figure 4.5). Does a category need occur and one looks for a product or service to meet it, which would be recall brand awareness, or does one see the product in the store and remember the need, which is recognition brand awareness?

Recognition brand awareness

In a number of purchase situations, it is seeing the brand itself in the store and recognizing it that reminds the consumer of the category

Figure 4.5
Brand awareness
strategy

need – Is this something I need or want? What goes on the consumer's mind is:

> Brand Awareness (in terms of recognition) reminds them of Category Need

This brand recognition can be either visual or verbal. In the store, merely seeing the package may key awareness of the brand. On the other hand, especially with telemarketing, *hearing* the brand name may key brand awareness. In either event, it is the recognition of the brand that constitutes the awareness, even though it may actually fail a recall test. As an example, think about how people shop in supermarkets. Market research consistently shows that very few shoppers actually use lists; and those who do will only have category reminders rather than brand names (e.g. bread, detergent, etc.). What happens is that as shoppers move up-and-down the aisles, when scanning the shelves they recognize brands (usually the package) and mentally decide if they need it or not.

What does this tell us about marketing communication? When brand awareness is likely to be based on recognition, one must be sure that the execution includes a strong representation of the brand as it will be confronted at the point-of-purchase. This means large visuals of the package for most packaged goods products (in the advertising, on coupons, etc.), and repetition of the brand name for products likely to be sold or solicited over the telephone.

Recall awareness

In other purchase or usage decision-making situations, the brand is not available as a cue. The consumer first experiences a need, and then must think of potential solutions. In this case the product or service must already be stored in memory. But more than that, it must also be *linked* in the target audience's mind with the category need. Just knowing the brand is not enough. It must become *salient* when the need occurs so that it is recalled from among the many brands someone may be aware of when they are ready to make a decision.

As an example, if you were to read a list of restaurants in your area, you would probably recognize most of them. However, when you decide to go out to eat, only two or three will come to mind, and you will make your selection from one of them. The owner of an Italian restaurant wants people to think of his restaurant when they are in the mood for Italian food. It doesn't help if the target audience is 'aware' of the restaurant when cued (recognition awareness); they must *recall* it when the appropriate need occurs (wanting to eat at an Italian restaurant). What must happen in the consumer's mind is:

Category Need (what is wanted) reminds them of Brand Awareness (recalled)

To achieve this sequence of effects it is important that marketing communication strongly associates the category need with the brand name, and in that order: need–brand. Ideally, this link will be repeated often in order to seed the relationship in the target audience's mind. Creative tactics for both recognition and recall brand awareness will be covered in more detail in Chapter 9.

Brand attitude strategy

The issue of brand attitude is an involved one, and well beyond the scope of this book. Nevertheless, a general understanding is essential for effective IMC planning. We will be taking as our model the Rossiter–Percy Grid (Rossiter and Percy, 1997), which looks at brand attitude strategy for advertising and other marketing communication in terms of two critical dimensions: involvement and motivation, as shown in Figure 4.6.

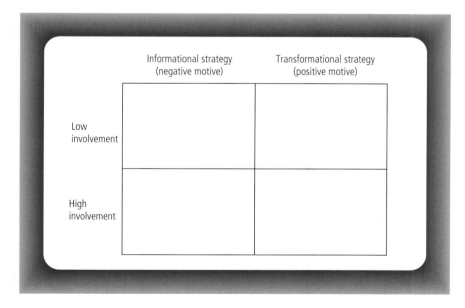

Figure 4.6
Brand attitude strategy: The Rossiter–Percy Grid

Involvement

It is generally acknowledged today that the level of consumer involvement in choosing a product or service will affect the choice, and that this is probably a function of the complexity of the attitudes held towards a particular product or service. Without going into the research that underlies this, we will simply define involvement in terms of the psychological or financial risk perceived by the target audience in the purchase or use of a product. In low involvement situations, trial experience will be sufficient because little or no risk is seen if the outcome is not positive. With high-involvement choices, there definitely will be perceived risk in purchasing or using the product or service.

An important point to remember here is that perceived risk is in the eye of the consumer. It will always be important to 'check the obvious,' and be certain whether there is or is not a perceived risk in the mind of the target audience. It is also good to remember that this perceived risk could vary by situation, even for the same person. For example, the choice of what wine to serve at a routine family meal may entail little risk, but the perceived risk could certainly increase when important guests are dining.

Motivation

Psychologists all seem to agree that everything humans do is driven by a small set of motives. Of course, they all don't agree on exactly what constitutes that set of motives, but in general there is not a great deal of difference. Again to keep things simple, we will be looking at a basic distinction between negative and positive motives. In terms of positive motives, we will want to consider *sensory gratification*, where the purchase is made to enjoy the product, or *social approval*, where the purchase is made in order to achieve personal recognition for buying the brand. There are three basic negative motives to consider: *problem removal* when the purchase is made to solve a problem, *problem avoidance* when the purchase is made to avoid a problem, or *incomplete satisfaction* where one is looking for a better alternative (see Figure 4.7).

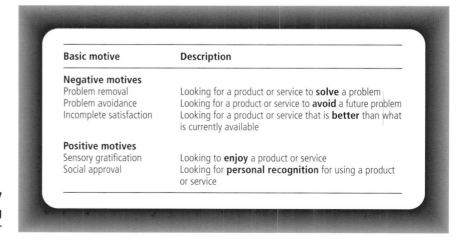

Basic motive	Description
Negative motives	
Problem removal	Looking for a product or service to **solve** a problem
Problem avoidance	Looking for a product or service to **avoid** a future problem
Incomplete satisfaction	Looking for a product or service that is **better** than what is currently available
Positive motives	
Sensory gratification	Looking to **enjoy** a product or service
Social approval	Looking for **personal recognition** for using a product or service

Figure 4.7
Motivations driving purchase behaviour

The important point to understand is that the reason why someone wants something, the motivation, causes attitudes to be formed in the first place. As a result, these motivations 'energize' the purchase or usage decision. In one sense it is like a circle. The consumer is motivated to buy something and choose a particular brand because his or her attitude towards that brand suggests it is the best solution to satisfying that motivation. With purchase and usage, the attitude based on the motive is strengthened with a good experience (or weakened with a bad experience).

To illustrate, if you have a bad headache, you will be motivated to do something about it (the negative motivation of problem–solution). You consider Advil the strongest and fastest working brand of pain reliever (the attitude associated with the motive), and take some. The headache goes away, and the attitude-motive link is strengthened. But motives are specific to attitudes. Continuing our example, if you have a sinus headache, while the general motive remains the same (problem–solution), the attitudes associated with *sinus* headaches may lead to the choice of another brand such as Sinutab.

This example shows not only how attitudes are dependent upon motives, but also how brand choices are linked to motives via attitudes. It also serves as a good example of how the brand awareness link must be carefully established. If your target audience makes a distinction between types of pain (i.e. their attitudes towards pain and hence towards brands), managers must be sure that the link between category need and brand awareness forged in the brand's marketing communication reflects these attitudes.

The Rossiter–Percy Grid

Given these dimensions of involvement and motivation, a 'grid' that reflects the interaction of the two easily follows. In effect, we are saying that if the fundamental criterion involved in choosing a product or service is the amount of perceived risk in the outcome of the decision and whether the need to be satisfied by the choice is negatively or positively motivated, then IMC planning must take into account the combination of involvement and motivation evidenced by the target audience. These strategic quadrants are represented by the 'grid' (as shown in Figure 4.6).

Before going further, we need to point out that the Rossiter–Percy Grid is *not* the same as the so-called FCB advertising planning grid. It too uses involvement (although defined differently), but a second dimension called 'think-feel'. The two should not be confused. Actually, the full Rossiter–Percy Grid also includes an overlay of the brand recognition–brand recall distinction within each quadrant. But even looking at the brand attitude component, there are significant strategic planning advantages to the Rossiter–Percy Grid over the FCB grid (Rossiter et al., 1991).

What are the strategic implications for IMC planning suggested by the four quadrants of the brand attitude grid? Depending upon where a brand's purchase or usage decision lies within the grid, creative tactics will differ significantly. For example, when a decision implies no risk, one does not really need to convince the target audience. All one need do is titillate, or create what Maloney (1962) has called 'curious disbelief'. This opens up the choice of media for delivering the message. On the other hand, with high-involvement decisions one needs to convince. This means more permanent media should be considered (as opposed, say, to a 15 second commercial).

When dealing with negative motives, one has a lot more latitude. Here the basic task is to communicate information that supplies the 'answer' to the need driven by one of the three negative motives. When dealing with positive motives, an 'emotional authenticity' is required in the executions. The target audience must sense that the feelings displayed are real and not contrived. This too will have significance for IMC planning. One of the reasons traditional advertising is generally more effective than other IMC options in building brand attitude is the broader availability of broadcast, especially television, to advertising. Of all the means of delivering marketing communication, television offers the greatest opportunity for eliciting emotional responses, as well as an advantage in portraying a sequence of emotions. All of this means television has built-in advantages when dealing with purchase decisions that are driven by positive motives.

To summarize, the Rossiter–Percy Grid help with IMC planning in the following ways:

1 It helps focus the manager's thinking about a brand in terms of the target audience's involvement with the decision and the motivation that drives their behaviour.
2 When involvement is low and the motivation is negative, a wide variety of options are open because the target audience does not need to be convinced (only interested), and the key is in the information provided.
3 When involvement is high and the motivation is negative, the target audience must be convinced by the message, so the communication options considered must be able to accomplish this.
4 When motives are positive, 'emotional authenticity' is the key to successful communication, whether involvement is high or low, and the communication options considered must be able to deal with this.

Beyond these general strategic implications, there are quite specific tactical considerations associated with each of the quadrants. These will be dealt with in Chapter 9. For the present, it is important to know that the brand attitude quadrants will inform executions for both advertising and promotion.

Summary

In this chapter we have looked at traditional advertising and its role in IMC. The key to understanding this role is the important distinction between advertising-like messages and promotion-like messages. All marketing communication where the primary objective is building brand awareness and positive brand attitude may be thought of as advertising, regardless of how the message is delivered. It differs from promotion in that promotion-like messages, while addressing both awareness and attitudes, has as its primary objective initiating immediate brand purchase intention.

There are four basic types of advertising: COBA, retail advertising, B2B advertising, and corporate advertising. COBA is brand focused and directed towards individual consumers, delivered via any of a broad range of media. Retail advertising involves both the store and the products or services it offers, and is generally local in nature. B2B advertising differs from the other types in addressing not only a customer base but also the trade and other aspects of the distribution system. Corporate advertising promotes the company rather than its products or services, and addresses a wide range of target audiences.

Brand awareness and brand attitude strategy are intimately involved in IMC planning. Brand awareness strategy addresses the important distinction between recognition and recall brand awareness. When the brand choice decision is made at the point-of-purchase, where seeing the brand stimulates a need for the product, a recognition brand awareness strategy is required. When this is the case, to be effective advertising must show the brand as it will be seen at the point-of-purchase. When brand choice follows in response to a need arousal, a recall brand awareness strategy is required. In such cases, advertising executions must link the need to the brand, and in that order, so that when the need occurs the brand will come to mind.

Brand attitude strategy follows from whether the purchase decision is low or high involvement, and driven by negative or positive motivations. These dimensions of choice are important to strategy because the creative tactics needed will differ significantly depending upon involvement and motivation. When involvement is low, it is not necessary to convince the target audience with the message, only to excite curiosity. But when involvement is high, the message must be convincing owing to the perceived risk associated with brand choice. When dealing with negative motivations, the advertising must provide information that will help address the problem posed by the category need involved. If the underlying motivation is positive, the execution must deliver an emotional authenticity that associates an appropriate positive feeling with the brand. The relationship between brand attitude strategy and involvement and motivation is summarized by the Rossiter–Percy Grid.

■ Review questions

1 What is the fundamental difference between advertising and promotion?
2 What is the primary role of advertising in IMC?
3 Why is television the strongest medium for COBA?
4 Why is it important to distinguish between different types of advertising?
5 Find examples of retail adverts that address the store's image and examples that deal with the products they sell.
6 Discuss B2B advertising and how it differs from other types of advertising.

7 How does branding strategy inform corporate image advertising?

8 Why is it important to understand if a purchase decision involves recall versus recognition brand awareness?

9 Why is it important to know if a purchase decision is high versus low involvement and negatively versus positively motivated?

10 Find examples of adverts for each of the four quadrants of the Rossiter–Percy Grid, and discuss why you selected them.

References

Bremans (1998) Marketing in the twilight zone. *Business Horizons*, 41(6 (November/December)), 69–76.

Clow, K.E. and Baack, D. (2004) *Integrated Advertising, Promotion, and Marketing Communication*. Upper Saddle River, NJ: Pearson Prentice Hall, p. 35.

Harvey, M. (1999) When the cause is just. *Journal of Business Strategy*, November/December, 27–31.

Jones, J.P. (1999) *How to Use Advertising to Build Strong Brands*. Thousand Oaks, CA: Sage, p. 2.

Maloney, J.C. (1962) Curiosity versus disbelief in advertising. *Journal of Advertising Research*, 2(2), 2–8.

Marketing News (2005) Fact Book, July 15, 27.

Myer, H. (1999) When the cause is just. *Journal of Business Strategy*, November/December, 27–31.

Pickton, D. and Broderick, A. (2005) *Integrated Marketing Communication*. 2nd edition, Harlow, UK: Prentice Hall.

Rossiter, J.R. and Bellman, S. (2005) *Marketing Communication: Theory and Practice*. French Forest, NSW, Australia: Pearson Prentice Hall.

Rossiter, J.R. and Percy, L. (1997) *Advertising Communication and Promotion Management*. New York: McGraw-Hill.

Rossiter, J.R., Percy, L., and Donovan, R.J. (1991) A better planning grid. *Journal of Advertising Research*, 31(5), 11–21.

Schumann, D.W., Hathcote, J.M., and West, W. (1991) Corporate advertising in America: A review of published studies on use, measurement, and effectiveness. *Journal of Advertising*, 20(3) (September), 38.

Starch, D. (1926) *Principles of Advertising*. Chicago: A.W. Shaw.

White, R. (1999) Brands and advertising. In J.P. Jones (ed.), *How to Use Advertising to Build Strong Brands*. Thousand Oaks, CA: Sage, p. 57.

CHAPTER 5

Traditional promotion

In the last chapter we introduced the fundamental distinction between advertising and promotion, emphasizing their *strategic* character. Advertising-like messages are strategically aimed at building brand awareness and positive brand attitudes, leading to a strong brand equity. This is reflected in the etymology of the word, 'to turn towards'.

Promotion-like messages are strategically aimed at driving short-term sales or brand usage. This too is reflected in the etymology of the word. The Latin root of the word is *promovere*, which roughly translates to 'move ahead'. Even though brand purchase intention is the primary objective of promotion, as with *all* marketing communication, it too must contribute to building brand awareness and brand attitude, something Prentice (1977) long ago referred to as 'Consumer Franchise Building' promotion. This is a point to keep in mind as we discuss specific types of promotion.

When most people think about promotion they are usually thinking about what has traditionally been called 'sales promotion', and specifically some incentive for immediate action. Sales promotion is generally defined along the lines of any direct purchasing incentive, reward, or promise that is offered to the target audience for the purpose of making a specific purchase or taking a specific action that will benefit those responding to the promotion. We will be taking a close look at several basic consumer and trade incentive promotion techniques later that certainly fit this traditional definition. But for integrated marketing communication (IMC) planning, it is necessary to look beyond this traditional understanding of sales promotion.

Rossiter and Percy (1997) introduced an interesting and important consideration in how one should think about promotion: the notion of *time*. Consistent with the importance of understanding how consumers make purchase or usage decisions (which we have already talked briefly about and will cover in more detail later in Chapter 11), they remind us that promotion-like messages should be integrated over time in relation to the target audience's decision process. This suggests that promotion-like messages may be helpful prior to the actual purchase or use of a product or service, if a consumer is looking for information about a brand prior to making a decision, during the actual purchase, or even after purchase.

Promotion-like messages and specific incentive promotional techniques should be considered for each stage in a consumer decision process, but it is not necessary to always include one. Promotion may be inappropriate at any one step, or while appropriate, may not be the best place to spend the brand's budget. If a promotion of some kind makes sense in order to accelerate the decision process, one must then choose a promotion that is appropriate for that stage.

Thinking about promotion in this general way, not as sales promotion but as part of marketing communication to help speed up the decision process whether or not an incentive is involved, it is impossible to consider promotion in isolation. In developing an IMC program, the manager should be thinking about whether promotion-like messages or a particular type of incentive promotion will be an effective *part of the whole* marketing communication effort. As we have been underscoring all along, this is what we mean by IMC – looking at all available communication options and using those which best help effectively and efficiently meet a brand's marketing communication objectives. In Chapter 10 we shall deal specifically with how advertising and promotion should be used together to maximize effective IMC. Now we shall turn our attention to specific incentive promotions. In the following discussions, as we talk about 'promotions' we will be referring to *incentive promotions* unless otherwise noted.

■ Basic types of promotion

Incentive promotions are generally divided into two broad categories: immediate reward promotions and delayed reward promotions. Immediate reward promotions are offers that provide something immediate, such as price reductions, bonus packs, free gifts with a purchase, etc. Delayed reward promotions defer the benefit of the promotion, and usually require the target audience to do something before they receive the benefit of the promotion. These would include such things as sweepstakes, refund offers that require a proof-of-purchase, frequent flyer programs, etc.

As we shall discuss below, different incentive promotions will have particular strengths for either attracting new users to a brand (trial objectives) or for gaining additional business from existing users (repeat purchase objectives). Generally speaking, immediate reward promotions are usually more effective because of their immediacy. This, of course, is consistent with the primary use of promotion-like messages to influence action now. When most people think of promotions they usually are thinking of consumer promotions, but promotions can be directed at the sales force and trade as well. In reality there are at least three major types of promotion that should be considered: consumer, retail, and trade.

Consumer promotion

Consumer promotions are developed by the marketer or its agency and directed towards the target audience in order to accelerate the decision process. Often these promotions are experienced at the retail level. Shelf talkers (messages found attached to a shelf in the store), in-store coupons or bonus packs, special displays, price-off offers, all are promotions received at the point-of-purchase. What makes them different from what could be an identical-looking retail promotion is that it was initiated and delivered by the marketer, not the retailer.

Retail promotion

To the consumer, there is not much of a difference between a retail promotion and a consumer promotion. All they see is a price incentive or special display. In both cases an inducement is offered to accelerate the decision process. But from a planning standpoint, there is a *crucial* difference. Retail promotions are generally independent of the marketer, initiated either by the distributor or the retailer. This often puts retail promotion *outside* the scope of IMC planning. To help bring retail promotion within at least the planning control of the marketer, more companies are turning to something called *tactical marketing*, which we shall discuss in Chapter 7.

The importance of coordinating retail and consumer promotion is underscored by research on consumer perceptions of promotional activity (Krishna et al., 1991). It has been found that consumers are reasonably accurate about sale price and deal frequency. This is significant in light of the general notion in the consumer behaviour literature that consumers tend to plan their brand choices and how much they buy based on when they expect a promotion. If consumers 'sense' when a product or service is likely to be on promotion, they are not making a distinction between a retail and consumer promotion. But, the retail promotion will certainly be a factor in the consumer's purchase or usage plans. If the marketer does not control or at least track these promotions, there is potential for conflict between the promotion objective of the retail store and the marketer. Even if a retailer insists upon control of their promotions, it is essential that managers stay informed about them and do their best to influence the message content and execution.

Trade promotion

Overall, as much as half of all marketing communications spending goes to trade promotion. Generally speaking, a trade promotion is a program of discounts aimed at increasing distribution or some sort of merchandising activity at the retail level. This may include everything from slotting allowances to sales incentives designed to reward individual retail salespeople for meeting specific sales goals. Later we shall look specifically at three basic trade promotion techniques.

■ Promotion to the consumer

As we can see in Figure 5.1, there are six basic types of consumer promotion (whether initiated by the marketer or retailer). These include coupons, sampling, refunds and rebates, loyalty or loading devices, premiums, and sweepstakes, games, and contests. There are, of course, many others. But for our purposes we shall only be considering these six basic techniques. It should be noted that not all types of promotion are permitted in all countries. For example, coupons as such are not permitted in Denmark.

Coupons

There are two types of coupons: brand sponsored (consumer promotion), and distributor or store sponsored and distributed (retail promotion). As

Promotion	Examples
Coupons	Coupon for reduced price delivered via FSI or other print media, also Internet
Sampling	Free distribution of product to home, in-store samples, free trial of product
Refunds and rebates	Automatic rebate on initial purchase price of expensive goods, or mail-in proof of purchase for refund
Loyalty and loading devices	Continuity programs such as frequent flyer or frequent stayer, multiple or bonus packs, price off marked on package
Premiums	Product-associated items such as Pepsi-wear, use of other products as premium with purchase
Sweepstakes, games, and contests	Free products or trips as prizes for mailing participation, entry for chance or prize for accepting product demonstration, 'scratch' cards or bottle caps identifying winners

Figure 5.1
Six basic consumer incentive promotions

mentioned earlier, however, this is *not* a distinction a consumer is likely to make, but one that must be considered in IMC planning. Basically couponing is an effective promotion technique which utilizes a variety of means for discounting the purchase price. Coupons are an excellent way of inducing trial for a new product. There is a danger in using coupons too frequently, however. Over 80% of coupon users stockpile coupons for the same brand, effectively lowering the price for all of their purchases of the brand. A growing trend in the use of coupons is more targeted couponing.

While there are some indications that marketers may be taking a harder look at the cost of using coupons, and that overall coupon distribution levels may have peaked, or even begun to drop slightly (Triplett, 1994), they remain very popular with consumers. In fact, consumers hold more favourable attitudes towards grocery product brands that offer coupons or other price incentives, and that feeling has been increasing. Nearly all households in a US study reported both using coupons at least some time, and feeling they are either very or somewhat helpful (Schlossberg, 1993). In another study, 72% of primary shoppers reported that using coupons as a way to save money on grocery bills, and 55% say they use them to help plan their shopping (Triplett, 1994).

Even though only 2% or 3% of the more-than-300-billion coupons that are distributed each year are ever redeemed, coupons remain an important promotion option. One of the suggested reasons for a possible decline in coupon redemption is a significant shortening of expiration periods in an effort by marketers to control coupon liability.

Traditionally coupons have been distributed via direct mail and newspaper FSIs (free standing inserts) or other print advertising, but today (at least in the US) the vast majority of coupons (86%) are in FSIs (Marketing News, 2003). Occasionally, coupons are included in packages of the couponed or sister brands. But as technology increases in both stores and homes, the use of electronic couponing is becoming more prevalent. Today there are on-line electronic coupon program services where all one need to do is select the coupons wanted and print them out (Stecklow, 2005).

Looking at the relative advantages of the primary delivery media for coupons, FSIs offer quick delivery at about half the cost of direct mail, but relatively no selectivity in reach. Coupons printed in advertising offer some selectivity in target audience, but a generally lower redemption rate. Direct mail offers highly selective and targeted distribution, but relative to other media is more expensive.

Sampling

Sampling is when the target audience is given an opportunity to actually try or use the product directly with little or no cost. It can range from an actual product sample, either in a regular size or a special sample size that has been developed for the promotion, or the use of a product or service for a limited time (e.g. a 30-day trial offer). The objective of sampling is to encourage trial of a product or service among a broader consumer base for an established product or service, or to introduce a new product or service. Because of market and media fragmentation, and the high cost of buying shelf space in stores, sampling has grown in popularity. Products with low trial or a demonstrable product difference are ideal candidates for sampling.

Samples can be delivered in a variety of ways, each with its own particular advantage and disadvantage. For example, sampling in-store or at a central location has the advantage of low-distribution cost, but it is difficult to control who receives the sample. Direct mail offers a very effective way of sampling either a very broadly based target market or a highly targeted market, but there are obvious limits to what one can efficiently sample through the mail. Door-to-door offers the only means of sampling products containing hazardous ingredients, but it tends to be inefficient and expensive. Overall, the most effective way of reaching a broadly based target market with sampling is through direct mail. In-store sampling is less expensive, but offers a more limited reach. Using more traditional advertising media to ask people to call or write for a sample is ideal for low budgets, but again has a very limited reach.

This would be a good place to point out that when a high-involvement product is offered on a trial basis, this is essentially 'sampling'. So if a company or business is given an opportunity to try a product before finalizing an order, this is a sample promotion even if it is not accompanied by a price incentive.

Refunds and rebates

A refund or rebate promotion is an offer that is made by a marketer to refund a certain amount of money, after purchasing a product, on the basis of proof-of-purchase. While most refunds and rebates are made directly to the consumer, they can be passed along by the retailer (e.g. automobile rebates used to lower the initial purchase price). These refunds and rebates can be either a specific amount or a portion of the actual retail value of the purchase, ranging from a certain percentage all the way up to a full refund of the purchase price.

Refunds and rebates are used to encourage purchase or trial of a product, and there are a number of ways of delivering the promotion message: everything from direct mail, FSIs (in newspapers or magazines), and in or on the package. The most common use for refunds or rebates is as a temporary sales stimulus or as a defensive measure to help counteract some competitive activity. Some of the strengths of using refunds or rebates include such things as:

- It effectively reduces the price *without* using the retailer
- It can be especially useful in stimulating interest in high-priced products or services
- There is a high level of non-redemption among those intending to apply for the rebate, reducing overall cost.

On the other hand, the value of refunds or rebates to the consumer is delayed, limiting their appeal. Many people perceive the effort involved as not worth it.

Loyalty and loading devices

Loyalty and loading devices are considered together because the aim of both is to help retain existing customers. Loyalty devices are promotions that are designed to reward a brand's customers for being loyal. They are designed to build repeat purchase for the brand and have the advantage of enabling the manager to develop a strong database of their loyal customers, which in turn can be used to monitor satisfaction over a period of time. We will be discussing databases in Chapter 7, when we talk about direct marketing.

Loading promotions differ in that, they are designed to take consumers out of their normal purchasing pattern by encouraging the purchase of such things as a larger size, a special bonus offer, or multiple packs. The reasons for wanting to do this can range from trying to upgrade the value or revenue of a purchase to a defensive measure against competitive strategy. For example, if a brand knows its major competitor is about to introduce an improved version of their product, a loading promotion will effectively take the brand's customers out of the market, making them less likely to try the competitor's improved product.

Some of the more common ways of implementing loading promotions are with such things as bonus packs, and cents-off and price-packs. *Bonus packs* are a particularly effective technique for moving additional product to the consumer, offering more of the product for the regular price. *Cents-off and price-packs* are an extremely effective and efficient promotion techniques, especially where the opportunity exists to stimulate brand switching, and as a strong defensive move when one is needed quickly.

Continuity programs are the most common loyalty promotion, one that requires the consumer to do something like save stamps, coupons, or proofs-of-purchase over a period of time in order to accumulate enough to qualify for a gift, trip, or a reward of some kind. But perhaps the best-known continuity promotion are frequent flyer programs of major airlines and frequent stayer programs offered by major hotel chains. The objective of continuity programs is to hold onto current users and to encourage occasional users to become more frequent users. A variation on continuity programs are points offered by credit card issuers for the amount charged, redeemable for products or services.

Again, the manager must consider the strengths and weaknesses of the various loyalty building and loading promotions available to them. Bonus packs, for example, while creating an immediate incentive to buy because the 'bonus' is immediate, are unpopular with the trade because they interfere with normal stocking and take up extra shelf space without adding additional profit for the retailer. Cents-off and special price-packs (where the discounted price is specifically marked on the package by the manufacturer) again offer an immediate value at the point-of-purchase, but tend to subsidize regular users more than encourage new trial or switching. Continuity programs do a good job of retaining customers and help build brand loyalty, but they do require long-term commitment both on the part of the target market as well as the marketer, who may find the cost in the long run much greater than expected.

Premiums

There are numerous types of premiums and just as many ways of delivering them. The goal of premiums is to influence consumers to take a specific action, with the premium as a reward. There are a wide variety of premiums one might consider. But it is very important to remember that the premium must appeal to the target audience, and they must perceive a value in the offer.

Additionally, the premium should have an obvious association with the product, and ideally reinforce the image of the brand and reflect its benefit. Premiums may be offered in connection with a one-time purchase or as part of a continuity program. The premium may require a mailed response, or be available at the point-of-purchase. When a premium is part of a package, it has the advantages of attracting attention to the product (usually with the enticement 'FREE!') and the reward is immediate, but it can occasion packaging problems and additional distribution costs. When a premium is available at the time of purchase (but not in or on the package), it too offers an immediate reward to the consumer and permits one to offer larger premiums, but it does require significant retailer support.

Premiums may also be 'self-liquidating.' This is where a premium is made available at a reduced price, usually 30–50% below regular retail prices, enough to cover the out-of-pocket cost of the merchandise for the marketer. While generally a low-cost promotion, and able to selectively target consumers via the type of premium offered, it does require advertising support to generate interest.

Sweepstakes, games, and contests

Sweepstakes, games, and contests offer the consumer a chance to win cash prize, merchandise, or travel in return for using the promoted brand or taking a specific action, such as visiting a dealer for a demonstration. Generally they are used to create interest in a brand or to provide a unifying theme for a group of promotions.

A significant concern with sweepstakes, games, and contests that is less of a problem with other types of consumer promotion is the legal aspects. As an attorney specializing in this area has put it, once you have decided upon your objectives and what type of sweepstakes, game, or contest might satisfy those objectives, the next step is to involve a legal expert (Lans, 1994). While we do not want to get into details (something way outside the scope of this book), perhaps it would be useful to relate some of the advice this attorney offers marketers in order to provide a sense of the potential complications involved.

The most important thing from a legal standpoint is the official rules of the promotion, which are regulated by the government and differ country to country. If a brand runs an annual promotion, even if the manager feels it is basically the same, it is best to check. Even seemingly insignificant changes may mean a new law applies. It is impossible to include a full set of rules on a package or in advertising, but an abbreviated set of the official rules must appear. In fact, marketing communication that includes a consumer sweepstakes should, at a minimum, include the following information: (1) no purchase necessary; (2) void where prohibited; (3) any age and geographic limitations for eligibility; (4) an end date for the sweepstakes; (5) that the sweepstakes is subject to complete official rules; (6) how consumers may obtain a copy of those rules; and (7) the name and address of the sponsor. Clearly, this is an area where expert help is required.

There are real weaknesses when using sweepstakes, games, and contests as a part of an IMC program. They do not require a purchase, the reward is not only usually delayed, but limited to only a small number of participants. But where they do work, they can help reinforce the image of a product or service at a relatively low cost. When well conceived they can also create excitement and interest.

■ Building brand attitude with consumer promotion

As pointed out at the beginning of this chapter, even though brand purchase intention is the primary communication objective for promotion, like all marketing communication, incentive promotion's as well as promotion-like messages must also address brand awareness and brand attitude. A well-conceived promotion will help enhance brand equity by communicating a positive brand attitude consistent with the brand's positioning. To quote Chuck Mittelstadt (1993), long-time consultant to the Interpublic Group of Companies, 'Promotions must be as creative as image advertising, and fully as effective in building brand equity'.

Each of the six basic consumer promotion techniques just reviewed offer opportunities for building positive brand attitude.

Coupons

Coupons are frequently used to introduce a new or improved product, and as such help initiate a positive brand attitude. But to be effective, it should be *tied to the introductory advertising*. This helps channel the good feeling occasioned by being offered a chance to try the new product at a discount with a positive message about the product itself. Even when used as a short-term tactic with established brands, this good feeling will occur *as long as the coupon is not expected*. When a brand regularly uses coupons they are no longer seen as a 'gift' from the company, but merely as the means of sustaining a lower price.

Regardless of whether a coupon is used for a new or established product, it is important to carry over the key benefit claim from the advertising to the coupon itself. If a brand is not currently advertising, the key benefit inherent in the brand's positioning should be conveyed *on the coupons*. This connects the positive reward of the discount with the brand's key benefit claim, reinforcing positive brand attitude. Additionally, this message will be reinforced each time the coupon is reviewed by the consumer, right up until it is surrendered at the store.

Sampling

Sampling is a promotion technique that in-and-of itself should stimulate a positive brand attitude. The consumer is being offered something for nothing (or a significantly reduced price), and especially for new products, this provides an opportunity to quickly establish a positive brand attitude. In one sense a person is already at least somewhat favourably inclined towards the brand or they would not accept and use the sample. But the sample itself will help nurture that initial positive attitude. The packaging and representation of the sample also offers an opportunity for building positive brand attitude.

Refunds and rebates

Refund and rebate offers made through traditional advertising media have a built-in opportunity of integrating the promotion and advertising message. Also, any offer that requires clipping something for mail-in provides a means of delivering the key benefit claim on the refund certificate itself. The offer should be worded in a positive way, linked to the brand, and importantly, *unique*. Too often there is very little imagination used in a refund or rebate offer. Most automotive rebate offers, for example, usually say nothing more than something like: 'Get 1,000 euros back!' It is important to avoid the impression that the offer is just another price-off deal.

Loyalty and loading devices

Like sampling, most loyalty and loading devices automatically effect brand attitude – or should. Loading devices such as bonus packs and cents-off or price-packs do *not* automatically contribute to an increase in positive brand attitude, and when misused (e.g. when offered too frequently) can have a *negative* effect on brand equity. How? If a brand has a premium image yet is often seen in price-packs, it will assume a lower-price image. Even a regular-priced brand can suffer from too frequent use of reduced price-packs. This is, of course, true of *any* price promotion if it is used too often, but especially with loading devices because the lower price is visually reinforced on the package.

Bonus packs offer a better opportunity, especially when the 'bonus' is offered by way of a larger package. This offers an opportunity on the package label to reinforce brand attitude, which coupled with the positive reward of the 'bonus,' should nurture or increase positive brand attitude. If multiple unit packaging is used, while the wrapper does offer some opportunity for a reinforcing brand attitude message, it will be discarded with use. Consideration should be given to a special package as well so the initial favourable attitude stimulated by the multiple bonus pack at the point-of-purchase will be reinforced each time the consumer uses the product.

Loyalty or continuity programs build positive brand attitude, and hence brand equity, in a different fashion. By their very nature, such programs require product use over time before rewards are forthcoming. This provides a good opportunity for reminding the consumer of the coming reward within a positive brand attitude message, either on the package, through advertising, or direct mail. On the other hand, if the requirements for earning a reward are seen as too difficult, or if the rules change over time, this can have serious negative consequences for brand equity. From the mid-1990s, airline frequent flyer programs have found themselves in just such a bind. Not only are reward levels increasingly more difficult to reach, but it also became more and more difficult to actually use frequent flyer miles for free flights because of high demand for seats. As a result, participants feel trapped in a program and cheated by the airlines, seriously affecting the brand equity of the airlines among their most loyal customers.

A good example of this problem is illustrated by recent changes in Delta Airline's frequent flyer program for their most frequent flyers. For many years, if one flew over 100,000 miles on Delta in a year you earned 'Platinum Medallion' status. Among other things, this enabled Platinum flyers to upgrade to first class when booking any flight within the US as long as one was available when the reservation was made. This was true even if the flight was booked at a low, discount fare. Then in the early 2000s, the policy was changed, and automatic upgrades at the time of booking were restricted to non-discounted fares.

While that was certainly fair, Delta then changed the program again so that Platinum flyers could only secure an upgrade if one was available five days before a flight; and only if one of a very few seats set aside for that purpose was open. As a result, fewer and fewer Platinum flyers, their most valued customers, were able to secure upgrades to first class. Then, they made things worse by redefining the number of miles needed to reach the Platinum level *down* to 75,000. While this may have had an initially positive effect on brand attitude for those now becoming Platinum flyers, it would be short lived.

All this did was make it even more difficult to secure an upgrade. Those very frequent flyers who travel over 100,000 miles a year saw their already reduced chance for an upgrade reduced even more; and the 'new' Platinum flyers quickly learned that they were not much more likely to secure an upgrade than before. There can be no question that this had a significantly *negative* effect on brand attitude for Delta among their most valued customers. Rather than 'rewarding' them, they in effect took away the primary benefit they enjoyed.

Premiums

Ideally a premium is chosen to reinforce the choice of the original product or service, appealing to the same motivation as the product or service. For positively motivated brand choices this means reinforcing the emotional response to the brand. When a brand decision is motivated by social approval, almost anything that will be seen by others and carries the brand's logo will help reinforce user brand attitude because it announces to the world the user's brand choice. Everything from jackets or other apparel with the brand's logo to things like insulated holders for beer cans might be used, but it is important that the premium too is consistent with the image projected by the brand.

Negatively motivated brand decisions call for premiums that are more directly related to the product or service offering the premium. For example, special folders for storing insurance policies or sun visors with a sunscreen provide positive, long-running association with the brand. As with positively motivated products, these premiums also should include the company logo or brand name. In this case it is to remind the user of the brand, not necessarily be noticed by others.

Selecting premiums congruent with motivation ensures positive brand attitude and the nurturing of brand equity. The most common mistake marketers make in selecting premiums is not relating it to the brand itself in a meaningful way, and not making certain it appeals to the same motivation that drives choice of the brand. But the *biggest mistake* a marketer can make is to offer a premium that is either inappropriate or unappealing to the target market. This may lead to negative attitudes towards the brand and a weakening of the brand's equity.

Sweepstakes, games, and contests

One of the more subtle benefits of a sweepstakes or contest promotion is that by its very nature it attracts people to the advertising or other sources used to announce the promotion. This is itself a good opportunity of associating the promotion with a strong brand attitude message. Beyond this, the sweepstakes, games, or contests themselves should be created around the brand's perceived benefit. The stronger the link between the motivation associated with the brand decision and the promotion, the more likely it will be reinforcing a positive brand attitude and corresponding brand equity.

For example, consider Mars' Bounty Bar. Bounty's positioning for many years has been based on the general theme of a tropical setting and 'a taste of paradise'. If they were to consider a sweepstake or contest where the prize was to be a holiday trip, what destination should the manager consider? The prize should be consistent with, and reinforce, the brand's positioning and benefit claim. That means offering as a prize a trip to somewhere like Tahiti or some other tropical 'paradise', *not* a skiing trip in the Alps.

■ Trial versus repeat purchase objective for promotion

While any type of promotion might be used to generate either new trial for a brand or to encourage more purchases from existing customers, certain promotions tend to be better suited for one objective versus the other. Those promotion types most appropriate for a trial objective are coupons, sampling, and refunds or rebates; those most appropriate for a repeat purchase objective are loyalty and loading devices, and sweepstakes, games, and contests.

Depending upon how they are used, premiums have strength for both trial and repeat purchase objectives. Offering an appropriate premium can have a strong attraction for consumers who regularly switch among brands within a category, providing an incentive to add an additional brand to the set they already purchase. On the other hand with current brand users, especially when dealing with products that have a very long purchase cycle (e.g. home appliances or computers), an attractive promotion could help initiate an earlier consideration of replacing an older product.

Before we review some of the situations where different incentive promotions might be effective, it would be well to point out that since promotions are generally used in a tactical sense to accelerate brand purchase intention, there are many, many unique ways such promotions might be applied. All we are attempting to do here is outline some of the conditions where a particular type of consumer promotion might be applicable. This should help further distinguish the particular strengths of the various types of basic consumer promotion.

Trial objective for promotion

While coupons, sampling, and refunds and rebates are especially effective in generating trial, this is not to say they are ineffective as repeat purchase promotions. Strategically, however, when trial is the objective, these three promotions should be considered. Of the three, sampling is probably the *most effective* promotion for generating trial, followed closely by coupons. Refunds and rebates, because they are less immediate, are somewhat less effective. But, they are perhaps the best means of accelerating trial of expensive products or services. They are also very useful in defending against strong competitors when the purchase cycle for the category is long.

Sampling is particularly effective where category or brand trial is low, especially if a brand has a demonstrable difference that will be readily apparent with use. It is also a good way of beating the competition to the punch when a new category is being introduced. As potential users consider a new category, sampling helps 'push' them into action, and with the sample brand. Sampling is also an effective technique when advertising may not be able to adequately demonstrate a brand's advantage. Is a hand lotion really less messy? Is the crust really crispier? Does someone really feel relief faster? If using a brand will easily and quickly demonstrate a positive benefit, sampling can be an effective way of making the brand's benefit claims believable.

While couponing is less effective than sampling in generating trial, it has the advantage of being much less expensive. The introduction of a new product or service is an ideal time to use coupons in stimulating trial, or when wanting to attract new users to the brand. The problem here, of course, is that current users will use the coupon as well. Figure 5.2 reviews favourable situations for trial promotions.

Repeat purchase objective for promotion

Strategic application of repeat purchase promotion tends to address more short-term issues than trial promotions do. Trial promotions are meant to bring in new customers for the long-term health of the brand. Repeat purchase promotions are generally used to alter the timing of a purchase, capturing users in the short-term to take them out of the market, or to accelerate purchase for some other tactical reason.

Promotion	Favourable situations
Coupons	• When brand has small budget • New product introductions
Sampling	• When brand has low trial but a demonstrable positive difference • When advertising cannot adequately demonstrate a brand's benefit
Refunds and rebates	• Incentive for trying expensive products or services • Defensive tactic against strong competition

Figure 5.2
Favourable
situations for trial
promotions

Of the repeat purchase promotions discussed, loyalty or continuity programs are the ones most directly aimed at creating and maintaining brand loyalty. The others are aimed at people who tend to switch among various brands, with the intention of attracting them to the promoted brand on their next category purchase. Again, if the promotion is well executed with building a more positive attitude in mind, the result will bring more frequent switching to the brand, resulting in more frequent usage.

All usage promotions, but especially premiums, can be conceived in a manner that targets particular segments of a market. The appeal of the premium can easily be matched to particular audiences, as can the prizes in sweepstakes, games, and contests. Both premiums and sweepstakes, games, and contests also have the potential of generating in-store merchandising activity such as point-of-purchase display, banners, special displays, etc. This has the advantage of both drawing switchers' attention to the brand as well as the opportunity of reinforcing key benefit claims. Sweepstakes, games, and contests also present a good way of providing a unifying theme for an IMC campaign.

Loyalty programs, and especially loading devices, are a good way of defending against competitor activity by removing people from the market. Loyalty programs help hold current brand loyal customers and retain switchers by building repeat purchase or use. Loading devices such as price-packs and bonus packs help attract switchers to a brand, and retard switching out to other brands. However, this can only be seen as a short-term, tactical application. For example, if a competitor is about to launch a new brand or otherwise challenge a brand, a bonus pack will temporarily disrupt the introduction by reducing category demand.

Repeat purchase promotions can be very effective, but one must guard against using them in a predictable or ongoing way (with the exception of loyalty programs, of course). They are meant to stimulate short-term usage, but the actual reward can only be a transition or aid to a more positive brand attitude. As with all promotions, they should contribute to long-term growth. Figure 5.3 reviews favourable situations for repeat purchase promotions.

Promotion	Favorable situations
Loyalty and loading devices	• To defend against switching • When a new competitor is about to enter the market
Premiums	• Capitalize on selective appeal • Encourages point-of-purchase display
Sweepstakes, games, and contests	• Provides unifying theme for a group of promotions • Reinforces brand's positioning and advertising • To gain in-store merchandising activity

Figure 5.3
Favourable situations for repeat purchase promotions

■ Promotion to the trade and retailer

We noted earlier that spending in trade promotion accounts for about half of all marketing communication expenditure, about twice that spent on consumer promotion. This trend is a function of many things, including a growing understanding by the trade of their power in the marketing mix. But perhaps the key reason has been the short-run emphasis of too many marketers attempting to use promotion to 'buy share' in order to satisfy immediate sales goals.

We cannot emphasize enough that this is *not* the way to deal with trade promotion. It is certainly true that without good distribution consumers do not have an opportunity to purchase. But it must be remembered that the brand's goals and the goals of the trade are not always the same. The trade makes its money from *category* sales. They are indifferent to what brands sell as long as their margins for the category are sustained. The brand, of course, is only interested in its own sales. So, while trade promotion must be seen as a cost of doing business, *strategically* it must be considered within overall IMC planning. This means integrating trade promotion with consumer promotion and advertising.

Figure 5.4 details a number of trade promotions. As already mentioned, trade promotions are usually a short-term incentive or deal that is offered to retailers or some other key participant in the distribution channel to stimulate stocking an item or to feature and/or promote a brand. These promotions depend entirely on trade cooperation for any sales increase.

Success for any brand depends upon trade or dealer support. The purpose of trade promotions is to in some fashion improve relations with the trade in order to gain and hold new distribution, build trade inventories

Promotion	Examples
Allowance	• Performance allowance • Trade coupon • Free product • Slotting fees
Display material	• Point-of-purchase • Special display
Trade premiums	• Dealer loaders • Sales goal incentives

Figure 5.4
Basic trade incentive
promotions

or to obtain trade merchandising support. There are three principal classifications of trade-oriented promotions:

● allowance promotions
● display material promotions
● trade premiums and incentives

Allowance promotions offer the trade something in return for purchasing or promoting a specific quantity of a brand, or for meeting specific buying or performance requirements. *Display material promotions* provide the trade or dealer with special in-store display material to use in featuring the promoted brand, often in conjunction with a trade allowance promotion. *Trade premiums and incentives* are promotions which offer the trade a free gift or a chance for an even higher-value prize in return for purchasing specific quantities of goods or meeting certain specified requirements.

There are both trial and repeat purchase trade promotions, just as with consumer promotion. Trial trade promotions are largely designed to gain an acceptance of a new product, or to encourage carrying an existing one. Repeat purchase trade promotions are used to ensure a product is stocked, as well as to get favourable shelf space. Various allowances are obvious usage promotions. Actually, all three types of trade promotion have application as repeat purchase promotion.

Before discussing the three basic types of trade promotion, we need to address slotting fees because they are likely to come out of the trade promotion budget. Slotting fees act like a trial promotion in that they are needed to secure distribution for a brand, but they are really now simply a cost of doing business. While one can understand that with an ever increasing demand to handle new products and line extensions, and their high-failure rate, the trade is demanding some help in order to deal with the overhead, the high fees charged are nonetheless worrisome. It has been estimated that as much as 70% of slotting allowances go directly to the retailer bottom line rather than to defraying costs.

Allowances

Allowances to the trade can take many forms, everything from direct price reductions on invoices to free goods. We have just mentioned slotting fees, and their virtual necessity for achieving distribution, especially for consumer packaged goods. As such fees increase, it makes it more and more difficult for those with small marketing budgets to compete.

A general weakness of most trade promotional allowances is that there is no guarantee that any significant portion of the money will find its way to the consumer, either through increased merchandising activity or lower prices. This is true of buying allowances, performance allowances, and even free goods. As a result, while it is very important that trade and consumer support be integrated, a manager must consider any consumer benefit a plus. Rather, trade allowances should be used for tactical purposes with the trade. For example, buying allowances and free goods help build inventories in support of consumer marketing programs (both promotion and advertising). Performance allowances, at least in part, will go to merchandising or retail advertising in support of the brand.

Trade coupons are actually coupons for the consumer, but distributed by the retailer rather than the marketer. They differ from retail promotions in that trade coupons are *controlled* by the marketer, not the retailer. Usually, the retailer pays for distributing the coupon in their advertising or other marketing communication and then is reimbursed by the marketer after the promotion. Because consumer promotions with coupons are keyed to trial, the same is true for trade coupons. Only in this case, it is not *trial* by the trade but by the consumer. Actually, it is a *repeat purchase* promotion for the trade, in the same sense as the other allowances we have discussed.

This is an important point for IMC planning. Retailers as a rulelike trade coupons because they help extend their own marketing communication budget. In this sense trade coupons can help secure trade cooperation within an IMC program. That is step one. But step two is the consumer response to the coupons. This must be considered in light of everything discussed about coupons as a consumer trial promotion.

Display material

Display allowances or material are usually used to generate special in-store merchandising activity for a new product or brand extension, but they are also used to stimulate trade support for consumer promotions. The importance of in-store merchandising is underscored by the fact that more than 70% of brand choices are made in-store (Advertising Age, 1995).

Basically, point-of-purchase refers to all those things that are used at the point of sale in order to attract the attention of the customer to the brand. The objective of point-of-purchase material is to draw attention to a particular brand or product on the shelf or wherever it may be displayed, or to provide information. It should encourage consumers to make an impulse purchase or trial decision, or to learn more about the item being featured. Sometimes it can even guide consumers to other areas of the store for cross-merchandising opportunities. Well designed point-of-purchase frequently acts as a trigger mechanism to remind the consumer of a brand's advertising.

One of the more interesting applications of point-of-purchase is interactive computer driven displays. The consumer interacts with a computer displayed within the point-of-purchase unit in order to gain information about a product or service. Through the computer the consumer can request a catalogue, ask questions, receive data in print-out form, and much more. Interactive point-of-purchase is used at automobile dealerships to provide consumers with information about specific models, in retail stores to access store catalogues, and they are even being introduced in fast food chains to place orders. The most common application, however, is where a high ticket, high margin purchase is involved, or where a purchasing decision process is more complex.

One of the advantages of using display materials as a trade promotion is that it encourages the trade to actually promote a brand in the store, because the incentive to the retailer is only available upon proof of compliance. It can also usually be quickly implemented, making it a useful tactical tool. The disadvantage is that it does require wide spread trade acceptance to be effective, and often must conform to various store guidelines for in-store merchandising.

Trade premiums and incentives

These last trade promotions centre more upon individual stores or personnel, and as a result are popular with the trade. Premiums offered to the trade are usually in the form of *dealer loaders*. Their goal is much the same as for consumer loading devices: to 'load up' the store or distributor with product. This is done with a product display where a premium is offered to the consumer, usually as part of the display. For example, a cooler might be offered at a very low price with the purchase of a 12-pack soft drink brand.

Incentives are offered to various levels of the trade, and for any number of reasons. Awards or gifts might be offered to individual counter or sales staff at retail for reaching a set level of sales for a brand, to a manager for store sales of a brand, or to staff for devising new or innovative ways of promoting a brand. Incentive programs are an especially good idea for new product introduction or for slow-moving products, and they have the advantage of being quick and easy to implement, as well as relatively inexpensive.

The problem with all trade premium and incentive promotions, however, is that many mass merchandisers do not allow them, or have rules that tightly restrict the type of programs acceptable.

■ Incentive promotion cost

Unlike advertising where the cost is fixed, at least in the sense of knowing what it will cost to produce and place the advertising, the cost of incentive promotions is *variable*. The eventual cost of a promotion will be directly related to the number of people responding to it. This will be true with trade and retail promotion as well as consumer promotion. For example, if a manager is expecting a normal 2% redemption on a coupon drop but experiences a 10% redemption, the cost of the promotion will have increased four to five times!

This will obviously have severe consequences for the brand's marketing budget. In such circumstances, it is rare that the additional business generated will be enough to cover lost revenue from otherwise-full-price purchases. The working margins for the brand will have been significantly lowered. With the surprise increase in cost from a too successful promotion, money will need to be found from other parts of the brand's budget, disrupting the IMC plan.

Managers must carefully consider the likely cost of a promotion, thinking through all of the possible consequences of a too successful promotion. Another 'cost' of a too successful promotion, for example, could be bad publicity following from an inability to meet demand for premium merchandise. Unless there is a prior history of a specific promotion's performance, research should be conducted to test its likely performance.

Summary

In this chapter we have looked at traditional promotion and its role in IMC, with special attention to incentive promotions. The primary communication objective for promotions is to stimulate immediate brand purchase intention. In terms of IMC strategy, promotion is used as a short-term tactic, and should not be used as an ongoing program that effectively lowers the price of the brand. The use of promotion should be carefully integrated over time in relation to the target audiences' decision process. And like marketing communication, promotion too must address brand awareness and brand attitude.

There are three basic types of promotion: consumer, retail, and trade. Consumer promotion and retail promotion are aimed directly at consumers. While it is important from an IMC planning standpoint to discriminate between consumer promotion initiated by the manufacturer versus the retailer, from the consumer standpoint there is no difference. Trade promotions provide incentives or merchandising activity for the trade, and make it the largest proportion of most brand's marketing budget.

Incentive promotions to the consumer, whether initiated by the manufacturer or retailer, fall into six basic types: coupons, samples, refunds or rebates, loyalty programs and loading devices, premiums, and sweepstakes, games, and contests. Coupons, samples, and refunds or rebates are used primarily to generate trial, while loyalty programs and loading devices and sweepstakes, games, and contests are used for stimulating repeat purchase. Premiums may be used for either trial or repeat purchase objectives.

Coupons make sense when the brand has a small budget, and for new product introductions. Sampling is a good promotion technique when a brand has a demonstratable difference, or when advertising cannot adequately demonstrate the brand's benefit. Refunds and rebates are effective for expensive products or services, and can be a good defensive tactic against a strong competitor. Loyalty programs are used to defend against switching and loading devices when a new competitor is about to enter the market. Premiums provide an opportunity for selected appeal, and can also encourage retailers to use point-of-purchase displays. Sweepstakes, games, and contests can provide a unifying theme for all promotional activity, and a chance to reinforce a brand's positioning in advertising. It also provides an opportunity for in-store merchandising activity.

Most consumer incentive promotion techniques will find their counterpart in promotion to the trade and retail. Basically these promotions fall into three categories. Allowance promotions, which include trade coupons, free product, and allowances for meeting performance goals. While not exactly a promotion, one must also consider slotting fees here. The second group includes various promotional display material, and the third category, trade premiums and incentives.

Finally, it must be remembered that there are costs associated with promotion, and when a promotion is too successful, the unexpected increased costs can have a significantly negative effect on the marketing budget.

■ Review questions

1 How would you describe promotion?
2 What is the role of promotion in IMC?
3 How do retail promotions differ from consumer promotions?
4 What are the similarities between trade promotion and consumer promotion?
5 Why are some incentive promotions more appropriate for gaining trial and others for repeat purchase?
6 When would you be likely to use a coupon rather than a rebate; and when a rebate rather than a coupon?
7 Discuss situations where it would be effective to use loading devices.
8 How can promotion be used to help build positive brand attitude?
9 What might be a good premium for a beer brand? What about for a major appliance; a tanning salon; a restaurant?
10 Why can a too successful promotion be harmful for a brand?

References

Advertising Age (1995) Report on a study of consumer buying habits, 20 October.

Krishna, A., Currin, I.S., and Shoemaker, R.W. (1991) Consumer perceptions of promotional activity. *Journal of Marketing*, 55, 4–16.

Lans, M.S. (1994) Legal hurdles being part of promotion game. *Marketing News*, 24 October, 15.

Marketing News (2003) NCH Marketing Services. *Inc. figures for 2002 with US*, 26 May, 3.

Mittelstadt, C.A. (1993). The coming era of image-building promotions, lecture given at Yale University, 3 March.

Prentice, R.M. (1971) How to split your marketing funds between advertising and promotion. *Advertising Age*, 10 January, 41.

Rossiter, J.R. and Percy, L. (1997) *Advertising Communication and Promotion Management*. New York: McGraw-Hill.

Schlossberg, H. (1993) Coupons likely to remain popular. *Marketing News*, 29 March, 1.

Stecklow, S. (2005) Obsessive coupon disorder. *Wall Street Journal*, 19–20 November, 5.

Triplett, T. (1994) Report of couponing's death has been greatly exaggerated. *Marketing News*, 10 October, 1.

CHAPTER 6

New media and other IMC options

Advertising and promotion define the two components of marketing communication, regardless of the medium used to deliver the message. Advertising-like messages are designed to 'turn' the target audience is toward the brand, building brand awareness and positive brand attitude, and promotion-like messages aim to 'move ahead' the brand by stimulating an immediate brand purchase intention.

In our discussion of advertising and promotion in the last two chapters we talked about each in terms of the traditional mass media generally associated with them. In this chapter we turn to some of the other ways in which advertising-like messages and promotion-like messages can reach their target audience. This will include the so-called 'new media' as well as other more non-traditional media, personal selling, and public relations.

In November of 2005, the *Wall Street Journal* reported on ten trends they felt were reshaping the advertising industry (Vrancia, 2005). The first is mobile marketing, which we shall address later, where adverts as text messages are sent directly to individual cell phones. Elaborate online campaigns now marry brand pitches with high-tech entertainment. For example, they describe a scenario where someone opens an e-mail that presents a fictional newspaper with a headline reading: 'Another slaying at Datadyne HQ'. There is a link that sends you to a video of an autopsy, and the camera pans down to a tag on the toe of the body with the person's name. A video game from Microsoft's Xbox is then advertised, with an invitation to send the link to a friend. If the link is forwarded, the person's phone rings and a recorded message from the video game's heroine announces, 'The job is done'. An e-mail then arrives from the heroine with a picture of another dead body, but with their friends name on the toe tag.

Product placements are now finding their way into the plots of entertainment programming. Innovative ways are being used to involve consumers in games or contests. Packaging and design are becoming more important. Adverts are now appearing in videogames. Spending on video game advertising was expected to grow from US $100 million in 2004 to more than US $500 million by 2007 (Interactive Advertising Bureau, 2004). Niche marketing is being directed to specific cultures and beliefs, with one executive of a firm that deals with predicting trends suggesting that 'the culture is the new media' (Vrancia, 2005).

New ways that are targeting consumers will permit customizing advertising, if not to individuals, at least to some common household denominator. Advertising is incorporating innovative new ways of delivering adverts, everything from single-advertiser issues of magazines to adverts with microchips embedded in them allowing for sound. And finally, as a result of all the changes in media, companies are looking outside of traditional marketing communication agencies, working with more groups, and giving assignments to smaller firms. This, of course, makes integrated marketing communication (IMC) even more important for effective communication of a brand's message; and, unfortunately, more difficult (Figure 6.1).

It is interesting to note that most of these trends in advertising involved non-traditional media; and those that do involve using more traditional media do so in very unique ways.

1. Sponsoring content and sending text messages directly to cellphones
2. Elaborate interactive e-mails integrating advertising-like messages and high-tech entertainment
3. Weaving product placement into plots of entertainment programming
4. Engaging consumers in games or contests
5. Attention to importance of product and package design, even for low- and mid-priced brands
6. Advertising in video games
7. Marketing to a specific culture and its beliefs
8. Better targeting: 'addressability'
9. Innovative ways of presenting advertising in print
10. Using more specialized agencies

Figure 6.1
Advertising industry
trends. *Source*:
Adapted from the
Wall Street Journal,
21 November, 2005

■ New media

There is no question that technology is changing the way in which people live. Inevitably this means new opportunities for marketing communication and how it might be used in an IMC campaign. As this section is being written, the world of Internet advertising has moved well beyond banner adverts; and mobile marketing has begun to make an impact. As you read this, things may have moved well beyond what we are about to discuss; just as what we are talking about here would not have been a part of a textbook written just 5 years ago.

Nevertheless, the really important point to bear in mind is that while 'new media' will continue to evolve and new means of delivering messages will be introduced, those messages will still be made up of text, audio, and visuals. Media changes, but how the mind processes the message remains the same. The strategic planning process remains the same. New media is only that; new ways of delivering a message to a brand's target audience that may or may not make sense as part of the brand's IMC program.

Internet

Global spending for advertising on the Internet was around US $18 billion in 2005, up over 28% from the previous year. This compared with around US $147 billion for television advertising, up about 4% (*Wall Street Journal*, 28 August 2006). Estimates are that online expenditures could grow to US $150 billion by the year 2015 (Guth, 2005b). Much of this growth is expected to come from web video adverts. While currently accounting for only a small proportion of web-adverts (around 2% in 2005), it is expected to grow significantly over the decade.

Yet, while Internet advertising shows strong growth, overall advertising spending has not experienced much growth over the same. If budgets experience the kind of cuts seen in the late 1990s and early 2000s, online advertising is likely to get hit just as hard as more traditional advertising (Guth, 2005a). Another potential roadblock to growth is the dislike of pop-up adverts. Users dislike pop-up adverts more than any other format, yet it is also the fastest-growing type of online advertising (Oser, 2004).

Despite the fact that the Internet is huge, the top 50 web companies account for nearly all Internet advertising spending, with most going to Yahoo, Google, AOL, and MSN. Like other media, this is largely a function of size, and the number of visitors they deliver. Daily user visits in 2005 ranged from 2.9 million at Google to 4.0 million a Yahoo (Angwin and Delaner, 2005). Google is testing the idea of offering diversified advertising, which would put them in direct competition with newspapers and online classified listing services. They now automatically scan the e-mail of their Gmail users (a free service Google offers), making money by charging advertisers each time a user clicks on their advert. Advertisers bid against each other in an online auction to have their adverts appear when a certain word appears in a search query.

Widgets, which are small computer programs that allow people to incorporate professional-looking content into their personal web pages on desktop computers, are seen by many major marketers as the next generation of advertising on the Internet. They see sponsoring widgets as a promising way to reach consumers because they integrate advertising onto their web pages. Widgets are considered a better approach than banner adverts and less annoying than video that takes over the screen. As of this writing, widgets are the only way a brand can get inside My Space pages. Reebok, for example, created a widget that allows users to display customized RBK shoes for others to critique (Steel, 2006).

Some other ways in which the Internet is being used to deliver online advertising include delivering advertising-like messages via video games; online radio where listeners can respond to an advert by clicking on a box at the station site to be directed to the advertised brand's Web site; entertainment programming created for the Web that weaves product endorsements into the storyline; the ability to stop video and click to purchase clothing worn by the actors; and in-text advertising, appearing on some mainstream journalistic Web sites, where a pop-up advert appears when the cursor is moved over a keyword.

Streaming video is also used to offer mini-movies where a brand features prominently. These videos are often cutting edge, and can quickly create an incredibly strong 'buzz'. BMW, on their BMWfilms.com site (separate from their home page), offer short streamed films produced by well-known producers and directors, and with well-known actors (Silberer and Engelhardt, 2005).

In addition to advertising on the Internet, promotion-like messages and specific incentive promotions are delivered on the Web sites such as

Fatwallet.com send out daily early-morning e-mail alerts for online bargains; sites like GottaDeal.com provide information about mail-in rebate; and sites such as CouponMountain.com and CouponCraze.com make it possible to print out coupons for both store and online retailers.

Mobile marketing

The new millennium saw an expanding use of Web-enabled mobile handsets. This was especially true in Scandinavian and Asian countries. While banner adverts appeared on cell phones as early as the year 2000 on the Pacific Rim, it did not immediately catch on in other areas because major carriers in the US and Europe feared it would not be acceptable to their customers. A recent study (Katsukura et al., 2005) reported that in the early 2000s, for example, roughly 55% of people in Japan had signed up for Internet access on their cell phones compared with only 12% in the US. But by the mid-2000s, major cell phone networks in the US (Sprint Nextel and Verizon) and the UK (Vodafone Group) had introduced advertising on their wireless information and entertainment services (Yuan and Bryan-Low, 2006). This was encouraged by advances in phone technology. Early cell phones were designed solely for calling, not downloading. But cell phones now offer large colour screens and data connections making them much like small computers.

The Mobile Marketing Association (2005) in the UK has defined mobile marketing as: 'The use of the mobile medium as the communications and entertainment channel between a brand and an end user. Mobile marketing is the only personal channel enabling spontaneous, direct, interactive and/or target communications, any time, any place.' But as pointed out by Vittet-Philippe and Navarro (2000), mobile marketing involves much more than simply mobile telephoning. The key is the target audiences' willingness to receive adverts on their mobile devices.

Advertising on mobile devices such as cell phones appeals to marketers because they can tightly targeted their messages, as well as control message environment and time of exposure. Additionally, the potential exists for better tracking of message exposure, and the construction of a database. Much like direct marketing (which is discussed in the next chapter), effective mobile marketing must be driven by consumer data (Peltier et al., 2003).

An interesting application of mobile advertising involves one of the oldest forms of advertising, outdoor. Outdoor advertising, in fact, has become the second fastest-growing form of advertising, behind the Internet. Billboards now have the ability to electronically beam information to cell phones.

■ Sponsorships and event marketing

Sponsorships play an important role in IMC, and involve a company or brand providing support for an event, organization, cause, or even a particular individual. In return, the company has the right to display its brand name or logo, linked to the sponsored activity or individual, and to use the sponsorship in their other marketing activities. This makes sense for the company's brand because it enables them to be presented in a favourable environment where it has the potential of benefiting from an already favourable attitude toward the sponsored activity. Of course, the sponsored activity or individual must be viewed positively by the brand's target audience. Otherwise, it makes no sense.

Event marketing is similar to sponsorships, differing only in that with event marketing a company supports a specific event rather than an on-going relationship. In effect, event marketing is a one-off sponsorship. For example, supporting a Tsunami Relief Concert would be event marketing, compared with sustained support of an organization dedicated to helping victims of natural disasters, which would be sponsorship. Sponsoring the World Cup would be event marketing; supporting a particular team throughout the season, sponsorship. In Europe especially, brands are major sponsors of football teams. In fact, worldwide most sponsorships involve sports (Meenaghan, 1998).

Unfortunately, while there are obvious potential benefits to sponsorships and event marketing, there is very little evidence that they have a measurable effect upon sales or a company's stock price. With sponsorships, there is always the risk of negatively perceived over-commercialization, or a negative association resulting from problems tied to the sponsored activity or individual.

The Olympic Games, perhaps the most 'sponsored' event in the world, illustrate these potential problems. In the run-up to the games, one is inundated with messages from 'official sponsors' of the games, as well as tie-ins with specific athletes that are participating in the games. If there are incidents that lead to negative publicity with a sponsor or Olympic athlete, it could dampen enthusiasm for the games. A disappointing performance by a country's team could re-bound negatively upon a sponsoring brand. Many studies have in fact shown very little positive lift from Olympic Games sponsorships (Crimmins and Horn, 1996; Kinney and McDaniel, 1996; Miyazaki and Morgan, 2001).

Nevertheless, if well conceptualized, sponsorships and event marketing can make a positive contribution to IMC. The key here is the same as with all other marketing communication: establish brand awareness and effectively build positive brand attitude. With brand awareness, the event or individual should have a clear association with the product (ideally), or the category need should be immediately linked to the brand name or logo.

To facilitate building positive brand attitude, there must be a clear association between the sponsored activity or individual and the primary brand benefit. Beer and sporting events make sense together because beer is associated with sports, and those attending sporting events are likely to be beer drinkers. The positive emotional benefits associated with sporting events by their fans will transfer to the brand. Tea and sporting events would not make sense. Nor would high-fashion brands like

Channel or Gucci make sense sponsoring sporting events, but a sports-wear brand like LaCoste, perhaps. LaCoste would certainly fit with golf or tennis, but not formula one racing or NASCAR. The brand manager must ask if there is a good 'fit' between the brand and the event; just as the event manager should ask if there is a good 'fit' between the event and the brand (Gwinner and Eatin, 1999).

■ Product placement

Product placement may be defined as the reference to or actual inclusion of a product or service within some context in return for payment or other consideration. That context may be anything from movies and television programs to video games or even books. While generally referred to as product placements, in actuality, of course, one is talking about *brand* placement. Nonetheless, we shall use the more common term, product placement.

There are many issues surrounding the use of product placement, including ethical concerns and whether or not they are effective. Rossiter and Bellman (2005), for example, take a strong stance against the use of product placement, going so far as saying they are 'ethically contemptible'; because there is no guarantee the audience will understand an attempt is being made to persuade them. Even if the audience does understand, they argue it is unethical because there is an *intention* to deceive on the part of the marketer.

Sutherland (2006) expresses concern that regulatory agencies such as the Federal Communications Commission in the US and the Independent Television Commission in the UK are paying less attention to product placements, even as their use increases. His point is that product placements could warp the public image of what brands are popular (among other things) because people are not likely to make the connection between a brand appearing in a movie or video game and the fact that the marketer paid to have it there. He fears a 'slippery slope' where this lack of attention by regulatory bodies will see us move from the correct 'communication in camouflage' to 'persuasion by proxy' to 'cash for comment'. It was not until the mid-2000s that the European Parliament's culture committee gave approval for product placements. Yet despite this, not all the EU countries are keen to adopt it. In the UK product placement has long been a controversial issue, and even with EU approval adoption is not expected in the near term. Even though many US television shows are seen in the UK, product placement in that programming is pixilated (digitally blurred out) (Hall, 2007).

Beyond the ethical concerns, there is an issue of whether or not product placement works. There are certainly many anecdotal stories about the effectiveness of product placements. An oft-told story concerns the 1986 movie *Top Gun* where Tom Cruise is wearing Rayban Aviator sunglasses. It is said that this led to a turn-around in the company's fortunes, which before the release of the movie was in financial difficulties (Fischer, 1996). Nevertheless, there are few empirical studies of product placement, and those that have been conducted are not encouraging (Johnstone and Dodd, 2000).

Assuming product placement can be effective, *how* the brand is placed will have an obvious impact. If a brand is clearly seen being used by a celebrity or specifically talked about, the potential effect will be greater than if it is simply part of the background (Semenik, 2002). If well placed, the most likely effect will be raising brand awareness and salience. But even this will require *conscious* attention to the brand.

The likelihood of product placement positively effecting brand attitude for significant segments of a brand's target audience is much more problematic. Even though the actual cost of a product placement in absolute terms is likely to be less than that for other forms of marketing communication, it is difficult to predict whether or not any positive effect will offset the cost of the placement. The key to effectiveness is the number of people *consciously* aware of the brand and positively associating it with the environment within which it is placed. While there may be implicit processing of the brand's placement, this will have *no* effect upon brand attitude or behaviour (Percy, 2006).

To be effective, product placements must stimulate explicit positive associations in memory with the celebrity or environment linked to the brand, and within the correct emotional context. If this occurs, the placement should contribute to brand attitude, because the audience may feel as if it has had a personal experience with what is going on. But this is a lot to ask of all but the most rabid fan of the principle actor or setting involved.

In any event, product placement does have the potential to build brand awareness and contribute to brand attitude. But it must be seen within a context consistent with the brand's positioning, attended to consciously, and positively linked to the appropriate emotional and explicit memories, as with any other effective marketing communication.

■ Packaging

Packaging is a critical element in IMC. Even though there is evidence that marketers are coming to realize that packaging is an important part of a brand's identity (Walczyk, 2001), the powerful role packaging can play in building and reinforcing positive brand attitude and equity is often underestimated by managers (Southgate, 1994).

In a study among brand managers, Chareonlarp (1997) identified a number of key emotional and psychological benefits associated with packaging. Basically, the findings may be summarized as the ability to attract attention and providing an expression of a brand's image: in other words, brand awareness and brand attitude, the key communication objectives for all marketing communication. And as with all other forms of marketing communication, the visual elements of a package, its 'message', should differentiate it from competitors.

Well-designed packages can attract attention at the point-of-purchase, a critical attribute for any product where the brand purchase decision follows from recognition brand awareness. Studies by the Point-of-Purchase Advertising Institute (2000) have shown that over 70% of brand awareness decisions in supermarkets are made in the store. A package, if effectively linked to the brand in the consumer's mind as a result of other marketing communication for the brand (especially advertising), and if visually impactful and unique relative to competitors, will be easily recognized at the point-of-purchase. Given the large number of package facings in a store vying for attention, packaging must be able to 'cut through' the competitive clutter.

But there is much more packaging must do. It should help reinforce the brand's image and key benefit. For many products the package is always there when the product is being used, providing an on-going reminder of the brand and an opportunity to reinforce its primary benefit. Products ranging from cold remedies to breakfast cereal to toothpaste to washing-up powder are used *from the package*. In a sense, packaging operates as post-purchase advertising. Rossiter and Bellman (2005) capture this idea in their definition of packaging, suggesting it may be thought of as 'take-away or leave-behind' communication vehicles. The advert shown in Figure 6.2 for Wyke Farms cheddar offers a very good example of how a product's package can be used to reinforce the brand's benefit. The advert underscores the brand's key benefit: it's *Just Delicious*. The package clearly reinforces this benefit. Every time the package is seen or handled, from the store to the refrigerator to serving, the consumer is reminded that Wyke Farms cheddar is 'just delicious'.

■ Trade shows and fairs

Trade shows and fairs fall somewhere between promotion and personal selling. Promotional incentives of some kind are often used to encourage attendance at trade shows and fairs, they are advertised through various media, and direct contact is made with customers and potential customers at the company's booth. Literally every industry has a trade show of some kind. They can be especially important for small marketers unable to advertise, and they play a significant role in the marketing communication for industrial companies. It has been estimated that between 20% and 25% of an industrial marketer's communication budget is spent on trade shows (Gopalakrishna and Williams, 1992).

Because of the personal interaction afforded by trade shows and fairs, they offer marketers a number of opportunities (Shipley et al., 1993). They provide a chance to identify and meet new customers, as well as entertain old ones. New products can be introduced, and existing products demonstrated. They also help raise the salience of a company and to enhance its image: brand awareness and brand attitude. The key advantage is that

Figure 6.2
A very good example of how a package can be used to reinforce a brand's benefit, in this case 'Just Delicious'. *Courtesy*: Wyke Farms

this may be all done in a relatively short period of time, and among nearly all of one's existing and potential customers. But as with all other forms of marketing communication, the trade show or fair, as well all of the advertising and promotion associated with it, should be consistent with other on-going IMC efforts.

There is some debate about the effectiveness of trade shows and fairs, even though there is no question that they provide a good opportunity for marketers and customers to meet in an environment where the one is imparting information and the other seeking it. Some have shown that they generate awareness and interest, leading to sales (Gopalakrishna and Williams, 1992), while others have questioned their value altogether (Sashi and Perretty, 1992).

Many define effectiveness in terms of leads generated that result in sales (Sharland and Balogh, 1996). This is certainly in line with one way managers who are heavily involved in trade shows and fairs look at it (Blythe and Rayner, 1996). Yet Shipley et al. (1993), as well as others, have found that the non-selling aspects of trade shows and fairs are highly valued by the managers involved with them. The problem would seem to be that there frequently are no set criteria for success, and this is complicated by no good measure of cost effectiveness. Additionally, when assessing trade shows and fairs managers are apt to look at them in isolation rather than as part of an overall IMC program.

■ Personal selling

In this section we are not so much interested in personal selling as such, but rather with the role of the salesperson in delivering and reinforcing a brand's positioning and marketing communication. How to be an effective salesperson is a subject for another book (e.g. Cialdini, 2001).

Personal selling may be looked at in terms of direct contact with consumers or a link to resellers or dealers in business-to-business marketing. In fact, personal selling is often the primary (if not only) form of marketing communication for industrial marketers. In either case, the message delivered must be consistent with that of the overall marketing communication program. It will differ from most other forms of marketing communication in an IMC program because the message moves *directly* from the marketer to an individual member of the target audience, providing an opportunity for interaction and modification of the basic message to address specific target audience concerns.

Rossiter and Bellman (2005) talk about personal selling in terms of six basic types: regular retail selling, small business selling, trade selling, high-end retail selling, technical selling, and telemarketing. The first two they describe as 'passive', where the sales exchange is largely initiated and controlled by the customer. The other four are 'active', initiated by the salesperson and where both the customer and salesperson are involved in controlling the exchange (see Figure 6.3). It is only these

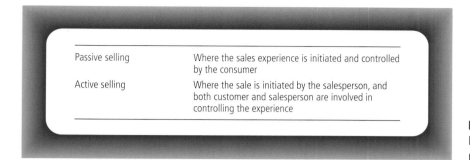

Figure 6.3
Passive versus active personal selling

'active' types of selling where marketing communication messages are involved.

The principal advantage of personal selling, from a marketing communication standpoint, is that it involves a two-way interaction between the salesperson and the customer, unlike the one-way communication of other marketing communications (with the exception of that involving interactive media). Personal selling provides an opportunity for customizing the message for an individual customer, and as mentioned above, the opportunity to adapt the message during the customer–salesperson interaction. Because of this, attention to, and involvement with, the message is likely to be high. Personal selling also offers a chance to demonstrate product benefits that might be difficult or even impossible to effectively convey with other forms of marketing communication.

The key advantage of personal selling in marketing communication unfortunately leads to its primary disadvantage, especially for IMC. Because of the flexibility and multiple delivery sources (the different salespeople) it is difficult to maintain message consistency. And given the nature of personal selling, relative to other ways of delivering a message, it is expensive and has a low reach. These advantages and disadvantages associated with personal selling in IMC are summarized in Figure 6.4.

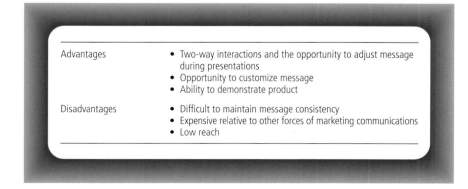

Figure 6.4
Advantages versus disadvantages of personal selling

Integrating personal selling into the development of IMC strategy can be difficult, for in many companies the sales force is not part of the marketing department, especially for consumer packaged goods. As Dewshap and Jobber (2000) point out, in packaged goods companies retailers are the brands for the sales force, unlike for marketing managers where the product is the brand. The focus is different, and they have separate budgets. Nevertheless, personal selling must be considered part of IMC planning, using a message that is consistent with a brand's other marketing communication.

In recent years there has been a realization that retaining existing customers is a more profitable strategy for the sales force than seeking new customers (not that a company should quit trying to gain new customers). This is what *relationship marketing* is all about. It also means that, with more long-term relationships in mind, there is a greater opportunity for personal selling to be used in reinforcing a brand's message.

While the ultimate objective of personal selling is to convince the target customers to stock or purchase the brand, like all marketing communication the message must address brand awareness and brand attitude objectives. With personal selling, the brand awareness objectives will be recognition. For brand attitude, there is a key difference. As already discussed, one has the opportunity of adjusting the message to maximize interest in the brands' benefit for a specific target customer.

Much personal selling is directed to the trade or in straight business-to-business situations, where the purchase motive is likely to be negative and an informational brand attitude strategy required. Additionally, the purchase decision is likely to be high. This means the salesperson must understand the target customer's *initial attitude* toward the brand because that understanding will be critical to framing the message for acceptance. The personal, interactive nature of personal selling allows for a certain amount of probing to ensure a good understanding of how the target audience sees the brand.

Interestingly, in these high-involvement cases, even if objectively a brand can deliver its key benefit better than the target customer believes it can, the salesperson should not try to convince them it will. They are not likely to believe the stronger claim, even if it is true. As long as the prospect is generally positive about the brand, talk about the benefit at the customer's level of belief. Research has shown that if when used a product turns out to deliver a benefit better than anticipated, overall brand attitude will *increase* (Kopalle and Assuncão, 2000). This results from the difference between the anticipation and actual delivery of the benefit.

But one must be careful here in the case of the trade. While getting the trade to stock a brand will likely involve negative motives, and an informational message strategy to 'close the sale', this may not be the case for the brand. When talking about the *brand itself* and its key benefit, if the purchase decision by consumers for the brand reflects positive motives, the message about the brand must incorporate a transformational strategy consistent with its overall marketing communication brand attitude objective. In other cases, especially when personal selling is direct to the consumer (e.g. with high-end luxury goods), when the motive driving the purchase decision is positive, the message strategy should be transformational. Here one need not be as concerned with the target customer's initial attitudes toward the brand, and the salesperson should feel free to present the brand in the best possible light.

■ Public relations

Where public relations, or as it is more commonly referred to, PR, fits within IMC is not an easy question to answer. Part of the reason is that neither academics or practitioners seem to offer a consensus as to the role PR plays with regard to an organization and its marketing activities. Rossiter and Bellman (2005) talk about PR as a 'general term now for all forms of manufactured publicity', but that does not get us very far. Many would argue, for example, that 'publicity' is only one part of PR. Is the advice a PR agency provides corporate management 'publicity', or the speeches they write for a CFO to give to the financial community? What about help with employee relations, or lobbying activities?

From a marketing standpoint, the word 'publicity' is perhaps a good choice. But many PR practitioners would like to distance themselves from any association with 'marketing'. They like to see what they do as more concerned with enhancing the image and reputation of an organization. The Institute of Public Relations defines PR as 'the planned and sustained effort to establish and maintain goodwill and mutual understanding between an organization and its publics'. While this definition would seem to distance PR from consumers and marketing, with an emphasis more upon the organization, obviously one of a company's most important 'publics' is the consumer. And as we saw in Chapter 3, an organization's image and reputation cannot be separated from the marketing of its products or services.

Regardless of how one chooses to define PR, it plays an important part in the marketing communication mix, and the messages it delivers to various 'publics' must be consistent with the message delivered by more traditional marketing communications. While some PR activities are clearly outside of the normal strategic planning for IMC, whatever activities are undertaken on behalf of an organization should take cognizance of the overall marketing communication program for that company's brands. While in this chapter we are only concerned with those areas of PR that have a direct effect upon marketing issues, we must still keep this in mind. Regardless of the PR activity, to the extent that it reflects upon the image and reputation of an organization or its products, it should be consistent with the overall IMC program.

Public relations strategy

One might think about public relations strategy in terms of being either *proactive* or *reactive*. *Proactive* PR involves planned activity designed to draw positive attention to a company and help build a positive image. This could include such things as cause-related marketing or 'green' marketing. The BP (British Petroleum) campaign from the mid-2000s focusing upon alternative energy sources is a good IMC example. Not only was PR involved in its traditional role, but corporate advertising was also used to underscore the company's activities in seeking energy alternatives to petroleum. *Reactive* PR results when a company experiences negative publicity and must deal with 'damage control'. This reflects what in social psychology is known as impression management, where one seeks to protect one's self by maximizing positive associations while minimizing negative associations.

Advantages and disadvantages

There are both advantages and disadvantages to using PR in marketing. Advantages include such things as low cost, the ability to reach very specific target audiences, avoiding 'clutter', and message credibility. (see Figure 6.5) Compared with other forms of communication, PR is much less expensive to use both in an absolute as well as relative source. Primarily, this is because there are no direct media costs involved. By its nature, PR activity can be directed to very specific target groups, and has the ability to reach highly segmented publics effectively. Because PR messages are not delivered via traditional media, they avoid the clutter associated with advertising-like messages. And because they are not seen as 'advertising', PR messages are likely to be seen as more credible.

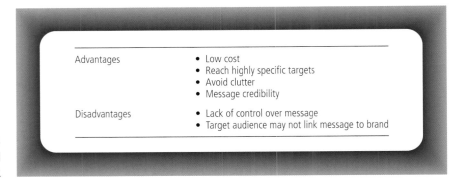

Figure 6.5
Advantages and disadvantages of PR

On the other hand, there can be disadvantages associated with using PR. Perhaps the greatest potential problem with PR is the lack of control. There is rarely a guarantee that a message will be exposed; and if it is, that it will necessarily be presented in the way the company desired. Also, owing to the fact that PR is not seen as 'advertising', the target audience may not make the desired link between the message and the brand or company.

Marketing public relations

In the mid-1990s it was estimated that 70% of PR activities were related to marketing (Harris, 1993). It was at this time that Thomas Harris introduced the term marketing public relations (MPR) to describe PR activities in support of marketing objectives. There is every reason to believe that the proportion of PR activities that could be described as MPR is even greater today. Harris specifically defined MPR as 'the process of planning, executing, and evaluating programs that encourage purchase and consumer satisfaction through credible communicators of information and impressions that identify companies and their products with the needs, wants, concerns, and interests of consumers'. In a sense, MPR helps define and communicate a brand's positioning, and Harris' definition outlines just this point.

When we discuss positioning in Chapter 11, we will see that effective positioning requires linking a brand with a need (defined as *category* need, a perceived need for a product in a particular category); and also linking the brand with a desired benefit. MPR, by identifying a company and its products with particular needs is helping to provide the link between a category need and the brand; and by identifying a company and its products with a want, links the brand with a desired benefit that satisfies that want.

This understanding of PR as MPR becomes even more important for companies that utilize source or endorser branding strategies. With such branding strategies, the company name is part of the brand name and acts as an endorser or guarantor for the product, as we have seen. When Nestlé adds its name to its Crunch bar, in a very real sense it is contributing Nestlé's image and reputation to the brand. The potential importance of MPR here is obvious. Any PR that helps build and nurture Nestlé's image and reputation enhances the image of the Crunch brand. On the other hand, PR for Mars is unlikely to effect the image of Snickers unless one knows that it is made by Mars. Snickers is what is known as a 'stand-alone' brand, as discussed in Chapter 2.

In any event, MPR must be seen as consistent with a brand's overall marketing communication, and ideally reflect the same visual and verbal 'feel'. This is why MPR must be considered within IMC strategic planning. When these objectives are achieved, the link between the MPR messages and the brand will be easily recognized, and help build positive brand attitude. The coordination between MPR and other elements of a brand's marketing communication is critical.

Some of the ways in which MPR can contribute to achieving a brand's overall communication objectives is through such activities as: media relations, corporate communication, sponsorships, events, and perhaps its most important activity, publicity. Maintaining good *media* relations helps to ensure a more likely acceptance for things like company press releases and feature stories, but it requires an on-going nurturing of editors and journalists. *Corporate communication* involves much of what was discussed in Chapter 3, and includes not only corporate advertising and directed communication to specific stakeholder groups, but also things like internal communication and company newsletters. Both *sponsorships* and *events* may be initiated as part of MPR, just as discussed earlier where they were more directly involved in brand marketing communication.

Publicity is what most people think about as PR, and it is by far the most frequently engaged in PR activity. In fact, publicity in one form or another is likely to be involved along with most other forms of MPR. Often people think of publicity as 'free advertising', especially since it uses mass media to deliver its message. An argument can certainly be made that MPR is (or should be) an advertising-like message, but it is certainly not free. There may not be an actual media cost, but there is an on-going cost for media relations in order to ensure the message will be broadcast and given favourable exposure. There are also costs for developing the message, and overall management. And of course, unlike advertising, there is no control over the content or when and how the message will be delivered.

Publicity does have the advantage of being seen as more objective than advertising because it is generally viewed as 'news' or information rather than an attempt at persuasion. While it is likely to reach far fewer people than other forms of marketing communication, it will likely be more persuasive among those who are reached. A Nestlé program for Nescafé provides excellent example of what we have been talking about. In 2002 they were involved in co-founding the Sustainable Agriculture Initiative, a group to work with local farmers in developing sustainable approaches to growing coffee. As a part of this program, in addition to providing technical agriculture assistance to farmers, they were also involved with improving worker housing, health care, and education. Out of this effort they are marketing Nescafé Partners' Blend, which is, as the label says, 'coffee that helps farmers, their communities, and the environment.' It is also reflected in a Web site, growmorethancoffee.co.uk. Figure 6.6 illustrates one way they are reinforcing the program with advertising, and the strong package reflecting the message.

■ Buzz marketing

While not exactly PR as such, buzz marketing is the term given to a new trend in word-of-mouth brand communication that emerged in the mid-2000s in an effort to better reach younger consumers. Companies were created to actively enlist the help of 'ordinary people' in talking about specific brands. One such company in the US (BZZ Agent) recruits people from the Internet to talk about their client's brands to friends and family. They are given free samples of the product, along with an outline of things they might say. For example, 3000 of these 'bzzagents' may be given a sample of a new perfume fragrance and asked to wear it, and to encourage people to talk about it. While they are encouraged to identify themselves as part of a marketing campaign, the 'buzz' created neverthe-less has more credibility than traditional advertising because it is coming from someone who is known.

COMMUNITY SPIRIT

After decades of civil war and natural disasters in El Salvador, farmers have united and gone back to what they do best: growing delicious coffee. **'María's story' by René Hernandez**

MARÍA ARACELI REYES, 42, IS A MEMBER OF THE CAFEMOR COOPERATIVE IN EL SALVADOR

A TIME OF TROUBLE

'I'm one of the 57 members of the Cafemor cooperative. My grandfather Bernardo Dominguez used to be president of the Association but he died in 1991, a victim of the 12 year civil war which ended in 1992.

It was a terrible period – we had to abandon our farm, leaving our four hectares of land behind. We lived a long time in the capital, San Salvador, where we sold vegetables in the street to help support the family.

In 1993 I married Jaime Nolasco, a forestry technician. We have two children: Jaime is 11 and Elias is 6. My new family and I returned to Morazan. My mother offered to pay me to look after her farm and I hired three men to help me and managed them like a true farm owner. The foreign experts from the project who were working with our cooperative advised us on our farming techniques and gave us an agricultural package as a gift, which included fertiliser.

EXPERT HELP

The gift was really important, as most of us couldn't afford to buy the fertiliser. Now the cooperative has the Fairtrade certification things are improving as we are guaranteed a minimum price for our coffee.

With Fairtrade, the cooperative receives an extra five dollars per quintal (a quintal is a local measure of 48kg) to invest in social work. We were only able to achieve certification by working together to fulfil the criteria. That's why we formed the cooperative to move things forward together. The experts helped us to organise ourselves and find other alternatives to survive should the coffee crop fail, such as rearing chickens and growing fruit trees on the farms.

❝ The experts have helped us to help ourselves: in unity there's strength **❞**

HOPE FOR THE FUTURE

I now have 100 chickens on my farm and orange, lemon, avocado and mango trees which I'll be able to harvest in a year's time. Today you'll see smiles on the faces of my children and I, but five years ago we were desperate. We didn't believe we'd be able to continue working on the farms, but necessity united us and the experts have helped us to help ourselves: in unity there's strength.

These days, we are also able to help the schools and health units in the communities. We've already been able to give school equipment and rucksacks to 250 students from the poorest families in the region. There's still lots to do, there are still children who receive their lessons beneath a tree. My motto is to serve and help. Today I am so happy because I feel we are moving in the right direction.'

EL SALVADOR

The tiny Central American nation of El Salvador, with its population of 6.4 million, has been in constant upheaval for a quarter of a century.

Following the 1980 assassination of Archbishop Romero, the country erupted into a civil war, which claimed the lives of 70,000 people.

In 1992, the UN brokered a ceasefire, which helped the country get back on its feet, only to be brought to its knees again by Hurricane Mitch and a series of earthquakes which claimed the lives of thousands.

With an economy traditionally dependent on the production of coffee, the country's finances have been held subject to the fluctuations in the price of the world's second-most widely traded commodity – and when the market turns downwards, it is the country's poorest people who are hit the hardest.

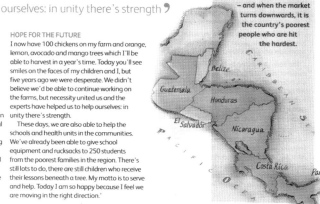

Figure 6.6

An excellent example of publicity reinforced by advertising where Nestlé talks about a joint program with they were involved in initiating with coffee growers in El Salvador. *Courtesy*: Nestlé, published in *Good Food* Magazine

Sustainable agriculture is one approach to bringing some stability to the region's farmers. This means helping meet farmers' and their communities' social, economic and environmental needs so that, in the long run they can become more self-sufficient and can build sustainable businesses. To discover more about sustainable coffee growing and how it can help communities like Maria's please visit *growmorethancoffee.co.uk*

Nestlé has stated its commitment to sustainability and in 2002 they co-founded the Sustainable Agriculture Initiative, a group that works closely with farmers to develop sustainable approaches to coffee growing. NESCAFÉ assists communities like Maria's in growing other crops, which help the farmers through times when there are fluctuations that affect the coffee price. The company also provides farmers with expert agricultural specialists who are on hand with advice to ensure the coffee crop is of good quality.

NESCAFÉ first started providing technical assistance to farmers over 30 years ago and now the three pillars of sustainability (social, economic and environmental) have been applied together to individual communities with a particular focus on smallholders who have been affected by changes in coffee prices.

A great example of this is in El Salvador where NESCAFÉ gives technical and financial support to a number of cooperatives to help their farmers become sustainable in the long term. So far NESCAFÉ has provided improved housing for workers at the mill, given technical agricultural assistance to farmers and built a learning centre and clinic which will be visited regularly by a doctor. An educational project involving 700 pupils is also underway. In addition, farmers have been given chickens to breed and help with growing fruit and vegetables for their own consumption and to trade at the local market to make extra money.

NESCAFÉ also recognises the important role that Fairtrade plays in guaranteeing smallholder producers a fair price for their product.

The beans harvested by four coffee cooperatives in the El Salvador programme are independently Fairtrade certified and will be used in the production of NESCAFÉ Partners' Blend. When you purchase this product it will make a direct and positive difference to the lives of farmers like Maria.

*NESCAFÉ has created a comprehensive website, **growmorethancoffee.co.uk**, which contains more information on Maria's life, NESCAFÉ's ongoing commitment and vision for PARTNERS' BLEND, plus information on how buying the product can provide the farmers of the El Salvador project with a sustainable lifestyle.*

Today I am so happy because we are moving in the right direction

Look for this Mark on Fairtrade products

Guarantees **a better deal** for Third World Producers

FAIRTRADE

fairtrade.org.uk

© 2005 SOCIÉTÉ DES PRODUITS NESTLÉ S.A., VEVEY, SWITZERLAND. TRADE MARK OWNER

Figure 6.6   *(Contd.)*

Figure 6.7
A good example of a campaign to create buzz for a brand. *Courtesy*: OMD and Henkel Got2B

A campaign for Henkel Got2B provides a good example of how buzz can be used in the launch of a new product with only a small media budget. Aimed at young people, the brand produced a commercial jointly with MTV, using one of their well-known VJ's as a spokesperson. This provided a strong, credible source for the brand's message, and put them in a perfect position to generate interest and word-of-mouth among teens and young adults (see Figure 6.7).

In other ways companies are using their web sites to encourage entertaining interactions to generate positive word-of-mouth about their brand. There are even auditing services that track 'buzz' about a brand on blogs.

Summary

In this chapter we have looked at alternative ways of delivering advertising-like and promotion-like messages. More and more, marketers are looking at non-traditional ways of delivering their message. While still a relatively small portion of the money spent on marketing communication, the so-called 'new media', especially the Internet, has shown dramatic growth. This growth, however, has been largely limited to the very largest Internet providers like Yahoo, Google, AOL, and MSN.

Advertising-like messages delivered through the Internet now go well beyond simple banner adverts or home pages, and are they being more targeted for interactive. Keywords used in searches and e-mail can now trigger related adverts. Promotions too are delivered over the Internet, with some web sites devoted only to online promotions. Mobile marketing enables advertisers to send messages directly to cell phones and other wireless mobile devices. With prior permission from cell phone users, messages can be highly targeted and exposure tracked. It is even possible to direct messages to cell phones from outdoor billboards.

Other alternative ways of delivering marketing communication include sponsorships and events, although there is little evidence that they offer a good return on investment. Nevertheless, when used within an IMC program they can help in building brand awareness and positive brand attitude. Product placement is another area of increasing use, but one that has aroused ethical concerns. There is also some questions as to their likely effectiveness. One non-traditional medium that does offer real potential, yet too often overlooked by managers, is packaging. For many products, especially fmcg, packaging offers an excellent opportunity for reinforcing not only the brand name but also the brand's primary benefit. Trade shows and fairs provide a very personal way of delivering a brand's message, and are widely used, especially by industrial marketers.

Personal selling is an area that is often overlooked in terms of IMC, yet it offers a good opportunity for reinforcing a brand positioning and message. The key is that the message must be consistent with the IMC message for the brand. It has the obvious advantage of personal interaction with consumers, which opens up the potential for customizing the message. But this obvious advantage can also lead to problems, because it is difficult to maintain consistency.

PR too should be considered as part of an IMC program. But it must fit within the overall brand communication strategy, even when it is addressing specific corporate communication issues. This idea has been talked about as MPR. It has the advantage of not being seen as advertising, but also the potentially serious problems associated with a lack of control over message content and how it is delivered.

■ Review questions

1 How is new media involved in IMC?

2 Do you feel the Internet or mobile marketing will emerge as the stronger new medium for IMC?

3 How would you use mobile marketing as part of an IMC program?

4 Discuss the ethics of product placement; and discuss their effectiveness.

5 Why is the package an important venue for advertising-like messages?

6 What are the strengths and weaknesses of trade shows and fairs for consumer packaged goods brands? What about for business-to-business marketers.

7 What role does personal selling playing in an IMC campaign?

8 How can public relations be used successfully in IMC?

9 What is the biggest weakness of public relations in terms of IMC, and how can this be overcome?

10 Find examples of buzz marketing, and discuss whether or not you think it works for the brand.

References

Angwin, J. and Delaner, K.J. (2005) Top web sites build up ad backlog, raise rates. *Wall Street Journal*, 16 November.

Blythe, J. and Rayner, T. (1996) The evaluation of non-selling activities at British trade exhibitions – an exploratory study. *Marketing Intelligence and Planning*, 14(5).

Chareonlarp, S. (1997) *An investigation of the representation of brand image through packaging, MSC Marketing Management Dissertation*. Birmingham: Astor Business School, Astor University.

Cialdini, R.B. (2001) *Influence: Science and Practice*, 4th edition. Needham Heights, MA: Allyn & Bacor.

Crimmins, J. and Horn, M. (1996) Sponsorship: from management ego trip to marketing success. *Journal of Advertising Research*, 36(4), 11–21.

Dewshap, B. and Jobber, D. (2000) The sales-marketing interface in consumer packaged-goods companies: a conceptual framework. *Journal of Personal Selling & Sales Management*, 20(2), 109–119.

Fischer, B.R. (1996) Making your product the star attraction. *Promo*, July, 58.

Gopalakrishna, S. and Williams, J.D. (1992) Planning and performance assessment of industrial trade shows: an exploratory study. *International Journal of Research in Marketing*, 9(19), 207–224.

Guth, R.A. (2005a) New media, beware: what's up now could be down. *Wall Street Journal*, 24 May, A7.

Guth, R.A. (2005b) New Microsoft service will rely on online ads. *Wall Street Journal*, 2 November, B2.

Gwinner, K.P. and Eaton, J. (1999) Building brand image through event sponsorship: the role of image transfer. *Journal of Advertising*, 28(4), 47–57.

Hall, E. (2007) Product placement faces wary welcome in Britain. *Advertising Age*, 8 January, 27.

Harris, T. (1993) *The Marketer's Guide to PR: How Today's Companies are Using the New Public Relations to Gain a Competitive Edge*. New York: John Wiley and Sons.

Interactive Advertising Bureau (2004) reported in *Wall Street Journal*, 21 November, 2005.

Johnstone, E. and Dodd, C.A. (2000) Placements as mediations of brand salience within U.K. cinema audiences. *Journal of Marketing Communications*, 6(3), 141–158.

Katsukura, A., Nishiyama, M., & Okazaki, S. (2005) Evidence from Japan: a preliminary scale development of consumer perception of mobile portal sites. *Advertising and Communication*, proceedings of 4th International Conference on Research in Advertising, Saarbruecken, Germany: Saarland University, 254–259.

Kinney, L. and McDaniel, S.R. (1996) Strategic implications of attitude-towards-the-ad in leveraging event sponsorship. *Journal of Sports Management*, 10, 250–261.

Kopalle, P.K. and Assuncão, J.L. (2000) When (not) to indulge in 'puffery': the role of consumer expectations and brand goodwill in determining advertised and actual product quality. *Managerial Decision Economics*, 21(6).

Meenaghan, T. (1998) Current developments and future directions in sports sponsorship. *International Journal of Advertising*, 17(1), 3–28.

Miyazaki, A.D. and Morgan, A.G. (2001) Assessing market value of event sponsoring: corporate Olympics sponsorships. *Journal of Advertising Research*, 41(1), 9–15.

Mobile Marketing Association (2005) What is mobile marketing, www.mmaglobal.co.uk.

Oser, K. (2004) Money, mayhem to be first with pop-ups. *Advertising Age*, 28 June, 51.

Peltier, J.W., Schibrowsky, J.A., and Schultz, D. (2003) Interactive integrated marketing communication combining the power of IMC, new media, and database marketing. *International Journal of Advertising*, 22, 93–115.

Percy, L. (2006) Are product placements effective? *International Journal of Advertising*, 25(1), 112–114.

Point-of-Purchase Advertising Institute (2000) *An Integrated Look at Integrated Marketing: Uncovering P-O-P's Role as the Last Three Feet in the Marketing Mix*. Washington D.C. Point-of-Purchase Advertising Institute. 10

Rossiter, J.R. and Bellman (2005) *Marketing Communication: Theory and Applications*. French Forest NSW, Australia: Pearson Education Australia.

Sashi, C.M. and Perretty, J. (1992) Do trade shows provide value? *Industrial Marketing Management*, 21, 249–255.

Semenik, R.J. (2002) *Promotion & Integrated Marketing Communication*. Cincinnati, OH: South-Western. 398

Sharland, A. and Balogh, P. (1996) The value of non-selling activities at international trade shows. *Industrial Marketing Management*, 25, 59–66.

Shipley, D., Egan, C., and Wong, K.S. (1993) Dimensions of trade show exhibiting management. *Journal of Marketing Management*, 9(1).

Silberer, G., and Engelhardt, J.F. (2005). Streaming media: a new way of online advertising. *Advertising and Communication*, proceedings of 4th International Conference on Research in Advertising, Saarbrucken, Germany: Saarland University, 254–259.

Southgate, P. (1994) *Total Branding by Design*. London: Kogan Page.

Steel, E. (2006) Web-page clocks and other 'widgets' anchor new Internet strategy. *Wall Street Journal*, 21 November, B4.

Sutherland, M. (2006) Product placement-regulators gone AWOL. *International Journal of Advertising*, 25(1), 107–110.

Vittet-Philippe, P. and Navarro, J.M. (2000) Mobile e-business (M-commerce): state of play and implications for European play. *European Commission Enterprise Directorate – General E-Business Report*, No. 3, 6 December.

Vrancia, S. (2005) Anywhere, anytime. *Wall Street Journal*, 21 November.

Walczyk, D. (2001) Packaging should be a critical element in the branding scheme. *Marketing News*, 35(23), 14–17.

Wall Street Journal (2006) reported in 28 August number.

Yuan, L. and Bryan-Low, C. (2006) Coming soon to cell phone screens – more ads than ever. *Wall Street Journal*, 16 August, B1.

CHAPTER 7

Direct marketing and channels marketing

There are two areas of marketing communication that are often mis-understood as simply ways of delivering a message rather than a *type* of message that deserves consideration on its own: direct marketing and channels marketing. The first is not new, direct marketing has been used in one way or another for centuries. Channels marketing, however, is a relatively new idea that combines tactical marketing and traditional co-op advertising. Each may be used with either advertising-like or promotion-like messages, although their primary application has been in the area of promotion.

■ The role of direct marketing in IMC

When most people think about direct marketing they think of direct mail. In fact, many marketers assume that they are the same. But direct mail is only one part of direct marketing, and while it is a very important part, it is not even the largest in terms of the money spent on direct marketing. In one sense, it probably does not really matter what is meant by direct marketing. But as Shultz (1995) has pointed out, what someone means when they say direct marketing may have absolutely no relationship to what others think is direct marketing. This is always a danger when terms are used loosely, and doubly so in integrated marketing communication (IMC) planning.

Consumers are unlikely to know or care what marketers call the messages they send, or the way they deliver them. But if managers are to be disciplined in their planning, they must. In fact, consumers think that nearly all the marketing communications they are exposed to is 'advertising'. This means everything from bumper stickers to coupons to refunds (Schultz, 1995). But for effective IMC planning, there must be an agreement on what is meant by such things as advertising and promotion (as already seen in earlier chapters), and what it means to include direct marketing as a part of an IMC program.

What then is direct marketing? According to the Direct Marketing Association, it is:

> An *accountable* system of marketing which uses one or more communications media to *effect a response*. It is an *interactive process* where responses from or about buyers are recorded in a *database* for building profiles of potential customers and providing valuable marketing information for *more efficient targeting*.

Obviously, the Direct Marketing Association has something rather definite in mind, and we shall now look more closely at several components of this definition (Figure 7.1).

The basic characteristics of direct marketing, implied by this definition, are that it asks for a response and that it can be highly targeted. In fact, it can be aimed at a single individual or a very narrowly defined group of individuals. In addition, every aspect of direct marketing must be tied to a

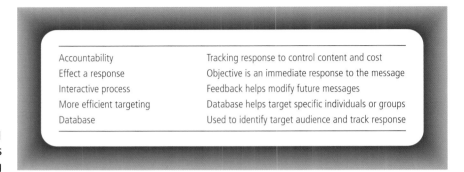

Accountability	Tracking response to control content and cost
Effect a response	Objective is an immediate response to the message
Interactive process	Feedback helps modify future messages
More efficient targeting	Database helps target specific individuals or groups
Database	Used to identify target audience and track response

Figure 7.1
Basic characteristics
of direct marketing

database so that statistical analysis can be used to access the effectiveness of any program. More on the importance of a database later, but let us briefly consider the other characteristics.

Accountability: Accountability is a key issue in direct marketing. While all marketing communication should be cost-effective, direct marketing is tightly controlled because of its dependence upon a database. With appropriate models, direct marketing offers the manager not only the opportunity of predicting and measuring responses, but also the ability to determine the actual costs associated with particular responses. Because of the database, managers can continually purge and update files to maximize the cost-effectiveness of their direct marketing programs.

Effect a response: The point has already been made many times that all forms of marketing communications must address brand awareness and brand attitude. But the primary job of direct marketing is to stimulate the target receiver to take some kind of action now: place an order, use a service, or make an enquiry. In this way it reflects the primary communication objectives of promotion-like messages.

Interactive process: All direct marketing is interactive in the sense that the response to a message becomes new information to be recorded in the database. This new information is then used in developing new messages to be used in future direct marketing efforts. When telemarketing or the Internet is involved, there is an opportunity for modifying the message during contact.

More efficient targeting: Since the primary goal of direct marketing is a response of some kind, the effort must be highly targeted. One is looking for a single individual or relatively small group of similar people, likely to respond favourably to the brand's message. Even when mass media is used for direct marketing, an effort should be made to target as specific an audience as possible.

Jerome Pickholz (1994), when chairman and CEO of Ogilvy-Mather Direct, suggested that there are two significant hurdles for direct marketing to overcome. The first is building a good database. The problem is that it must be built over time, and as Pickholz reminds us, this can be a real problem for marketers who are looking for immediate solutions. The second hurdle is the cost. Despite the fact that studies show direct marketing helps to build business, the cost per response can seem way out of line. As again Pickholz points out: 'It's hard for marketers accustomed to a $20.00 cost per thousand to acclimate themselves to a $500 CPM, no matter how much more effective the medium has proven to be.' But the nature of direct marketing does allow for close monitoring of costs, and provides the needed flexibility to evolve increasingly more cost-effective programs.

Difference between direct marketing and traditional advertising

There are a number of ways that direct marketing differs from traditional advertising and several are detailed in Figure 7.2. Perhaps the most important difference between direct marketing and traditional advertising is that rather than trying to stimulate brand purchase intention via brand attitude through multiple exposures to the message, direct marketing usually makes only one attempt to generate a response. And as we have already discussed, while brand purchase intentions is rarely a specific objective for advertising-like messages, it is always an objective with direct marketing. The target audience is always asked to do something, and do it now.

	Direct marketing	Traditional advertising
Message delivery	Single exposure	Multiple exposures
Target audience	Individual	Mass
Distribution	The delivery medium serves as the marketplace	Distribution is used to define the marketplace
Primary communication objective	Brand purchase intention	Brand awareness and brand attitude
Accountability	Direct	Indirect

Figure 7.2
Differences between direct marketing and traditional advertising

Another difference is the personal nature of direct marketing. Because the target audience can be tightly targeted, direct marketing rarely addresses a mass audience. One speaks directly to members of the target audience about their particular needs, *and never in the third person*. Also, the focus of direct marketing is generally on existing customers (Reichheld, 1996).

Distribution is also considered in a much different light. With direct marketing, distribution itself can become an important brand benefit (e.g. not sold in stores). Direct marketing also uses the delivery medium (direct mail, telemarketing, broadcast) *as the marketplace*, whereas with traditional advertising distribution is used to define the marketplace. For example, direct marketing is really the only way many companies and others distribute their products.

In terms of communication objectives, while both brand awareness and brand attitude must be objectives, advertising will be more strongly oriented towards brand attitude goals while direct marketing clearly means to stimulate immediate brand purchase intention, the same as promotion. Yet just as we saw that promotion can and should help support brand equity, direct marketing too can help build brand equity.

One final difference is related to the issue of accountability in direct marketing and databases. In a very real sense direct marketing may be seen as 'interactive'. Based on information about the target audience a specific message is tailored to it, which in its turn repays the marketer with new information about the target market, either through a purchase response or request for information. All of this is tracked and measured, providing a record of a program's effectiveness. One of course tracks and measures the effects of advertising, but the accountability is not nearly as tight (although continuous tracking programs for advertising have made significant gains in measuring response to advertising).

In many ways, direct marketing is much like personal selling (Tapp, 1998). Before the 'sales call' one gathers as much information as possible about the customer. With direct marketing, this is found in the database. And like personal selling, direct marketing communicates directly to individuals, and the message can be tailored for them.

When to use direct marketing

Direct marketing can be an important part of IMC planning. But one must remember that it is merely *one* way to deliver marketing communication. While it has become an increasingly used tool, this does not mean that direct marketing need necessarily be a part of any particular IMC campaign, only that it should be considered when appropriate. Direct marketing is not appropriate for every type of product of service. In fact, it is almost never a good way of marketing most fast moving consumer goods (fmcg). While direct marketing can be effective for some low-involvement products, its primary use is with high-involvement products.

This does *not* mean that consumer-packaged goods marketers do not use marketing communications tools that may look like they are part of a direct marketing campaign. This is where the definition is important. Does the inclusion of an 800-number in advertising constitute direct marketing? Probably not, in most cases. What about direct mail coupons? Again, probably not. As we have seen direct marketing is a way of delivering a message that asks for an immediate response, is highly targeted, but importantly, is based on a database. An 800-number in an advert is probably a convenience for enquiry, not the primary objective of the marketing communication; and the mass mailing of coupons generally is not highly targeted. When considering the use of direct marketing in IMC planning, it should be within the bounds of its definition.

There are three questions a manager must ask when thinking about using direct marketing in an IMC program (see Figure 7.3). First of all: Does direct marketing make sense? Are there situations where a direct response is desirable? Is all or part of the target audience concentrated and easily identifiable? This would certainly be the case, for example, with customers for military aircraft or some specialized manufacturing equipment. But what about consumer markets? As we have just noted, the *key* is likely to be whether or not the purchase decision is high involvement.

- Does direct marketing make sense given the brand and its communication strategy?
- Is a good database available for identifying the target audience?
- What is the best way to deliver the message?

Figure 7.3
Questions to answer when considering direct marketing

Again, this does *not* mean direct marketing is never appropriate for low-involvement products. But it does mean that one should take a closer look if marketing low-involvement products, *and apply the definition*. Of course too, we are assuming these low-involvement products are available through traditional mass merchandising chains of distribution. Many catalogue and other marketers deal with low-involvement products, but direct marketing is their *only* (or primary) means of distribution. These marketers, if they indeed only distribute via direct marketing, are not involved with IMC.

If direct marketing does make sense, the second question that must be asked is: Is there a good database available for the target market? If direct marketing has been a part of previous marketing programs, a list is probably available. Many businesses retain customer and prospect lists. If not, lists of businesses and consumers are generally available to rent, covering almost any product category or selected demographic group. If nothing satisfactory is available, consideration could be given to developing custom lists. This, of course would only work if there were time to develop the list.

As the definition implies, a database is required for direct marketing and we will be dealing with this issue in more detail later. To underscore the importance of a database in direct marketing, it has been suggested that the quality of the list used accounts for 40 percent of the effectiveness of a direct marketing effort, compared with the headline or primary thrust of the message which account for another 40 percent, and the remainder of the message, only 20 percent (Lamons, 1992). Without a good list, direct marketing is unlikely to be effective.

The last question to ask is: How do I deliver the message? Basically, there are four media to choose from: direct mail, telemarketing, mass media, and interactive media. As a rule, only *one* form of media will be used in direct marketing when it is part of an IMC program. Messages in other media in an IMC program may play a secondary role by alerting the target market to the direct marketing efforts, but the nature and cost of direct marketing usually dictates a single, primary medium for delivering the message. An exception would be when different segments of the market are more easily reached by one medium over another. The strengths of each of these four basic media for different direct marketing tasks are highlighted in Figure 7.4, and discussed next.

Figure 7.4
Strengths of basic direct marketing media

Media	Strength
Direct mail	Greatest flexibility
Telemarketing	Provides immediate feedback
Mass media	More broadly based audience
Interactive	Largely self-selecting

Direct mail

We have already remarked that direct mail and direct marketing are often thought to be merely two ways of saying the same thing. But direct marketing is a *type* of marketing communication, not simply a way of delivering a message. Direct mail is, however, a key medium in direct marketing. It provides the greatest flexibility in targeting audiences, and provides the greatest latitude in creative options.

According to Stone (1996), direct mail has a number of advantages over other direct marketing media:

- There is greater *selectivity* with direct mail enabling more precise targeting.
- *Virtually unlimited choice of format* available.
- A greater ability to *personalize* the message.
- If someone opens and reads a piece of direct mail (a big 'if'), there is *no direct competition* for their attention.
- Because the marketer controls the mailing dates, whom it is mailed to, and what is said, direct mail offers *more control*.
- And finally, it offers a *unique capacity to involve the recipient*.

Everything from product samples to corporate gifts, brief postcards to involved messages and catalogues, can be delivered via direct mail.

Telemarketing

The telephone today probably accounts for the largest amount of direct marketing activity, but not all of that activity would be called telemarketing. Direct marketing requires an immediate response, and the telephone (especially 800-numbers) offers a convenient way for this to be accomplished. Telemarketing, however, also implies telephone contact with the target market in order to deliver some kind of message. In a more detailed definition, Stone and Wyman (1986) have said that telemarketing:

> 'Comprises the integrated and systematic application of telecommunications and information processing technologies with management systems to optimize the marketing communications mix used by a company to reach its customers. It retains personalized customer interaction while simultaneously attempting to better meet customer needs and improve cost effectiveness.'

You can see how closely aligned this definition is with the Direct Marketing Association definition of direct marketing: it enables immediate responses, it can be highly targeted, and it makes use of the best database technologies. It also underscores telemarketing's most positive advantage over other forms of direct marketing: immediate feedback. This is especially helpful in marketing high-involvement products because it permits the message to be customized to a prospect's concerns and questions as they arise.

Telemarketing does have a potentially significant drawback. By its very nature, it is non-visual. This means if your product requires visual recognition or understanding, telemarketing cannot be used. Also, in the US beginning in the early 2000s consumers were able to 'opt-out' of receiving telemarketing calls by supplying their telephone numbers to a central database.

Mass media

Direct marketing can use any mass media, the same media used by traditional advertising and promotion. The fundamental difference is the way in which the media is purchased and used. Direct marketers are looking for media that will deliver the optimum number of *immediate responses* for the least amount of money, and the use of space will be dictated by a different creative style. The use of the four major types of mass media in direct marketing is outlined next.

Television: While in the past direct marketing on television was generally confined to the early hours of the morning, it is more and more finding its way into prime time. Still not much of a factor in over-the-air television, among other reasons because it does not offer precise enough targeting, it is becoming increasingly a part of satellite and cable television. One reason for this is the somewhat-better targeting potential owing to cable channels devoted to highly specific topics (e.g. history, home and garden, sports, etc.) and the ability to run longer commercials – 60-second, 90-second, and even 2-minute commercials are not uncommon. The longer commercials, of course, permit more copy, a necessary ingredient when television is used for high-involvement products. The ultimate long commercials are 'infomercials', which are program length and run up to 30 minutes or longer. They look like regular programming, and their use is growing (Cleland, 1995).

Television commercials, and especially longer commercials and infomercials, are a good way to direct market high-involvement products where a demonstration is necessary or desirable.

Radio: As might be correctly surmised, radio is not often considered for direct marketing. The obvious reason is the difficulty in effecting an immediate response to the message. Radio is generally a 'passive' medium, listened to while driving or engaged in some other activity, making it difficult to switch attention and find pen and paper to write down a telephone number or address in order to respond to the message.

Nevertheless, radio does have the advantage of being able to tightly target specific audiences, and it is relatively economical. It also provides almost instant access for a message. Radio commercials can be quickly produced and aired; even within a day or two if necessary. These are very real advantages, but one must be sensitive to the creative challenge involved in facilitating a response (e.g. repetition of an address or telephone number, made easy to remember with, say, a mnemonic device).

Newspaper: The primary use of newspapers in direct marketing is for the distribution of various pre-printed inserts, principally free-standing inserts (FSIs). The advantage of using newspaper for direct marketing is that almost any length printed message may be inserted, and it does not need to be printed on newsprint stock; almost any paper stock can be used. Another advantage is timeliness. Newspapers are distributed daily, so a message can be scheduled for delivery on any specific day. The disadvantage is that newspapers reach an ever shrinking market, and circulation is not targeted (except, perhaps, geographically). This means newspaper should only be considered when a broad-based target audience, within specific geographic boundaries, is appropriate.

Magazines: Compared with newspapers, magazines offer the opportunity for rather focused targeting. There are magazines and trade journals aimed at almost any type of audience one might require. Where newspapers utilize FSIs, direct marketing through magazines generally will use on-page messages in the magazine itself, often with a bound-in postal reply card. There may even be stand-alone cards that by themselves carry the message (known as 'blow-ins').

In IMC planning, the inclusion of magazines to deliver direct marketing falls somewhere between highly targeted direct mail that is designed to reach specific audiences and newspapers that deliver a broad-based, geographically targeted audience. The need for specificity of target audience and cost will determine which of the three is more efficient for a printed message.

You may be wondering here why we are talking about mass media when a point was made about the need for using a database in direct marketing. In this case, a database is used to identify specific media used by the target audience, and their response to the offer is tracked by medium, and this new information added to the database.

Interactive media

Although interactive media plays a relatively small role overall in today's marketing communication programs, as discussed in the last chapter it is growing and will likely continue to grow. Technological advances almost guarantee it. Nevertheless, there are serious questions about the extent to which it is likely to ever play a really large role in direct marketing.

Perhaps the earliest example of interactive direct marketing was television shopping programs such as the Home Shopping Network in the US. While not technically 'interactive', it certainly conditioned a large number of households to television shopping, and as CD-ROM-equipped televisions become more common, shopping networks will become truly interactive. For those with CD-ROM-equipped home computers, CD-ROM catalogues are available now for interactive shopping.

Of course, the real star of interactive media is the Internet and other new media. There is no question that marketers are becoming more comfortable with the Internet. But as Harry Rosenthal, when president of Sundance Catalogue reminds us, getting people to browse through the catalogue isn't the problem, 'getting them to buy is hard because they might not be direct response buyers (Miller, 1995).' This is an important point. Just because someone buys over the Internet does not mean that they respond to direct marketing appeals.

The database in direct marketing

As the definition of direct marketing implies, a database is at the heart of a direct marketing operation. Before discussing the database in direct marketing, however, something should be pointed out. Not all uses of a database in marketing constitute direct marketing. In fact, in its broader application, use of databases in marketing is often referred to as 'database marketing'. One growing use of database marketing is in the retail area. A study of nearly 300 retailers (including large mass merchandisers as well as smaller retailers) revealed that two-thirds were using database marketing programs, and an additional 40% were planning them (Miller, 1995). They were used for everything from general promotions and information mailings to preventing customer defections and support for special promotions. Mall marketers too are using database marketing as an aid for their smaller, less sophisticated retailers (Shermach, 1995).

But not all database marketing is direct marketing. And a database is *not* just another name for a mailing list. A mailing (or telephone) list is indeed essential to a database, but a database is much more. One definition of a database describes it as 'a shared collection of interrelated data designed to meet the varied information needs of an organization.'

This data will generally combine the names of customers and prospects (including how to contact them) along with particulars about their buying or usage behaviour and other information. Obviously this can be a powerful tool in isolating very specific target groups.

The most effective use of a database is when it is a closed-loop system, according to Robert Kestinbaum (1994) when head of a large direct marketing company. In his words, one knows 'who has been contacted at what time, and at what cost', and by looking at the costs, evaluate the results. This ensures accountability. It also permits updating and re-evaluating the database.

Building a database

The steps that go into building and maintaining a database are shown in Figure 7.5. The first step is to *develop a list*. This can be done in any number of ways. If there is no customer list, the first step is to develop one. Regardless, managers should comb through all available marketing data; it may be surprising what is already on hand. Sales forces keep records, there may be warranty cards, charge records, etc. If there is time, one could survey the market. A quick start is possible by simply renting or buying a list that corresponds to the target market.

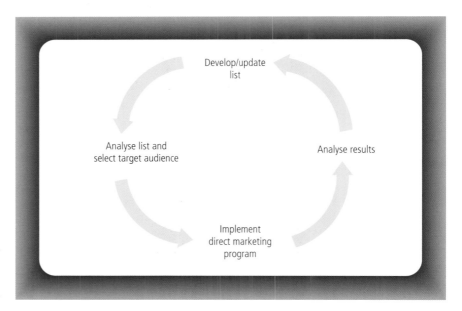

Figure 7.5
Steps in building and maintaining a database

But having a list is not enough, it must *analysed*. What information does it contain? Should the entire list be used? What does the list imply about the type of offer or means of response? Who are customers, whom prospects? Once the content of a database is understood, it is time to *use* it to implement a direct marketing program. Once the program has run, *the results must be analysed.* It is not enough to simply use a database as a source for contacting customers or prospects. One must study the effectiveness of the list. Is there any information in the database that explains why some people may or may not have responded to the message?

Developing and using a list does not make a database. One must constantly *update* all of the information. Keep track of who does, and who does not respond, to what type of messages; what are the purchase rates and patterns. In effect, retain and track the details of every direct marketing program and the response. In a very real sense one is always building a database.

Effective use of a database

Since the definition of direct marketing includes the use of a database, when to use a database in one sense is the same as when one should consider using direct marketing. This has already been discussed. What we want to briefly cover here is how a manager can use a database to help make direct marketing decisions. Figure 7.6 outlines four situations where information in a database can help guide strategic decisions as to whether or not to include direct marketing in a particular IMC program. The first situation is where it is known that people on the list make *multiple or repeat purchases* of a product or service, especially where there are high gross margins. It also helps if the purchase cycle is neither too short nor too long. If the purchase cycle is too short, even if a person is a regular customer, the margins generally will not support specialized direct marketing. If the purchase cycle is too long, unless one knows it is time for the customer to repeat, too much of the direct marketing effort could be wasted on people not in the market at the time of the campaign.

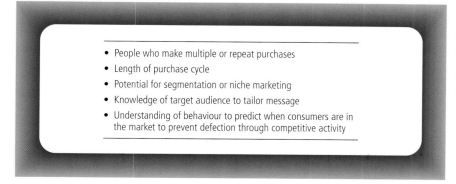

- People who make multiple or repeat purchases
- Length of purchase cycle
- Potential for segmentation or niche marketing
- Knowledge of target audience to tailor message
- Understanding of behaviour to predict when consumers are in the market to prevent defection through competitive activity

Figure 7.6
Information in database that helps identify opportunities for direct marketing

A second situation is where specialized niche marketing or *segmentation* makes sense. Direct marketing is meant to be highly targeted, and a database can reveal important segments. Of course, this assumes that the brand has compiled the relevant dependent segmentation variables in its database. Because so much is known about the customers and prospects in the database, it offers unique opportunities for *increasing business* among them. An obvious example here would be to use the database for cross-selling. Beyond this, by knowing customers well, it is possible to tailor messages to reduce switching behaviour or increase their current usage or purchase of the brand. Finally, with a good database one can predict when customers are most likely to be in the market, and prevent defections by competitive attempts to lure them away. This is why 'quick-lube' outlets send a reminder card after three months, or a bank reminds customers a savings instrument is about to mature.

Analyzing a database with these points in mind will help pinpoint potential direct marketing applications. If information that might help target particular segments is not in the database, thought should be given to what it might take to add it.

■ The role of channels marketing in IMC

Channels marketing is a term that refers to marketing communications geared to assisting the marketer at all levels of trade. The term 'channels marketing' evolved out of the importance of trade-oriented promotions. The two principal components of channels marketing are co-op advertising and tactical marketing. While cooperative or co-op advertising has been around for a long time, tactical marketing is something relatively new. Co-op advertising is essentially an arrangement between a marketer and a retailer to cooperate when selling the marketer's brand or service. It consists of advertising programs that are really nothing more than extensions of the marketer's basic marketing communication plan, funded in whole or part by the advertiser, and designed to assist the retailer in selling the brand or service.

Tactical marketing, however, is a channel-oriented marketing communication system that is designed to alter the terms of marketing in favour of the marketer and leverage incremental support from the trade (particularly retailers) by offering them specific advertising and promotion paid for by the advertiser on an *earned* basis. Simply put, the concept is to offer the retailer comprehensive customized advertising and promotional support in exchange for incremental sales features, distribution and/or store space.

Co-op advertising

While co-op advertising and tactical marketing may appear quite similar, as they should since tactical marketing is an outgrowth of basic co-op principles, the difference lies in the nature of how these techniques are applied. Co-op programs are usually broad in scope and passive in nature. In a typical co-op arrangement, a brand's entire retailer base is eligible to participate, with retailers earning a certain budget for advertising or promotion based on sales volume. The marketer provides set material for use by the retailer, and then reimburses the retailer for its use on a periodic basis up to the limits of an established budget.

Generally the retailer takes advantage of the money and marketing communication as they see fit. To counter this, marketers should make a special attempt to encourage greater retailer participation or a particular strategic shift in retailer activity by manipulating allowances or methods of allocating funds. For the most part, however, traditional co-op programs are fairly straight forward.

Tactical marketing

Tactical marketing is always a *proactive* effort. When tactical marketing is considered, a brand is looking for specific and incremental support from a given retailer. In return for this support, the marketer will create a specific program tailored to the needs of that retailer, and will fund and implement the program. With tactical marketing the *marketer* controls the entire process from beginning to end.

Tactical marketing concepts grew out of the need for brands to provide a more individualized execution than was possible with most co-op programs. In traditional co-op advertising, the marketer reimburses the retailer or pays them all or part of the cost of the advertising or promotion. As retailers became more and more powerful through consolidation and the formation of buying groups and with the expansion of national chains via mergers, they began using co-op advertising as a profit centre to offset their operating costs. Frequently funds went to increasing store margins and other non-advertising functions. With an increasing power advantage, retailers began forcing marketers to participate in retailer initiated programs which may or may not have been to the advantage of the marketer or its brands. In effect, the marketer had lost control of co-op programs to the retailer.

As a result of this situation, the tactical marketing concept was developed as an alternative retailer marketing system that could provide the marketer a means of extending brand support at the retail level with control flexibility, while providing complete coordination and production services to the retailer. This means that a retailer could take advantage of marketing communication provided by the marketer, but also in more of a partnership. Tactical marketing also enlarges on the more traditional print orientation of co-op programs by providing the retailer access to television and radio commercials, direct marketing, sponsorships, outdoor, and other IMC options. But perhaps most importantly in terms of IMC, a specific marketing communication plan customized to particular retailers is utilized, one consistent with the overall IMC strategy.

Overall, while co-op advertising programs tend to be general, passive, and standardized, tactical marketing is specific, proactive, individualized, and highly participatory.

Summary

Direct marketing and channels marketing are more than just ways of delivering a message. They also define a specific type of advertising-like or promotion-like message. In the case of direct marketing, this means a message that seeks an immediate response, and one that is part of an interactive process, tightly targeted, within an accountable system, all driven by a database.

Direct marketing is like traditional promotion in that its objective is an immediate response and the results can be measured directly. But, it is not promotion. Direct marketing may utilize both advertising-like and promotion-like messages. It differs from traditional advertising not only in terms of seeking an immediate response, but in using a single exposure versus multiple exposures, addressing a highly targeted versus more broadly based target audience, and using its delivery system as the marketplace versus using the distribution chain to define the marketplace.

Managers need to address three questions in considering the use of direct marketing as part of an IMC program. First of all, does it make sense given the brand and its communication strategy. Second, is a good database available to identify the target audience. Then, if it fits within the brand's overall communication strategy and a good database is available, what is the best medium to use in delivering the message. Here there are four basic options: direct mail, telemarketing, mass media, and interactive media. Direct-mail offers flexibility, telemarketing the opportunity for immediate feedback and the chance to adjust the message during the call, mass media can reach a broader audience (while still tightly targeted), and interactive is self-selecting.

A strong database is critical for effective direct marketing. One builds a strong database by developing a list, analyzing it, and selecting a target audience. A program is implemented, and results then become a part of the database, which is re-analysed, leading to a better targeted audience for the next effort, which will provide new information for the database, and on it goes. The database is continuously updated and refined as more information is acquired from and about the target audience.

Channels marketing grew out of a recognition by marketers of the need for more control over traditional co-op advertising. With co-op, there is an arrangement between a marketer and retailer to cooperate in joint advertising and promotion for the brand. While the advertiser may bear most or even all of the cost of the program, they have little control over implementation. Channels marketing differs in offering the trade-specific programs paid for by the advertiser or on an earned basis. This is important for IMC because it means the message will be consistent with other marketing communication for a brand since it is developed and controlled by the marketer.

■ Review questions

1 How would you define direct marketing?
2 In what ways is direct marketing similar and in what ways different from other ways of delivering advertising and promotion?
3 Why is a database critical for direct marketing?

4 What is the fundamental difference between direct marketing and traditional advertising?

5 Describe some situations when it might make sense to include direct marketing in IMC for a fmcg.

6 Discuss when you would use direct mail rather than telemarketing for a direct marketing program; and when you would use telemarketing rather than direct mail.

7 When does it make sense to use mass media in direct marketing?

8 How would you go about building a database for a new product?

9 Why are co-op advertising programs not always good for a brand?

10 How does co-op advertising differ from tactical marketing?

References

Cleland, K. (1995) More advertisers put infomercials in their plans. *Ad Age*, 18 September, 50.

Kestinbaum, R. (1994) Editorial. *Journal of Direct Marketing*, 8(3), 2–3.

Lamons, B. (1992) Creativity is important to direct marketing too. *Marketing News*, 7 December, 10.

Miller, C. (1995) Marketers find it's hip to be on the Internet. *Marketing News*, 27 February, 2.

Pickholz, J.W. (1994) From the practitioners. *Journal of Direct Marketing*, 8(2), 2–6.

Reichheld, F.F. (1996) *The Loyalty Effect*. Cambridge, MA: Harvard Business School Press.

Schultz, D.E. (1995) What is direct marketing. *Journal of Direct Marketing*, 9(2), 5–9.

Shermach, K. (1995) Large and small retailers see value in database marketing. *Marketing News*, 25 September, 8.

Stone, B. (1996) *Successful Direct Marketing Methods*. 5th edition Lincolnwood, IL: NTC Business Books.

Stone, B. and Wyman, J. (1986) *Successful Telemarketing*. Lincolnwood, IL: NTC Business Books, p. 5.

Tapp, A. (1998) *Principles of Direct and Database Marketing*. London: Financial Times Management Pitman.

IMC messages

SECTION III

In the first two sections of this book we have explored the general context of IMC, where it fits within corporate and brand strategy, and its various component parts. In this section we turn our attention to the message itself, the importance of understanding how it is processed and techniques needed to ensure that it happens. IMC is made up of advertising-like and promotion-like messages that may be delivered in a variety of ways, as we have seen. These messages are no more than a collection of words and pictures, without meaning for a brand, until successfully processed.

In Chapter 8 we shall discuss message processing, and learn how difficult it is to get a target audience to successfully process marketing communication. To begin with, it is the job of the media carrying the message to make it available to the target audience. Once exposed, it is up to the execution itself to attract and hold attention, and encourage learning the brand name and key benefit (at minimum); and for high involvement decisions, to accept the message as well. At each of these steps, emotion will be involved, informing how the message will be processed.

Maximizing the likelihood of message processing and satisfying a brand's communication objective is the job of creative executions in IMC. While it is creative instinct and genius that brings marketing communication to life, especially advertising, effective executions require much more than a great creative idea to be successful. A great creative idea could be entertaining, but may not satisfy the brand's communication objective. An idea that is not consistent with the executional requirements associated with a brand's communication objective and strategy cannot be successful. In Chapter 9 we shall be addressing some of these requirements, and looking at creative techniques that are known to help facilitate message processing, and specific creative tactics associated with brand awareness and brand attitude communication objectives.

There is a large and significant body of knowledge in psychology covering the ways in which words and pictures are used in the execution of a message that leads to successful processing. These fundamental creative techniques should be understood by everyone involved in the development, execution, and evaluation of IMC. They provide the foundation from which the creative mind must build its magic, insuring not only a memorable and unique execution, but one that is likely to satisfy the brand communication objectives and positively influence brand choice. A number of these techniques are also discussed in Chapter 9.

CHAPTER 8

Message
processing

Processing is the general term that applies to the short-term attention paid to marketing communication, and what follows. It occurs with *each* exposure to a message execution, however delivered: via traditional advertising or promotion, the package, even the product itself, or just hearing the brand name. In fact, any reference to the brand. Processing reflects how the target audience deals with the message being delivered in an integrated marketing communication (IMC) campaign. It is obviously dependent upon exposure to the message, and if successfully processed will lead to the desired response.

This process follows what McGuire (1969) referred to as an *information processing paradigm*. William J. McGuire was one of the founding fathers of attitude change theory, and he described six processing steps that must occur for any message to be persuasive. He was referring to any type of persuasive communication, and this would include advertising. The six steps were: the message must be presented to the target audience, they must pay attention to the message, comprehend what is presented, yield to the argument, retain that agreement, and then act on it.

Perhaps the most important point to understand about McGuire's information processing paradigm is that it involves *compounding probabilities*. This is why persuasive communication is so difficult. What it means is that if one is 50% successful at each stage of the process, less than 2% of the target audience will actually act upon their positive intention formed as a result of processing the message: this is the nature of compounding probabilities. If 50% are presented the message and 50% pay attention, that is 25% of the target audience; another 50% comprehend what the message is saying, meaning 12½% of the total target audience; 50% yield, or 6¼% of the target; 50% form a positive intention, a bit over 3% of the target; and 50% act upon that intention, just 1½% of the target audience. This should dramatically underscore the difficult job IMC has in effectively communicating with its target audience.

■ Communication response sequence

In an IMC sense, these six steps of the information processing paradigm may be thought of as a communication response sequence where exposure leads to processing that brings about a communication effect leading to the desired target audience action:

Exposure→Processing→Communication Effect→Target Audience Action

It is the job of IMC to ensure that all of the various executions in a campaign are contributing to this process.

Good planning will ensure exposure. The manager is responsible for scheduling media in such a way that the target audience will have ample opportunity to see and hear the messages. An important consideration at this first stage in IMC planning is how many opportunities, at minimum, will be necessary to ensure that enough processing of the message occurs to drive the desired communication effect. It may require several exposures before enough attention is paid to learn something about the brand's primary benefit; and even if a positive intention is formed, additional messages may need to be processed in order to keep that intention salient until an actual purchase is made. This can be true even with current users of a brand. If a brand is not routinely and frequently purchased, even users may need to be regularly reminded.

■ Message processing responses

The communication response sequence is triggered by exposure to any part of an IMC campaign, as well as to the brand itself during usage. In fact, as Rossiter and Bellman (2005) have pointed out, even exposure to the marketing communication of competitive brands could influence processing for a brand. For example if two competing brands are associated in memory, exposure to the competitor's marketing communication could trigger a sequence such as: 'Ah, this is the brand that claims to be better than my brand, but nothing can top my brand' for a brand loyal. Or for more casual users of the brand, perhaps: 'This is the brand that claims to be better than the one I'm using. I wonder if it is? Maybe I'll give it a try'.

The point is, processing of information about a brand can be initiated by exposure to a wide variety of sources. Thus exposure to anything related to a brand has the potential for initiating processing of information about it. One cannot control the advertising or other marketing communication of competitors, but it must be taken into account when developing one's own.

Processing itself is made up of four different responses that can follow from exposure: attention, learning, acceptance, and emotion (Figure 8.1). With the exception of emotion, which is involved with the other three, these responses reflect stages of McGuire's information processing paradigm (attention, comprehension, and yielding).

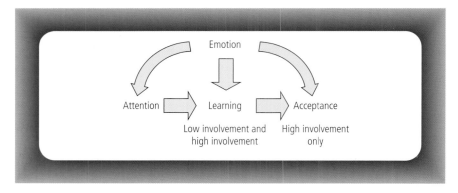

Figure 8.1
Processing responses

Attention is necessary before any of the other processing responses can occur. Without *conscious* attention being paid to the message (and again we mean message to include any reference to the brand) it will be impossible to *fully* process the message. While some have tried to argue that low attention or even subconscious attention to marketing communication can be effective, with the exception of emotional responses, it is very unlikely; and with only unconscious attention, impossible (Percy, 2006). Full processing occurs in working memory (which we shall discuss later in this chapter) where the new information that has been attended to is consciously integrated with existing knowledge and assumptions about the brand. Certain very low level learning is possible with low attention or subconscious attention, but it will not have an effect upon attitudes or preferences; which is what *full* processing is all about. But more on this subject later.

After attention comes *learning*, where some information is picked up from the execution and is stored in memory. With effective processing of the message this will include at least the brand name and the key benefit. With low involving products, for potential buyer's learning is really all that might be necessary in order to stimulate a tentatively positive attitude toward the brand and an interest in trying it. With existing users, relearning of the brand and benefit from an IMC execution serves to reinforce brand awareness and positive brand attitude. When we say 'relearning' we do not mean users have necessarily forgotten the brand, only that as they process the message it is consistent with existing memory for the brand, and makes it salient.

With high-involvement products, the target audience must not only learn what the message is trying to communicate, they must also *accept* the message. In processing the message, they must take what they have learned and integrate it with all of their knowledge and assumptions about the product category and competing brands, and believe that what the message says fits with this. If it does, this will initiate the formation of a positive brand attitude for potential new users, and help reinforce or build brand attitude for users.

The fourth response in processing is *emotion*. At some level there is an emotional response to everything one encounters in life, so that necessarily includes marketing communication. It is important to understand that emotion will be involved in attention, learning, and acceptance; and in some cases, along with attention, may be all the processing that occurs. After attending to the message someone may have a negative emotional response and *never* learn anything, including the brand name. A person may simply hate the advert, package, etc. On the other hand, someone may only have a positive emotional response and connect it with the brand, which itself could be enough to drive preference if it is a low-involvement product (especially transformational). We shall be looking at emotion in some depth later in this chapter.

Processing of messages, once it moves beyond attention, has the potential to initiate, reinforce, or increase communication effects for a brand. For those unfamiliar with a brand, at the very least brand awareness will occur. Users of the brand will likely have their brand attitude and purchase intention reinforced; potential users familiar with the brand may have their attitudes toward the brand strengthened, and a purchase intention initiated. At the same time, if marketing communication for a competitor brand is being processed, there is the potential for those communication effects to interfere with the communication effects for the first brand. This would be the case in the example above for the casual brand user whose interest in another brand was initiated by advertising. Their existing positive brand attitude for the brand they use, built and sustained by processing the brand's IMC, was interfered with by processing the other brand's advertising.

While a very simple example, this is what is going on all the time in the market. The target audience is processing messages from a wide variety of sources for a number of brands in a category, with resulting communication effects: they are aware of many brands, they have at least some tentative positive brand attitudes, and for some have formed purchase intentions. The stronger a brand's marketing communication, the greater chance it has of 'inoculating' the target audience against competitor messages. This is something McGuire (1969) talked about, how processing strong positive messages over time will build attitudes more resistant to the arguments of others.

In a sense, processing is where the target audience takes over from the marketing manager. It is the manager who provides the opportunity for exposure, but the target audience must then process the marketing communication before anything else will happen. True, the manager can help facilitate the likelihood of processing with effective creative executions, and we shall be looking at how this can be done in the next chapter. But in the rest of this chapter we want to look specifically at just how the target audience process messages. When managers understand how a message is processed, they are in a much better position to develop more effective strategic IMC plans.

Attention

Our primary concern is with the *initial* attention paid to marketing communication. Once initial attention is achieved, it is up to the execution itself (the advert, package, brochure) to hold attention and ensure further processing. While the notion of attention may seem obvious, there is nonetheless a great deal of debate in the fields of neuropsychology and neurology over just what constitutes 'attention'. In the last 50 years over a dozen different theories of attention have been proposed. Although no single theory has emerged, perhaps the work that has enjoyed the strongest influence on the meaning of attention is that of Broadbent (1958) and his filter theory. This theory basically posits that people have the ability to block or weaken the messages coming to the brain from their sense organs. It is not exactly clear how this is done, but there is ample evidence that it does occur. The result is that the content of consciousness in working memory after being filtered by attention is very limited.

Today, attention is no longer seen as a simple process that enhances perception, but rather a complex process that helps us better understand what is going on around us, and provides strategies, as well as control of, how information is processed (Gregory, 2004). In terms of marketing communication, we do not need to be concerned over the neural arguments, but we do need to understand that there is a difference between conscious and unconscious attention, and that most unconscious attention will not lead to a full processing of a message.

Unconscious processing is automatic, and reflects something psychologists talk about as 'bottom-up' processing, which deals unconsciously with signals from our senses. This is in contrast to 'top-down' processing, which calls upon the associations already in explicit or declarative memory (conscious memory) to help interpret the signals coming from our senses. However, just because someone is not aware of something does not necessarily mean they do not consciously processed it. As someone flips through a magazine or glances at a television commercial, they are probably not aware that they are paying attention to the content. Do you consciously think to yourself 'that is an advert and I am not interested'? Unlikely, but your behaviour can indicate that you did pay some attention because you keep turning the pages, or leave the room to get something to eat. Visual input into working memory (bottom-up processing) was recognized as an advert or commercial (top-down processing) and the decision was made to not further process the message.

But people do pay unconscious attention to much of what is going on around them; they just tend to ignore it. For example, research suggest that our visual system is filtering out some information even if neurologically it is being held at an unconscious level. This is especially likely if one's attention is focused somewhere else. The frontal-parietal network simply filters out some information. In a classic example of this, Simons and Chabris (1999) showed a group a film of people tossing a basketball back-and-forth, and asked the participants to count the number of passes. About a minute into the exercise someone dressed in a gorilla costume walked directly in front of the screen, yet incredibly 70% of those in the study did not notice the gorilla! When the exercise was repeated, and the participants were asked to look for the gorilla, they had no trouble seeing it.

With marketing communication, to be effective *conscious* attention is required, with one exception. Generally speaking, emotional responses are processed unconsciously. But as we shall see later in this chapter, they interact in working memory with conscious, declarative memory.

Learning and acceptance

In processing marketing communication messages, after gaining attention, the target audience must 'learn' something. At the very least, the marketer must communicate the brand name and the primary benefit associated with that brand. With low involving product decisions, that is really all that is necessary. But as we shall see later, for high-involvement decisions, the simple learning of the brand and the benefit will not be enough. The target audience must also accept the message as true.

Within a neurological or psychological context, learning means the stimulating of pre-existing synapses in the brain. It is rare that learning will involve something totally new, and the creation of a new synapse. Learning involves the integration of new information with existing knowledge and assumptions. In processing marketing communication, if one pays attention and continues to process the message, they are 'learning' at least something. But what they are 'learning' may not be new information. They may simply be learning that they already know those things about the brand. For example, people familiar with a brand will recognize it and learn that the message is about that brand, and they will bring into working memory other associations they have with that brand, and integrate it with what they are processing from the message (top-down processing, as discussed earlier). If the benefit has not already been associated with the brand in memory, what they do associate with that benefit will be brought into working memory and integrated with what they know about the brand. Then either a new memory will be formed coupling the benefit with the brand, an association with the brand will be rejected, or the message will simply be 'forgotten'.

In a psychological sense, all of this is 'learning'. The reason it is important to understand this is because when developing marketing communication executions (packages, adverts, etc.) one must be aware that the images used and the benefits presented will be understood within the framework of already existing knowledge and assumptions about those images and textual content.

Learning and brand awareness

Learning in the sense that we are using the term refers to rote learning. Rote learning is basically a passive process, and occurs automatically whether we are aware of it or not (Langer et al., 1978). Because of the nature of rote learning, a certain amount of repetition is usually required before new memories for the learned response are retained. Part of that repetition comes from the consistency in message and execution that is part of IMC.

Those unfamiliar with a brand must obviously 'learn' the brand name, but this does very little good if they do not also associate the brand with the appropriate category need. The response that must be learned will depend upon whether recognition or recall brand awareness is required, as discussed in earlier chapters. What must be learned with brand recognition strategies is that the brand will be associated with the need in such a way that when the brand is seen at the point-of-purchase it is immediately linked with the need. With recognition brand awareness, seeing the package or hearing the brand name should always elicit in the target audiences' mind the question: 'Do I need any of that now?' On the other hand, brand recall learning requires the brand be the response to the need. When the need occurs, it should elicit from the target audience the brand as satisfying that need.

The key to learning the appropriate brand awareness association is something Tulving (1983) talked about as *encoding specificity*. As he defined it, 'successful retrieval depends on achieving a match between the information encoded at the time of learning and the information that is available at the time of retrieval.' With marketing communication this means that the execution must present the brand in the same way that it is most likely to be presented when a brand choice is made. For brand recognition learning, the target audience must be able to recognize the brand at the point-of-purchase. As discussed above, this means the execution must show the package as it will be encountered, and within the context of the product category. For brand recall learning the need must be clearly shown with the brand as the solution, and in that order, so that the connection is learned in such a way that the brand name is retrieved from memory when the need occurs. We shall be dealing with creative tactics in more detail in the next chapter.

Learning and brand attitude

The key to learning for building positive brand attitude is to learn the brand's primary benefit, and link it in memory with the brand. Remember, that benefit, at least in some form, will already be associated with other things in memory. The job of a brand's marketing communication is to highlight the degree of the connection between the brand and the benefit; and the job of individual executions (things like the package, adverts, in-store collateral, etc.) is to tie in other positive associations with the benefit from memory in order to reinforce the positive nature of the benefit.

If the primary benefit for a brand of soluble (instant) coffee is 'great coffee taste', using images in executions that are likely to elicit this benefit will facilitate making that connection, and making it stronger as new memories are formed. For example, suppose the brand used a picture of an espresso machine in the background, with a steaming cup of coffee in the foreground alongside the package. The image of the steaming cup of coffee would be likely to elicit positive memories among the target audience of coffee's aroma, and this will be reinforced more positively by the association with coffee made by an espresso machine. Additionally, using a cup, not a mug, should activate more high quality association in memory. All of this is then linked to the brand, and a new memory formed. People know that soluble coffee really does not taste as good as fresh-brewed espresso. But because this is a low involving decision, all that is necessary is to create a positive feeling that it just might be good tasting coffee. When seen in the store, that positive feeling will be retrieved as they think to themselves: 'I wonder if it really does taste that good. I think I'll try it and see.'

For high-involvement decisions, however, this sort of simple rote learning will not be enough to drive positive brand attitude. To begin with, because of the risk involved, more than one benefit will usually need to be learned. Learning about the primary benefit is what will help hold the target audience's attention, and interest them in processing the rest of the advert. Assuming the primary benefit is important to them, they will then be looking for more information before beginning to form a positive brand attitude and possible brand purchase intention.

To facilitate learning when dealing with high-involvement decisions, it is important to understand the target audience's existing knowledge and assumptions about the brand and product category. In order to process and learn the brand's benefit they must be pitched in the execution at a high level, but not so high that it is dismissed as unbelievable. Knowing where this line is drawn is critical because the message should not undersell either. This idea reflects something that Sherif and Hovland (1961) long ago talked about in their assimilation-contrast theory. People hold definite beliefs about things, and if an advert for a high-involvement product makes a claim, that claim will either be accepted or not based upon these existing beliefs. If a new hybrid automobile makes the claim that it is more powerful than a BMW, the target audience is likely to dismiss it out-of-hand. Such a claim would fall into what Sherif and Hovland called their 'latitude of rejection'. How could a hybrid be more powerful than a BMW?

But what if this new hybrid really was more powerful? If that were the case, marketing communication would need to gradually build toward that claimed benefit, perhaps with a refutational strategy. This can be accomplished by pitching the claim in what Sherif and Hovland call the 'latitude of indifference', an area between what is clearly felt to be true and definitely not to be true. Perhaps the claim could be made that because of new technology this new hybrid has significantly more power. Unless the target audience believes a hybrid can never have much power, this claim could fall into their latitude of indifference: they don't necessarily agree, but they don't necessarily reject it either. They would be open to processing the message, especially if not having enough power was a significant concern among potential hybrid buyers. You can see from this example how important it is to know what the target audience's existing attitudes are when dealing with high involving decisions. If they are to successfully process the message, learning the desired benefit, it is critical to understand where their latitude of rejection lies in order not to overclaim.

In summary then, as with brand awareness, all that is required for low-involvement persuasion is rote learning of the brand benefit in order to initiate positive brand attitude. The brand name has already been learned (brand awareness learning), and it is only necessary to associate that brand in memory with its benefit. The actual response learned will be that the brand has the benefit. Because it is a low-involvement decision, the benefit is only temporarily held in memory until the product is actually purchased. But with high-involvement decisions, persuasion requires acceptance, not just learning, of the brand's benefit. The target audience must *personally agree* with the benefit claims being made for the brand.

This thinking follows directly from low- versus high-involvement models of decision-making. In psychology, low-involvement decisions follow a cognitive-conative-affect model and high-involvement decision a cognitive-affect-conative model (where cognitive reflects learning, affect attitude formation, and conative behaviour). This has been translated in the marketing and communication literature to various low-involvement choice models and the traditional hierarchy-of-effect model.

In low-involvement models, such as Ehrenberg's Awareness-Trial-Reinforcement model (Ehrenberg, 1974), one first becomes aware of the brand, then on the basis of a tentatively formed favourable attitude ('I think I might like that') the brand is tried. *After* trial, more permanent attitudes are formed. Trial of the brand will either reinforce the initial positive attitude or bring about a rejection of it. One does not necessarily need to accept that the message is really true because there is little, if any, risk involved. If the person does not like the product after trial, they simply do not buy it again. On the other hand, when dealing with high-involvement decisions, a hierarchy-of-effects model holds. One becomes aware of the brand, but because of the risk associated with making a bad choice, a *definite* positive attitude must be formed prior to trial. The buyer must be convinced they will like the brand before buying. These basic models are illustrated in Figure 8.2.

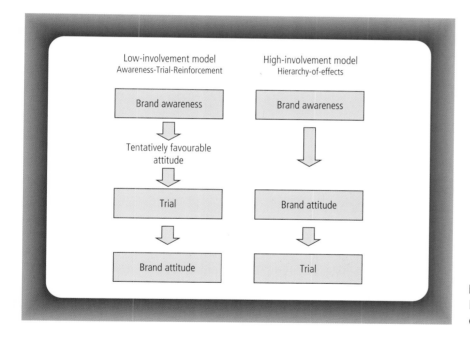

Figure 8.2
Basic consumer decision models

An experience of *Wine Enthusiast* magazine in the USA offers an excellent example of the need to consider every aspect of marketing communication in terms of how the message is likely to be processed (Strum, 2004). Wine retailers often use ratings and reviews at the point-of-purchase for wines on offer. The value of these ratings comes from the consumer's perception of the credibility of the reviewer or publication offering the rating. Thousands of wine retailers used the ratings from the *Wine Enthusiast* taste panel on 'shelf-talkers' (those small notices fixed to a store shelf with an announcement or promotion).

But, there was a problem. Retailers brought to the magazine's attention that its logo was presenting a problem. The logo used the word 'Wine' in large letters, stacked over the smaller 'Enthusiast' (Figure 8.3a). When the logo was used with a rating on a shelf-talker, the word 'Wine' was clearly visible, but the key word 'Enthusiast' that identified the magazine, and the source of the rating, was so small as to be barely perceptible. Consumer seeing the shelf-talker would process only the word wine and the rating.

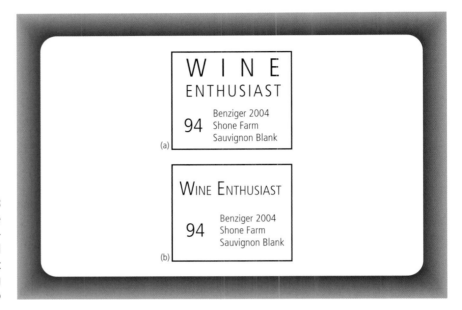

Figure 8.3
(a) Original Wine Enthusiast shelf-talker. (b) Revised Wine Enthusiast shelf-talker using new logo

This was obviously not what the retailer wanted to convey; and the magazine was receiving no exposure. The retailers wanted consumers to understand that the *Wine Enthusiast* had rated the wine highly, and in effect was recommending it. All the consumer was processing, however, was that the wine was rated highly by 'someone'. This may have been sufficient if the purchase was low involvement, but most wine purchases are likely to be high involvement. The buyer wants to be sure the wine will be good; especially for special occasions. In response to this problem, the *Wine Enthusiast* redesigned their logo (Figure 8.3b). With the new logo, ratings can be quickly and easily processed and linked to *Wine Enthusiast*; and with the new logo, the magazine had a new face, as we see in Figure 8.4.

Emotion

We have seen that processing marketing communication requires attention, learning, and for high-involvement decisions acceptance as well. But processing also involves emotion. In fact, emotion is a critical component of all message processing, and it is essential for managers to understand the role it plays. Emotion operates in two fundamental ways as it influences how marketing communication is processed. Firstly, there

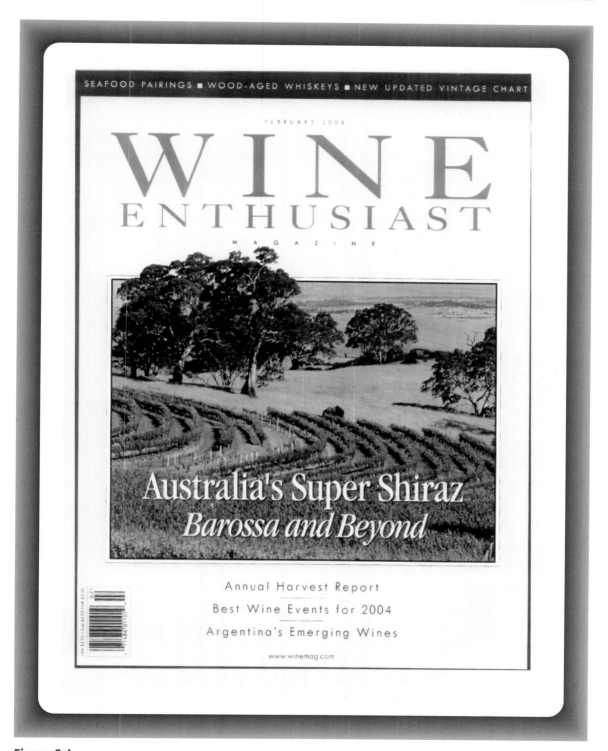

Figure 8.4
An example of how changing the masthead enabled wine ratings from the *Wine Enthusiast* magazine to make more of an impact at retail. *Courtesy*: Wine Enthusiast

Figure 8.4 (*Contd.*)

are emotional associations in memory linked to just about every object and experience in a person's life, and these emotional associations will be activated by the text and, especially, the images used in an execution. Secondly, when there are people shown in an execution, the emotion expressed by those people will stimulate a corresponding emotion in anyone paying attention to it (something known as embodiment).

The way these two emotional responses mediate the processing of marketing communication will be discussed below, but first it would make sense to look at just what is meant by an 'emotion'. To begin with, it is important to understand that emotions and feelings are *not* the same thing. An in emotion is the unconscious underlying process that embodies all of the components that go into making up an emotion, while a feeling is only the 'conscious' expression of that emotion. Damasio (1999) has described this difference well: 'The full human impact of emotions is only realized when they are sensed, when they become feelings, and when those feelings are felt. That is when they become known, with the assistance of consciousness.'

Most people who study emotion described it in terms of three different components referred to as the 'reaction triad': physiological arousal, motor expression, and subjective feeling. To illustrate this, suppose you came across a coiled snake on a path as you were walking through the woods. Before you are even conscious of the snake, your limbic system is at work signalling the body to release adrenaline and the heart to beat faster (physiological arousal), you 'freeze' (motor expression), and only then do you become aware of the sense of danger and fear (subjective feeling). All of these responses are part of emotion. While the first two have little practical value for marketing communication, subjective feeling certainly does. It is these 'feelings' with which we are concerned.

Our conscious response to an emotion, our feelings, become a part of the cognitive process that leads to logical thinking. It helps increase attention and learning when consistent with the relevant underlying motivation driving behaviour and choice in the brand's product category. Damasio (2003) has stated that reasoning is influenced not only by conscious signals, but also by unconscious signals from the neural networks associated with emotions. This means that along with a person's knowledge and experience with a brand, the emotional associations with these memories will influence brand choice.

Recent studies in neuropsychology using neuroimagery with positron emission tomography (PET) scans and functional magnetic resonance imagery (fMRI) that measure brain activity when information is being processed have confirmed the role emotion plays in brand choice decisions. In one study (McClure et al., 2004) brain activity was measured with fMRI as people made a choice between two colas. When they did not know what they were drinking, the only areas of the brain that were active were those associated with taste perception. But for those whose favourite brand was Coke, when they were asked to choose between Coke and Pepsi, knowing what they were tasting, those areas of the brain associated with emotional memory were active when they stated their preference.

Clearly, if managers can measure and understand the emotional associations with brands and with their marketing communication executions they will have a powerful tool for developing more effective messages; messages more likely to be positively and fully processed. Gaining this understanding is not as difficult as one might think. Measuring emotional associations is done by simply asking about the *feelings* associated with something. According to Bradley and Lang (2000), people become conscious of their emotions when asked, and are quite capable of describing their feelings when asked to think about it.

Emotional associations in memory

Few, if any objects or experiences are emotionally neutral. Everything one experiences and forms long-term memory traces of will have an emotional component. Adverts, packages, and other marketing communication for a brand will activate not only cognitive, conscious associations from memory (declarative, or explicit memory as we shall see later in the chapter when we talk about memory), but also unconscious emotional associations (nondeclarative emotional memories) with the brand. These memories are stored in the amygdala, part of the limbic system, and located in the paleomammalian region of the brain.

As one begins to process marketing communication, the emotional memories associated with the imagery used in the execution, as well as the brand itself, will proceed into conscious working memory, and it will arrive *ahead* of whatever conscious memories are activated. These emotional memories help 'frame' the knowledge and assumptions activated in conscious memory (largely from the hippocampus), and inform how the message will be initially processed. One of the most important jobs in IMC, which we shall be underscoring in the next chapter, is insuring a consistent look and feel among all of the various executions in different media. This helps ensure that the same emotional memories are activated in the processing of the messages.

This means that when an advert or other marketing communication for a brand cues either positive emotional associations with the brand or with the imagery in an execution, those unconscious emotional memories will mix with conscious memory and enable a person to become aware of the fact that they are emotionally aroused. For example, they may experience a good feeling, or even a happy feeling. Out of the processing that occurs, new associations in memory are possible and likely. Any emotional learning, if linked to the brand, as well as learning associated with the benefit in the message, will be in play and ready to be activated when exposed to new advertising for the brand, when the brand is seen at the point-of-purchase, even when just 'thinking' about the brand. Effective marketing communication, utilizing common executional elements within an IMC campaign, will ensure this happens.

Still, it must be remembered that while positive emotional associations in memory will provide an initial positive context within working memory for processing the message, it does not have the strength to override negative conscious elements in the processing (e.g. noticing that the price of the brand has increased significantly). But in all other cases these positive emotional associations will facilitate positive processing of the message and the formation of new positive memories: in other words, learning.

Interpersonal emotion

The second area of emotion important to understand in the processing of marketing communication is interpersonal emotion and the notion of *embodiment*. Other people's emotions influence our own by virtue of the information they convey. This is thought by some social and evolutionary psychologists to be part of our natural response to our environment in order to survive. Sensing fear or anger in someone conveys potential threat or danger; happiness, safety or comfort. When people are shown in adverts, on packages, storefronts, or in other marketing communication, and they convey particular emotions, those perceived emotions will tend to influence parallel emotional responses in the target audience.

This is known as embodiment. In other words, people will embody, that is take on or initiate, the emotional behaviours of others as perceived in their facial expression, body posture, or prosody (tone of voice). As Niedenthal et al. (2005) have defined it, embodiment means 'the bodily states that arise (e.g. posture, facial expression, and use of the voice) during the perception at an emotional stimulus, and the later use of emotional information (in the absence of the emotional stimulus)'. In effect, the emotions exhibited by people in, for example, an advert, will be 'felt' by those attending to it, and that emotion will become part of the processing in working memory of that message. This will be available for later use when processing other messages about the brand.

The most important component in assessing someone else's emotional state is their facial expression, and this has been studied more than any other aspect of emotional expression (deGelder, 2005). It seems that people have a very efficient system for recognizing and processing the emotional content of facial expressions. And, as with emotional memories, the amygdala is at the heart of how emotional expressions are processed (Wright et al., 2002).

When looking at someone's facial expression, it is the eyebrows, mouth, and eyes that convey emotion. Based upon a study of schematic faces representing happy vs. threatening faces (as illustrated in Figure 8.5), Lundqvist and Öhman (2005) found that V-shaped eyebrows conveyed a threatening emotion while Λ-shaped eyebrows were seen as friendly. They also found that a U-shaped mouth conveys a happy feeling while a ∩-shaped mouth was seen as unhappy. Using eye tracking, they also determined that the most important facial cue communicating threat or anger was the eyebrows, and for communicating a happy feeling, the mouth. Subsequent work using image analysis of real faces supported these findings.

This of course has direct implications for executions in marketing communication. To communicate a positive, happy emotion requires attention

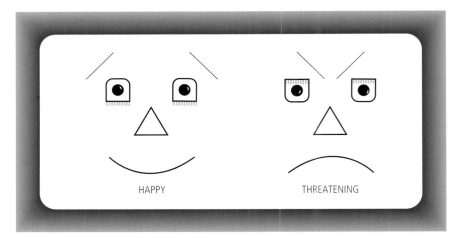

Figure 8.5
Happy versus threatening schematic faces. *Source*: Adapted from Lundqvist and Little (2004)

to a true 'smile'. Rossiter and Percy (1997) pointed out the need for depicting an authentic emotion, critical for transformational strategies. But, this is not easy to effect. Even experienced actors have difficulty realistically projecting an emotion that is not truly felt, and this is especially true of smiles. This is because of the evolutionary importance of smiles. The facial muscles that control smiles are affected by two distinct neural systems. The evolutionarily older one originates in the striatum and exerts an involuntary control over facial muscles, reflecting truly felt emotions (Fridland, 1994). The second, in terms of evolution, is newer and involves voluntarily controlled muscles (Gazzaniga and Smylie, 1990). As a result, the use of the intentionally controlled muscles for a smile that an actor may use in smiling might not reflect a true positive emotion.

These voluntary smiles need only involve the mouth, and are consciously seen and interpreted as a smile, as the work by Lundqvist and Öhman (2005) has shown. The truly felt positive emotions such as happiness will also involve the muscles around the eye, and this will initiate an embodiment of the emotion. Such smiles are known as 'Duchenne Smiles' after the 19th century French anatomist Duchenne de Boulogue. A true Duchenne Smile is an unintentional emotional signal that occurs spontaneously upon the experiencing of the positive emotion of joy or happiness, reflecting a true emotional state. This is what one is looking for when using people in marketing communication and one wishes to elicit a positive emotional response (essential for transformational brand attitude strategies).

■ The role of memory

One must be concerned with memory in any consideration of IMC because of the very nature of IMC. With multiple messages, delivered through different media, how these messages are processed and stored in memory will be critical to the overall effectiveness at the campaign. It is essential that as different messages are processed they become part of a unified memory for the brand. Even though various messages, and various aspects of individual messages, may be processed differently, they must be associated in memory with the brand, and available for subsequent processing when the brand is being considered.

In this chapter we have referred a number of times to 'conscious' and 'unconscious' processing, and will deal with this in more detail below. In many ways what we are really talking about here when talking about processing and its result is *memory*. Conscious processing involves the use of what psychologists call declarative or 'explicit' memory. Unconscious processing involves what is known as nondeclarative or 'implicit' memory, and generally reflects what we have talked about as 'bottom-up' processing. It is important to understand that even if there happens to be unconscious processing of marketing communication leading to implicit memory (unlikely in any case), those memories cannot inform brand attitudes or choice. The only exception here are nondeclarative emotional memories (Percy, 2006).

Declarative and nondeclarative memories recruit different brain systems and use different strategies for storing memory (Heilman, 2002). One's declarative memory is for facts, assumptions, and events, the sorts of things that one can bring consciously to mind as either a verbal proposition ('that is an expensive, luxury product') or a visual image (in our mind's eye we 'see' the product). Nondeclarative memories also come from experiences, but they are expressed in terms of unconscious changes in behaviour, not as conscious recollections. With the exception of emotion, nondeclarative memories are generally inaccessible to the conscious mind. Such memories tend to involve knowledge that is *reflexive* rather than *reflective* in nature (Heilman, 2002). Importantly in terms of IMC and brand learning, once something is stored in nondeclarative memory, that unconscious memory *never* becomes conscious.

Unconscious processing

There is a great deal that people process, but are unaware of it. It is impossible to consciously attend to everything in our environment; and much of our behaviour is unconscious. This is what enables a driver to stop at a red light, a person to type, or to play the piano. One does not consciously think: 'That light just turned red, what should I do?' One simply applies the brake. In typing or playing the piano, one does not consciously recall where the letter 'g' is located on the keyboard or where the note b-flat is on their instrument. They automatically type the letter or play the note. This is called procedural memory, a key part of nondeclarative or implicit memory, and behaviour associated with it is unconscious.

There are other forms of nondeclarative, or unconscious, memory, and some have tried to argue that it in fact can have a positive effect in processing advertising and other marketing communication. They suggest that messages are processed unconsciously, and this is an additional 'power' of advertising, having a subtle, unconscious effect upon brand attitude and behaviour. As already pointed out, this is impossible neurologically. The neural systems involved are separate from those involved in conscious processing and behaviour, and implicitly processed information does not recognize the use of higher-order, conscious manipulation.

Often these proponents of unconscious processing point to the work of Zajonc and his colleagues, and his notion of 'mere exposure'. Indeed, there are such things as priming effects (Zajonc, 1968; Murphy and Zajonc, 1993). For example, having seen or heard words or pictures briefly, even subconsciously, it can increase the likelihood of using them later (Kalat, 2004). But priming effects are largely a response to familiarity among a set of otherwise unfamiliar alternatives. As we have pointed out elsewhere (Percy, 2006), even if there is unconscious processing of advertising, there is simply no reason to expect a priming effect because of the other brands, as well as attitudes toward the 'primed' brand, will be recalled from *conscious* memory during brand choice.

Before leaving this subject, however, we must be careful to point out that we are *not* suggesting that something that is not fully attended to will not be consciously processed. People frequently process things consciously without paying attention to it or necessarily knowing it at the time. What we have been talking about here is processing that is *neurally* unconscious.

Conscious processing

People respond 'consciously' to everything they are exposed to and to which they actively attend neurologically. Psychologists like to talk about this in terms of *cognitive response*, which is nothing more than a conscious activity that goes on when actively processing information. Even though someone may not consciously be aware of everything that is being processed, they are associating in working memory the new information (e.g. exposure to an advert or seeing a brand on the shelf) with all the relevant knowledge and assumptions already stored in declarative memory. This is top-down processing, and involves declarative, explicit memory; our conscious memory.

People bring to brands and their marketing communication attitudes and beliefs, associated with their expectations, and experiences; and this will all inform how they think about that brand and process information about it. This follows from the two fundamental types of conscious memory: semantic memory and episodic memory (Tulving, 2002a,b). Semantic memory may be thought of as 'fact-based', and will include a general knowledge and understanding of brands and products. Episodic memory is 'event-based', and will include a person's experience with brands and products. This would not only include using the brand, but memories of an event that was sponsored by the brand. Together both semantive and episodic memory combine to form declarative, conscious memory, and are integrated with new information as it is processed in working memory to form and build new memories linked to the brand.

In terms of cognitive response theory, it is assumed that people will try to make sense out of what they are experiencing: looking at a product display in a store, reading an advert in a magazine or watching a commercial on television, or attending an event sponsored by a company. How they make sense of what they are experiencing is by accessing the appropriate declarative memories from both semantive and episodic memory. It is the job of IMC to be sure a consistent base of knowledge and experience is available for making judgments about a brand (brand attitude) and making choices (brand purchase intention).

Summary

In this chapter we have discussed what is involved in processing marketing communications. It is important for managers to understand this because every aspect of IMC must be conceived to maximize the likelihood that a message will be positively processed, leading to the appropriate target audience action. Information is processed hierarchically, following the six steps of McGuire's Information Processing Paradigm. The message must be presented to the target audience; they must be attend to it, understand what is presented and yield to the argument; they must retain that agreement and then act upon it.

The important point here is that the process is hierarchical, involving *compounding probabilities*. This means each step in processing information is dependent upon the successful completion of the previous step, and the percentage of the target audience positively responding at each step is multiplied over the six steps. So if 60% of the target audience is exposed to a message and 45% pay attention, that means only 27% of the target audience is even available to learn something; and so on through the last step, acting on the message.

For IMC planning, McGuire's Information Processing Paradigm has been reconfigured into the Communication Response Sequence, where *exposure* is followed by *processing* in order to achieve the desired *communication effect*, which should lead to *target audience action*. Obviously, the target audience must have the opportunity to see or hear an execution (exposure), and this is the job of media planning, the final step in the strategic planning process for IMC. Once exposed, the message must be processed, and successful processing involves: attention, learning, acceptance, and emotion.

Conscious attention is required in order to fully process the message. One may not necessarily be aware of the message at first, but neurologically it must activate conscious processing in working memory, which will then lead to active, conscious learning. At minimum for successful processing, the target audience must learn the brand name and primary benefit. With high-involvement decisions, because of the risk involved in making a bad choice, the target audience must except the message as true. With low-involvement decisions acceptance is not necessary because there is no real risk involved. The target audience need only think the message might be true in order to be motivated to try the brand.

Mediating attention, learning, and acceptance is emotion. People have emotional responses to everything with which they come in contact, and this includes marketing communication. These emotional responses, along with already existing nondeclarative emotional memories linked to the brand and to elements within an execution, will all be at work to attract and hold attention, and facilitate learning and acceptance. New memories are then formed based upon what has been processed, mediated by those emotions. These new memories are then available, with the emotional associations, when brand purchase decisions are made.

This last point is important. By its nature IMC will most often involve multiple messages being delivered through various media. The need for a consistent look and feel over all IMC executions will be discussed in the next chapter. But additionally, it is critical that the processing of each message leads to a unified memory for the brand. Even though each message is processed individually, they must be associated with the brand consistently in memory. These memories become part of the knowledge and assumptions about the brand, stored in declarative, explicit memory. This is our conscious memory, and is required for attitude formation and purchase behaviour.

Although some have tried to argue for unconscious processing of marketing communication, while some messages or parts of messages may be processed unconsciously and enter nondeclarative, implicit memory, those memories cannot inform attitudes or brand behaviour. It is impossible because different brain systems are involved. Emotion is the only component of nondeclarative memory that has any effect upon IMC message processing.

■ Review questions

1 What must happen for a message to be successfully processed?
2 Why is it so difficult for marketing communication to result in a brand purchase?
3 How can processing advertising for a competitor help a brand?
4 Can unconscious processing of marketing communication be effective for a brand?
5 Discuss attention and its role in message processing.
6 What is the role of learning in building brand awareness?
7 How does learning differ for high versus low involving product decisions?
8 What is the role of emotion in message processing?
9 Discuss the two ways in which emotion can effect the way in which marketing communication is processed.
10 Look at some adverts and record your 'feelings' as you look at them. Where do they come from? What is it about the executions that elicit those emotions?
11 Why is it important for managers to understand the role of memory in processing marketing communication?
12 What is the difference between semantic and episodic memory? Find examples of advertising that are likely to involve each.

References

Bradley, M.M. and Lang, P.J. (2000) Measuring emotion: Behaviour, feeling, and physiology. In R.D. Lang and L. Nadel (eds.), *Cognitive Neuroscience of Emotion*. Oxford: Oxford University Press, pp. 242–276.

Broadbent, D. (1958) *Perception and Communication*. London: Pergaman.

Damasio, A. (1999) *The Feeling of What Happens*. San Diego, CA: Harcourt.

Damasio, A. (2003) *Looking for Spinoza*. Orlando, FL: Harvest Books.

Ehrenberg, A.S.C. (1974) Repetitive advertising and the consumer. *Journal of Advertising Research*, 14(2), 25–34.

Fridland, A.J. (1994) *Human Facial Expressions: An Evolutionary View*. New York: Academic Press.

Gazzaniga, M.S. and Smylie, C.S. (1990) Hemispheric mechanisms controlling voluntary and spontaneous facial expressions. *Journal of Cognitive Neuroscience*, 2, 239–245.

deGelder., (2005) Nonconscious emotions: New findings and perspectives on nonconscious facial expression and its voice and whole body context. In L.F. Barnett, R.M. Niedenthal, and P. Winkielman (eds.), *Emotion and Consciousness*. New York: The Guilford Press, pp. 123–149.

Gregory, R.L. (2004) *The Oxford Companion to the Mind*. 2nd edition. Oxford: Oxford University Press.

Heilman, K.M. (2002) *Matter of Mind*. Oxford: Oxford University Press.

Kalat, J.W. (2004) *Biological Psychology*. 8th edition. Belmont, CA: Wadsworth.

Langer, E., Blank, A., and Chanowitz, B. (1978) The mindlessness of ostensibly thoughtful action: The role of "placebic" information in interpersonal interaction. *Journal of Personality and Social Psychology*, 36(6), 635–642.

Lundqvist, D. and Öhman, A. (2005) Caught by the evil eye: Nonconscious information processing, emotion, and attention to facial stimuli. In L.F. Barnett, P.M. Niedenthal, and P. Winkielman (eds.), *Emotional and Consciousness*. New York: The Guilford Press, pp. 97–122.

McClure, S.M., Li, J., Tomlin, D., Cypert, K.S., Montague, L.M., and Montague, P.R. (2004) Neural correlates of behavioural preference for culturally familiar drinks. *Neuron*, 44, 379–387.

McGuire, W.J. (1969) The nature of attitudes and attitude change. In G. Lindsey and E. Aronson (eds.), *The Handbook of Social Psychology*. Vol. 3. Reading, MA: Addison-Wesley.

Murphy, S. and Zajonc, R.B. (1993) Affect, cognition, and awareness: Affect priming with suboptimal and optimal stimuli. *Journal of Personality and Social Psychology*, 64, 723–739.

Niedenthal, P.M., Barsalou, L.W., Riz, F., and Krauth-Gruber, S. (2005) Embodiment in the acquisition and use of emotion knowledge. In L.F. Barret, P.M. Niedenthal, and P. Winkleman (eds.), *Emotion and Consciousness*. New York: The Guilford Press, pp. 21–50.

Percy, L. (2006) Unconscious processing of advertising and its effects upon attitudes and behaviour. In S. Diehl and R. Terlutter (eds.), *International Advertising and Communication*. Wiesbaden, Germany: Deutcher Universitäts-Verlag, pp. 110–121.

Rossiter, J.R. and Bellman, S. (2005) *Marketing Communications, Theory and Applications*. French Forest, NSW, Australia: Pearson Education Australia.

Rossiter, J.R. and Percy, L. (1997) *Advertising Communication and Promotion Management*. New York: McGraw-Hill.

Sherif, M. and Hovland, C.I. (1961) *Social Judgement*. New Haven: Yale University Press.

Simons, D.J. and Chabris, C.F. (1999) Gorillas in our midst: Sustained in attentional blindness for dynamic events. *Perceptions*, 28, 1059–1074.

Strum, A. (2004) The changing face of Wine Enthusiast. *Wine Enthusiast*, May, 10.

Tulving, E. (1983) Elements of Episodic Memory, Oxford: Oxford University Press.

Tulving, E. (2002a) Episodic memory: From mind to brain. *Annual Review of Psychology*, 53, 1–25.

Tulving, E. (2002b) *Elements of Episodic Memory*. Oxford: Clarendon Press.

Wright, C.H., Martis, B., Shin, L.M., Fischer, H., and Rauch, S.L. (2002) Enhanced amygdala responses to emotional versus neutral schematic facial expressions. *Neuroreport*, 13, 785–790.

Zajonc, R.B. (1968) Attitudinal effects of more exposure. *Journal of Personality and Social Psychology Monographs*, 9(2, part 2), 1–27.

CHAPTER 9

Creative
execution

In the last chapter, we looked at how marketing communication is processed. Now we will be looking at the creative tactics that should be used in order to optimize the likelihood that a message will be processed. First, we shall discuss some general principles and creative tactics that reflect our understanding of how certain aspects of a message execution can significantly affect how well it will be processed. We shall be addressing the ways in which the words and pictures used in an execution can maximize attention and learning. Research in psycholinguistics and visual imagery have yielded a great deal of knowledge about how the way in which something is said, or the characteristics and the images used in visual communication, can affect the likelihood someone will pay attention and learn something from the message. We will be reviewing a number of these findings that have a direct bearing on marketing communication.

Following this, we will be looking more specifically, at the creative tactics needed to address brand awareness and brand attitude objectives, and how consistency across different integrated marketing communication (IMC) executions will enhance the overall power of a brand's marketing communication.

■ Gaining attention

How much attention someone is likely to pay to marketing communication is generally a function of the way in which words and visual images (pictures and illustrations) are used in an execution. Additionally, for print, the size of the execution and its focal point will influence the degree of attention paid; and for broadcast (both television and radio), the length of the commercial. But attracting attention is only the first step. Executions must also *hold* attention so the message can be processed. In this section we will be discussing some of the creative tactics that can help both attract and hold attention (summarized in Figure 9.1).

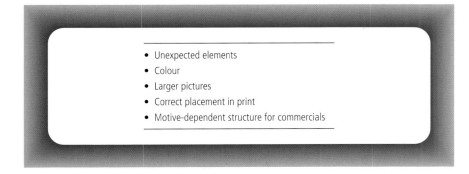

- Unexpected elements
- Colour
- Larger pictures
- Correct placement in print
- Motive-dependent structure for commercials

Figure 9.1
Creative tactics for gaining attention

Unexpected elements

According to Myers (1994), one of the easiest ways to attract attention in print is to use letters in unexpected ways or by altering the spelling of words. A very good example of this is the provocative logo for the French Connection UK (FCUK). In broadcast, the repetition of particular sounds can help draw attention to a brand name or slogan, and reinforced it in memory.

The reason unexpected things attract attention is that people are accustomed to experiencing things in certain ways, and when there is a departure from the norm, interest is aroused. People tend to notice changes in things that are out of the ordinary. If you were to hear someone say 'you placed the em*phasis* on the wrong syl*lable*,' stressing the second syllable rather than the first in emphasis and syllable, your attention would be immediately drawn to what was said. In marketing communication this can easily be done in the voice track by simply placing more emphasis on a particular word where it would not be expected.

Colour

For all print media, four-colour (i.e. full colour) attracts more attention than two-colour, which attracts more attention than black and white. This is true for both consumer as well as business and trade marketing communication. One sometimes hears arguments from marketing practitioners that black and white adverts will attract attention because they 'stand out' from clutter. However, there is nothing to support this idea. In fact, attention to black and white adverts in consumer magazines is about 30% less than full color adverts; and the advantage is even greater in newspaper. With business-to-business advertising, color adverts draw about 50% more attention than black and white (Rossiter and Bellman, 2005).

Size of picture or illustration

In print advertising the picture or illustration will draw most of the attention of a reader. For example, about 70% of the time looking at print adverts is spent looking at the picture (Rossiter, 1988). Research has consistently found that the larger the picture size in an advert, the more it will be processed (cf. Franke et al., 2004). There is an old rule-of-thumb in advertising that attention to print adverts will increase at a rate of about the square root of its size. This would mean that an advert with a picture or illustration four times larger than that in another advert should receive twice the attention (the square root of four being two).

Picture size is especially important for low-involvement transformational advertising where traditionally the picture is the most important element of the execution. But a key point to bear in mind is that when talking about picture size we are referring to a picture or illustration with a single dominant focal point (Franke et al., 2004). In other words, a single picture, not several, making up the size and the visual content; and in that single picture, only one central image.

Print placement

While not strictly a creative tactics, where adverts are placed within a magazine can have a significant effect on how much attention will be paid to it. Back cover placement will gain the highest attention, followed by the inside covers; and cover position in business-to-business publications will have very high-attention value (Rossiter and Bellman, 2005). Paradoxically, having another advert on a facing page will actually *increase* attention slightly, while editorial content will significantly hurt attention to a nearby advert.

Format

With print advertising, the trend to smaller newspaper page size does not appear to have any affect on attention to adverts within, nor does the page size of magazines impact the attention paid to its adverts. Interestingly, the size of a banner advert on the Internet does not affect attention (Ahn and Edwards, 2002).

The length of commercials, for both radio and television, is directly related to attention. The longer the commercial, the greater the attention (Ritson, 2003). The number of cuts in a commercial does not seem to affect the attention, even though as the number of cuts rise above the average of 13 per 30 commercial, the level of *arousal* does increase. While this does not seem to affect attention, it does impact learning.

The key to *holding* attention with television commercials is a function of the pattern or structure of the execution. Communication for informationally driven commercials should use a *two-peaked pattern* where the category need is presented first, the brand identified in between, and the benefit provided in the second peak. In this way the target audience recognizes the need, associates the brand with that need, then 'stay tuned' to learn how the brand can satisfy that need. With transformationally driven commercials, the execution should reflect a *raising* pattern, beginning with brand identification and followed by a building of positive emotion, ending with a definite 'kick' (Rossiter and Percy, 1997).

■ Facilitating learning

It is, of course, not enough to simply pay attention to marketing communication, one must also 'learn' what it is trying to say. Critically, this means learning the brand and its primary benefit. There are a number of ways to facilitate learning based on the way words and pictures or illustrations are used within the creative execution. In this section we shall review a number of ways in which attention to how words and pictures are used in an execution can increase the likelihood that someone will continue to process the message (after attending to it) and learn the brand and its benefit (summarized in Figure 9.2).

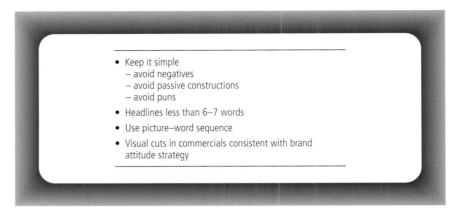

Figure 9.2
Creative tactics for facilitating learning

- Keep it simple
  – avoid negatives
  – avoid passive constructions
  – avoid puns
- Headlines less than 6–7 words
- Use picture–word sequence
- Visual cuts in commercials consistent with brand attitude strategy

Keep it simple

There is a large body of research that has found that using familiar words in familiar ways will facilitate learning (Paivio, 1971). The more complex or difficult a sentence, the greater the likelihood there will be difficulties in processing, and hence learning. This means avoiding passive sentences and long or complicated sentence structures. One should avoid the use of puns (verbal or visual) unless you are certain they will be *readily* understood by the target audience. The English are very fond of using puns in advertising, but to be effective the point must be understood immediately.

The headline for a BMW advert reads: 'Bigger boots. Move Welly.' What is the benefit here? In the UK 'welly' would be understood as short for wellingtons, which is the generic for rubber boots. What associations are being activated from memory by the words 'boots' and 'welly'? How does this relate to 'bigger boots'? Does this reinforce the benefit of '1,385 litre of boots space' in the 3,300, where 'this large, uncluttered space provides a variety of flexible storage options' (as detailed well into the copy)? One must be very careful with puns. If used they must quickly be seen as conveying the 'real' meaning.

It is also a good idea to avoid using negatives. A great deal of research has been done that says it is more difficult to process negatives used in phrases or sentences. The problem is that to correctly understand a sentence using a negative requires two-step processing. One must first process the negative word, then 'reverse' the meaning. This is certainly not to say one should never use negatives, but it does mean that one must be careful the meaning is quickly and easily understood. In addition to the potential problem associated with two-step processing, when negatives such as 'not' are embedded in a sentence, it is very easy for the eye to simply miss it unless one is carefully paying attention.

Use short headlines

Using short headlines is important because of the way people read. They do not read each word one at a time, but rather process *groups* of words.

Those groups are made up of fewer than six or seven words, depending upon their length (Wearing, 1973). Look at the following headline:

Shoes Designed to Move You

The moment you glanced at the headline, you processed it at once. It was not necessary to 'read' the words, it was understood as a unit. On the other hand, with larger headlines the eye will initially only register a group of words, with perhaps taking meaning from a few scattered words near the edge of the group. Look at the following headline:

Everything Your Skin Needs Most to Face Winter

To understand what it says requires one to be motivated to spend time processing it.

The implications of this for advertising are obvious. If someone is flipping through a magazine, each page will attract at least momentary attention in order to see if there is anything there worth holding their attention. But if there is a short headline, less than six or seven words, even with brief exposure if the eye falls on the headline its content will be processed and communicated. Copy on posters and outdoor, as well as on packages, should also be short in order to ensure processing at a glance.

Picture–word sequence

The order in which the eye attends to the pictures or illustrations and words in marketing communication will affect learning. In a study reported by Brainerd et al. (1987), it was found that when people confront a picture–word sequence rather then a word–picture sequence, learning increases. Contributing to this phenomenon could be the fact that pictures are known to have superiority over words in learning (Eyesenk, 1977; Bryce and Yalch, 1993). People tend to automatically engage with pictures, and they seem to elicit more elaboration from memory than words. Myers (1994) has made this point with a very good example. If you were to read about a new soap that would make you beautiful, you would no doubt be a bit sceptical. But if you saw a picture of a beautiful woman holding a bar of that new soap, the image of the beautiful woman would help reinforce the claim, and you would be more inclined to believe it.

But one must be careful not to take this idea of a picture–word sequence literally, at least for print, and this includes the Internet. It does *not* mean, for example, that a picture or illustration must be at the top of the page, with the headline and copy at the bottom. What it means is that the eye should be drawn to the picture or illustration first, then the headline. This is in generally not a problem because the eye is more likely to be initially drawn to the visual. However, this can always be checked with eye-tracking.

This same idea also applies with television. When important points are to be made by people in a commercial, by voice-over or printed boards on screen, they should be immediately *preceded* by an appropriate visual element that elicits reinforcing memories that will help facilitate the processing of the verbal claims (Young and Robinson, 1989, 1992; Rossiter and Percy, 1997).

Pacing of commercials

In our discussion of format and attention earlier, we talked about the optimum patterns in commercials for gaining attention. Another aspect of this concerns the pacing, or the number of visual cuts in the execution. While the increase in arousal associated with more than the average of 13 cuts per 30 commercial may be good for transformational advertising where the emotional 'feeling' is so critical, it definitely is *not* for informational executions. With higher numbers of cuts, only peripheral, executional content is likely to be learned. This is fine for transformational strategies where the benefit is in the emotional response to the execution itself. But with informational strategies, it is necessary to process and learn the content of the message, and this cannot happen when the number of visual cuts is much more than the average.

Interestingly, it is often argued that viewers today, and especially younger viewers of the so-called 'MTV-generation', are conditioned to fast-cut visuals. That may be true, but that does not mean they are processing much beyond sensual stimulation. In fact, at an MTV-rate of 20 or more cuts per 30 commercial, loss of attention among 18–34 year olds is actually *greater* than among older adults (MacLachlan and Logan, 1993).

■ Consistency in IMC executions

One of the most important, and often most difficult, tasks for IMC is ensuring consistency in executions within and across the different types of marketing communication a brand is using, as well as over time. *Everything* connected with an IMC campaign should have a similar 'look and feel'. That means everything from adverts to direct mail to collateral to packaging to posters to the sides of delivery trucks to business cards and letterheads – everything.

The target audience should be able to immediately identify any execution within a campaign, and over time, as belonging to the brand. This is an important part of a brand's identity, and the more consistent the executions, the more readily brand awareness and communicating the brand benefit will be achieved. In fact, in time the inclusion of the brand name would not even be necessary. People will associate in memory the 'look' of the brand's marketing communication with the brand. Yet it is surprising how many marketers do not seem to understand this. Too often a brand's advertising changes completely within a campaign; and it is not at all unusual for a brand's promotions to have nothing visually in common with its advertising (or in terms of the benefit).

A consistency in execution does *not* mean everything must look exactly the same. It is a 'feeling' that ties everything together, and this evolves over time. In fact, some variation in execution is essential to maintain attention and interest, and to help forestall wear out. What is needed is a *unique* look or feel to everything that is done so that the target audience recognizes a brand's marketing communication even before they see the brand name.

The long-running campaign for Silk Cuts tobacco in the UK (up until all tobacco advertising was banned in the early 2000s) was one of the best examples of what we are talking about. For years the brand's advertising never included the brand name. The adverts were always some variation of scarlet silk and a 'cut'. Of course, it took many years of advertising following this 'look' *with* the brand name to seed the association in memory before it could be dropped from the advertising. The advert shown in Figure 9.3 illustrates this, and represents the last of Silk Cut's advertising in the UK (it isn't over until the fat lady sings, as they say, and she is singing). We are not advocating that one's goal should necessarily be to reach a point where the brand name is no longer used (after all, there are always new people entering the market), only that it reaches the point

Figure 9.3
One of the best examples of consistency in advertising over time enabling a brand's advertising to be recognized without using the brand name. *Courtesy*: SilkCut

where the target audience would know it was the brand advertising even if the brand name was not used.

The key to consistency is the *visual* feel. This is because the visual memory for the imagery associated with the brand actually elicits faster brand identification than the brand name itself. This is because visual memory is superior to that of memory for words. When the visual imagery is also associated in memory with the benefit, or if the associations reinforce the nature of the benefit, the consistency over time will ensure communication of the brand and its benefit with even a brief glance.

Visual look must be unique

The very reasons for a consistent look among all the parts of an IMC campaign argue for its uniqueness. If there is any chance that the target audience may confuse the brand's marketing communication with a competitor's, the problem is obvious. Yet there is an incredible amount of similarity between competitive brands' advertising. Pick up any magazine and one will see how similar is the look and feel of advertising for competing brands is. This is especially true of retail, bank, automotive, fashion, and cosmetic advertising.

What is needed are *unique* executions that have the same look and feel, and over time become firmly associated in memory with the brand. If competitors copy a brand's 'look' after it is firmly associated with that brand, misattribution is likely to occur, and the competitor's similar looking advertising will merely reinforce the brand that 'owns' the look. Because of the nature of memory, once a brand is associated with a particular look or feel, any time that imagery is encountered it will stimulate associations with the brand. Good IMC planning can help ensure a unique and consistent look and feel for all of a brand's marketing communication.

■ Specific creative tactics for brand awareness and brand attitude

In Chapter 4 we introduced brand awareness and brand attitude strategies. Now we are going to explore the creative tactics that should be used in developing executions in order to optimize the likelihood that they will be correctly processed to effectively implement the appropriate strategy. While we shall be generally talking in terms of traditional advertising, it should be remembered that the same creative tactics apply to promotion-like messages (in terms of awareness and brand attitude); and also that it does not matter if it is a typical advert, brochure, in-store display, or package. These are the creative tactics necessary to ensure that brand awareness and brand attitude communication objectives are reached.

Brand awareness creative tactics

You will recall from our earlier discussion of brand awareness strategies that the correct brand awareness objective depends upon the role awareness plays at the time the purchase decision is made. The brand will either be recognized at the point-of-purchase, reminding the consumer of the need, or a need will come up and the brand must be recalled from memory: recognition brand awareness versus recall brand awareness. The creative tactics involved will be different, depending upon the specific brand awareness objective (Figure 9.4).

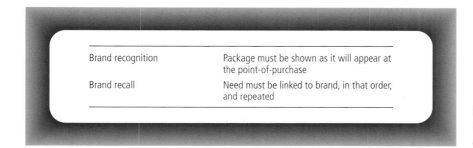

| Brand recognition | Package must be shown as it will appear at the point-of-purchase |
| Brand recall | Need must be linked to brand, in that order, and repeated |

Figure 9.4
Brand awareness creative tactics

Brand recognition

With recognition brand awareness, the package (or a symbol or logo for the brand if that is how it is recognized at the point-of-purchase) must be *clearly* presented in the execution in order to ensure visual iconic learning (Kosslyn and Thompson, 2003). It is not enough to only show the product, unless the product is sold *without* a package. This can become a difficult creative problem when dealing with transformational products, where the package can easily get in the way of emotional presentation of the benefit. Nevertheless, it is critical because that visual image of how the product will be recognized at the point-of-purchase must be stored in memory and linked to the appropriate need so that when it is seen in the store it will trigger that need.

If the package is not sufficiently exposed, there is every chance that one's marketing communication will not be associated with the brand; or even mistakenly linked to another brand. This is especially true for new product introductions, or when trying to reach new users. As a rule of thumb, the package should be attended to for two seconds if it is to be 'learned' and recognized later. This means being able to *hold* attention in print, and to be exposed for *at least* two seconds in a television spot or Internet advert (or any other new media). In addition to visual recognition, you will remember from Chapter 4 that occasionally auditory recognition may be needed. The tactics are the same, except that the name must be *heard* as it will be heard during the sales process; and *repeated* to ensure exposure time.

Regardless of whether it is visual or auditory brand recognition, one must be sure that the category need is obvious. With established product categories, the appropriate need is usually understood. But with new products, or new brands in an established category, the need must be clearly evident. In either case, within the execution the *package* should trigger the need, not the other way around, because it will be the package that is recognized first at the point-of-purchase and 'remind' the consumer of the need for the product.

As a footnote to the discussion of the creative tactics needed for effective recognition brand awareness, a study by Henderson and Cote (1998) identified four visual elements that significantly increase the likelihood that something will be recognized. First, there should be some sense of curvature; second, generally, but not exactly, symmetrical; third, some degree of repetition in the design; and finally that it represents some recognizable object. In designing packages and brand symbols or logos these points should be kept in mind, especially if recognition brand awareness is involved.

Brand recall

With recall brand awareness, the need occurs first, and the brand must be recalled from memory. This means that the creative execution must establish in memory a link between the need and the brand such that when the need arises, the brand name will come to mind as satisfying that need. The key is that the association is learned in that direction: need first, followed by brand (Nelson et al., 2003). This is generally done in the headline and repeated in the body. Because this is a more difficult learning process than that involved with recognition learning, this *association* must be repeated to ensure learning.

A visual could be used to establish the category need, but this is not always easy to do because the need must be immediately apparent. The visual would need to be immediately and correctly 'labelled' in the target audience's mind when they see it in the advert because it is that verbal 'label' that is most likely to be used in working memory when the need actually occurs, not the image of the need. If you decide to go out to eat at a Chinese restaurant, you are likely to be thinking about Chinese food, not seeing visual images of Chinese food, although some images may follow. But the initial need is likely to be considered verbally. Advertising for a Chinese restaurant will want to associate the desire for Chinese food with the name of the restaurant: strategically, 'when you think about Chinese food, think about us'. This is the link that should be established (obviously much more creatively). And while it is certainly appropriate to use strong visual images of Chinese food in the advert, this will primarily operate on brand attitude. The *need* should be labelled.

One way to help boost brand recall awareness is by using a celebrity presenter in the execution. However, the important thing to understand is whether or not the target audience easily recognizes the person, and that person is held in high regard by them. If they are famous and positively regarded in their eye, then research has shown that the visibility of the celebrity can be transferred to the brand (Holman and Hecker, 1983). That, however, is the key. The celebrity's visibility *must* be linked to the brand.

Brand attitude creative tactics

In Chapter 4 we briefly introduced the Rossiter–Percy Grid and pointed out how it helps define brand attitude strategy for marketing communication by looking at the level of involvement in a purchase decision and the underlying motivation that is driving behaviour in the brand's category. This results in four distinct quadrants defined in terms of low versus high involvement and negative (informational) versus positive (transformational) motives. The reason these considerations are so important is that each are directly related to the way in which a message will be processed. And as it happens, the creative tactics needed to facilitate the processing of the message are different for each quadrant (Figure 9.5).

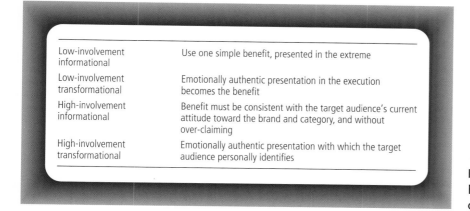

Low-involvement informational	Use one simple benefit, presented in the extreme
Low-involvement transformational	Emotionally authentic presentation in the execution becomes the benefit
High-involvement informational	Benefit must be consistent with the target audience's current attitude toward the brand and category, and without over-claiming
High-involvement transformational	Emotionally authentic presentation with which the target audience personally identifies

Figure 9.5
Brand attitude creative tactics

The specific creative tactics associated with each quadrant of the grid are designed to optimize the likelihood of a person successfully processing the message. This means being able to communicate the benefit around which a brand is positioned within its marketing communication, and ensuring that the optimal emotional associations are triggered to facilitate message processing in working memory. We will first take a look at the creative tactics appropriate for the brand attitude strategy quadrants, and then review how emotion is handled within an execution to encourage processing.

Low-involvement informational

This is the quadrant for low-involvement decisions involving negative motives. Because the decision is low involvement, one simple benefit in the message is enough. This benefit should be presented in the extreme because the target audience does not really need to believe the claim. All that is necessary is something Maloney (1962) has called 'curious disbelief'. This is a perfect description of what one is trying to accomplish with low involving brand attitude strategies, and especially low involving informational marketing communication. One is looking for the consumer to think: 'I wonder if it can really do that? It would be great if it did!' Because it is a low-involvement decision, there is no risk in trying. The Aqua Sphere advert shown in Figure 9.6 offers a perfect example of what we are talking about. Here is an execution that takes the simple benefit of clear vision while swimming and illustrates it in the extreme. Would things really be that clear? It doesn't matter, the point is made, and in a memorable way.

In fact, with informational messages the target audience does not even need to like the execution. One of the classic examples of this is a long-running Charmin toilet tissue campaign in the US during the 1980s. In this series of commercials, women would attempt to squeeze packages of Charmin because it was 'squeezably soft', and every time they did, Mr. Whipple, a store clerk, would appear and say 'Ladies, please don't squeeze the Charmin!' Research showed later that this was considered by consumers as one of the all-time most obnoxious commercials, but it nevertheless moved the brand to number one in the category (Freeman, 1989). How can such a thoroughly disliked campaign still be effective for the brand? By using such an extreme presentation, it also sharply focused on the benefit. When shopping, consumers were much more likely to see Charmin and wonder if it really was that soft, rather than think about the obnoxious Mr. Whipple.

Benefit focus In all marketing communication, how one focuses upon the benefit must be consistent with the underlying motivation. Informational versus transformational brand attitude strategies require different ways of supporting or drawing attention to the key benefit claim. When dealing with low-involvement informational brand attitude strategies, the focus is *directly* upon the key benefit claim which is expressed in terms of the subjective characteristic of the brand: for example, 'fast acting', 'the latest technology', 'softer skin', etc.

Source characteristic When dealing with low-involvement informational brand attitude strategies, the perceived source of the message must be seen as credible, and as an *'expert'*. We put the word 'expert' in inverted commas because we are using it in its broadest sense here, not just in terms of technical expertise. For example, a mother is an 'expert' at getting children's clothes clean. When there are people in an advert, they will generally be seen as the source of the message, and in this quadrant should be perceived as an 'expert' in the product category. When there are no people, the company or brand itself will be seen as the source.

Low-involvement transformational
In this quadrant we are dealing with low-involvement decisions, but the underlying motivation driving behaviour in the category is positive. The real key here is getting a positive emotional response to the

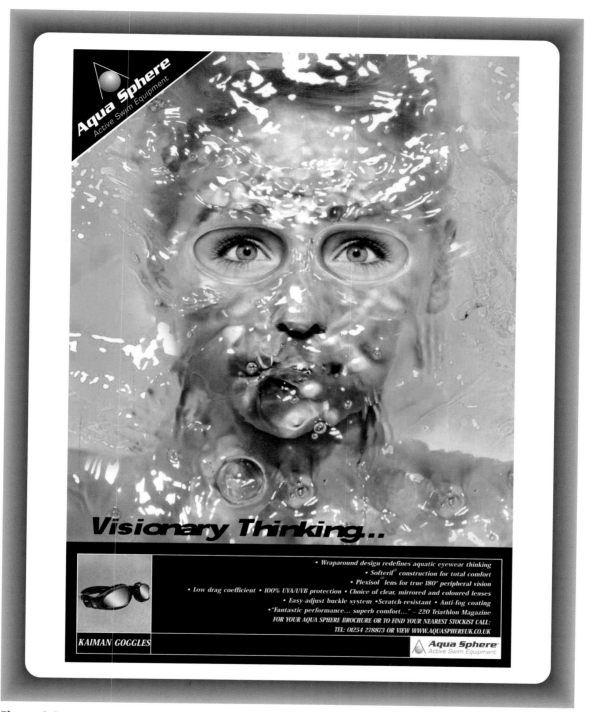

Figure 9.6
A good example of low-involvement informational advertising, presenting a single benefit and in the extreme. *Courtesy*: Aqua Sphere

execution, because in a very real sense the brand benefit is in the execution itself. This requires a presentation of the benefit in an emotionally *authentic* way. If there are people in the advert, they must look real and natural, not posed. If they do not, the emotional response to them will not seem real.

The target audience must immediately connect emotionally with what they see, and the feeling they get in a very real sense becomes the benefit for the brand. At the point-of-purchase or when the brand decision is made, you want the consumer to re-experience that same positive feeling for the brand. Because it is a low-involvement decision, that should be enough to drive purchase. This is why only one benefit should be presented, because the benefit is tied so closely to the emotional response. It would be impossible to process two independent emotional responses at the same time.

The advert shown in Figure 9.7 for McCain Potato Gourmet is an excellent example of emotionally delivering the benefit of 'great taste' in authentic way. Looking at advert, one's reaction is: 'Wow does that look good!' It is a clear presentation of a single benefit. At the point-of-purchase, when the target audience sees the McCain package, the positive emotional experience from the advert will come to mind, and the desire to see if it really will taste as good as it looked should motivate purchase.

While all brands should seek a unique 'look and feel' to their marketing communication, it is *critical* for transformational brand attitude strategies. Unfortunately, too-often advertising for different brands of fashion products, cosmetics, and beverages (among others) effect the same image. One look through a women's fashion magazine is enough to illustrate the point. But no matter how well executed the emotional presentation is, if it is similar to another brand, in effect both brands are offering the *same benefit*. One can experience that same positive feeling with either brand.

Unlike low-involvement informational advertising, transformational advertising *must* be liked. Think about it. You may not need to believe that Hägan-Das ice cream will make you feel passionate or that a Wonder Bra will make you sexy to enjoy the feeling that it just might. But, you do have to have a positive response to the execution. Otherwise, how could you experience a positive emotional reaction? In effect, what is going on is the target audience takes a positive emotional feeling stimulated by the execution and associates it in memory with the brand. This requires a complete positive experience with the message.

Benefit focus When dealing with positive motives, the benefit is the relevant *emotion*. One can either use the subjective characteristic of the brand in support of the 'feeling' you will get using the brand (e.g. 'tastes so great you'll think you are in heaven') or a pure expression of the positive emotion, usually visual. In the low-involvement transformational case, either focus upon the emotional benefit is appropriate.

Figure 9.7
An excellent example of low-involvement transformational advertising, delivering here the benefit of 'great taste' in an emotionally authentic way. *Courtesy*: McCain

Source characteristic The key source characteristic for transformational brand attitude strategies is attractiveness, and for the low-involvement quadrant the *likeability* component of attractiveness. This should be obvious given what we had just discussed. If there is only a picture of the product, to elicit a positive emotional response you must instantly 'like' what you see; if it is a person, they should not only appear 'real', but also likable.

High-involvement informational

As we already know from the last chapter, when dealing with high-involvement purchase decisions it is necessary for the target audience to not only pay attention and learn something from the message, they must also *accept* it. Perhaps the single most important creative tactic for this quadrant is to make sure the message is consistent with the target audience's current attitudes: both toward the product and the brand. Unlike with low-involvement decisions where the consumer is likely to suspend belief about the benefit claim until trying the product, with a high-involvement decision too much is at risk. The target audience must be convinced that the benefit claim (or claims) is true before risking purchase.

It order to ensure that the message does not over claim (which is not only acceptable but also desirable with low-involvement decisions) it is essential to understand what the consumer is or is not likely to believe. If the message over claims, or is inconsistent with the target audience's beliefs and attitudes, they will counterargue the message and not accept it. Benefit claims should be made that fall within and what Sherif and Hovland (1961) call a person's latitude of acceptance, as discussed in the last chapter. For all of us, there are things we readily believe; and then there are gray areas where we are not quite sure whether we do or not, but are open minded (what Sheriff and Hovland call the latitude of indifference). Beyond that, we reject the claim (our latitude of rejection). The job of high-involvement informational marketing communication is to the ensure that the key benefit claim used in the message is at the *upper end* or the latitude of acceptance (do not inadvertently under claim), and that any other benefit claims used in support also fall at the upper end, or within the latitude of indifference.

In terms of execution, the key benefit claim should be immediately apparent, in both headline and visual. Regardless of where the key benefit claim is placed within the execution, it and any linked visual should be the first thing that confronts the target audience's attention. It will attract their attention because it will be addressing something important to them. If they are in the market, it will be this key benefit, communicated through the headline and visual, that will encourage processing the entire message to see what it is all about. It must 'hook' the target audience immediately, while the additional benefit claims in the body copy will help convince them of the desirability of the brand.

Finding good examples of advertising for products in the high-involvement informational brand attitude quadrant is never easy. However, the advert for Amtico Floors shown in Figure 9.8 is an exception

Figure 9.8
A really good example of the creative tactics needed for an effective high-involvement informational advert, with the key benefit in the headline and visual to draw the reader into the copy. *Courtesy*: Amtico Floors

providing a really good example of the creative tactics needed for an effective high-involvement informational advert. It targets the key important benefit in both the headline and the visual, floors with water resistance, which attracts attention and leads into the body copy. In the body copy additional benefits are presented: slip, dent, and stain resistance, wide range of design; and a source for more information. The advert presents a clear message designed to convince someone looking into new flooring to consider Amtico Floors.

Benefit focus The focus on the key benefit for high-involvement informational executions, as in the low-involvement case, will be to either draw attention directly to a subjective characteristic of the brand that is seen as important by the target audience, or by using the key benefit claim as the solution to a problem that is known to be important to the target audience. The focus on the other important benefits used in the copy should use specific attributes of the brand in support of the subjective characteristic: for example, 'with a 5.8-litre engine you have all the power you need' (the objective attribute, a 5.8-litre engine, supports the subjective characteristic of 'all the power you need').

Source characteristic Credibility is the key characteristic for the perceived source. As in the low-involvement informational case, the source must be seen as an *expert*, again as either a technical expert or as a 'user' expert. But because the message must be accepted, the additional credibility component of *objectivity* is also required.

High-involvement transformational

Just as with low-involvement transformational marketing communication, the execution here must be seen as emotionally authentic. But unlike high-involvement informational executions, even though the decision is high involvement the benefit claim should be expressed in the extreme. Here you want to over claim in the sense of communicating an intense and *personal* feeling. This is the key. When the target audience sees the execution they must think: 'yes, that is what *I* want'.

It must be 'real' to the individual, not necessarily in the sense of reality but in terms of their wishes, dreams, or desires. Most four-wheel-drive trucks, for example, are purchased by men who never drive them off-road. But they want to experience the 'feeling' of masculine adventure portrayed in the advertising for such vehicles. Women who see glamorous images portrayed in advertising for high-fashion perfume purchase it in order to experience the 'feeling' that is elicited by the imagery in the advert. In neither case is the image in the advertising likely to reflect their reality, but it is nevertheless 'real' for them. High-involvement transformational advertising must elicit such highly authentic emotional responses. Identifying personally with the image is in effect their acceptance of the key benefit claim.

Because the decision is high involvement, for some transformationally driven purchase decisions some information may also be needed. This will not be the case for high-imagery products like fashion or jewellery, but could be for such things as (say) a holiday cruise. In an IMC sense, for such cases the strong imagery may be conveyed via television with the same imagery reflected in print, along with some functional support benefit to help facilitate message acceptance. Just as with high-involvement informational executions, the key benefit (here in terms of the strong emotionally arousing imagery) must be noticed first, attracting attention via a sense of: 'They are talking directly to me'. That will lead them into whatever *brief* copy might be needed. Ideally, this copy will direct them to a Web site, toll-free number, or retail location for more detailed information. And wherever they might be directed, the information there must be consistent with the emotional response aroused by the original message.

The advert for FCUK shown is in Figure 9.9 offers a very good example of what we are talking about. The advert creates, especially through its provocative logo, a strong positive emotion, but only for those who want to be a part of that 'feeling'. This emotion becomes linked in memory with the brand for them, and is reinforced as they shop the retail stores and wear their fashions.

Figure 9.9
A very good example of high-involvement transformational advertising. *Courtesy*: French Connection UK

Benefit focus In high-involvement transformational executions, as with low-involvement transformational, the benefit focus will be either a subjective characteristic in support of the positive emotion, or simply the emotion. If some additional information is needed to help with the acceptance of the message, present either a straight expression of a subjective characteristic, or use the specific attribute in support of a subjective characteristic.

Source characteristics As with low-involvement transformational strategies, the key source characteristic here is attractiveness, which means the source should be likable. But in this case it must also be seen as *similar* to the target audience in their perceived emotional state. This is what helps the target audience personally identify with the message. The perceived source either implies the way they wish to see themselves (e.g. someone who wears Channel perfume if only the package is shown), or the people in the execution reflect their perceived image of themselves using the brand. Again, their 'similarity' is unlikely to reflect reality, but rather the 'feeling' they wish to experience.

■ Eliciting the correct emotional response

In the last chapter we discussed the important role emotion plays in the processing of marketing communication. To help facilitate the correct emotional association with the key benefit, the emotional response to an execution must be consistent with the underlying motivation involved. Depending upon whether it is a positive or negative emotion that is driving behaviour, the nondeclarative emotional memory associated with the category need will differ. In fact, given the nature of how we experience life, the emotions associated with satisfying a behavioural motivation will follow a sequence or change in emotional response, and marketing communication should reflect this (Figure 9.10).

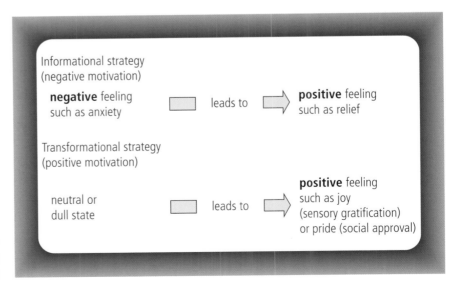

Figure 9.10
Emotional response
sequence

The idea of a sequence of emotions being involved in the processing of marketing communication was first introduced by Rossiter and Percy (1987), and is based on Hammond's (1970) re-conceptualization of Mower's theoretical work in the area. Mower (1960) looked at how unlearned emotional states relate to motivating behaviour in terms of a simple pleasure–pain dichotomy. Hammond then built on this idea, considering the relationship between emotion and motivation in terms of approach and avoidance behaviour. When people find themselves in a 'painful' situation, as it increases, fear is excited; as the situation decreases, it is inhibited, and one feels relief. On the other hand, when someone is experiencing 'pleasure', as it increases hope is excited; but if it decreases that hope is inhibited and they feel disappointment.

This distinction has a direct bearing on what creative tactics should be used in marketing communication because it implies different tactics will be necessary, depending upon whether positive or negative motivations are involved. The emotional portrayal of the motivation in an execution must not only be consistent with the motivation driving behaviour but it also should reflect the *sequence* of emotions involved in the elicitory behaviour driven by positive motivations as positive feelings are increased; and in the inhibitory behaviour resulting from negative motivations as negative feelings are decreased, leading to a positive feeling.

All of this is actually a lot simpler than it may seem from this brief theoretical discussion. If we think about informational brand attitude strategies, the negative motivations involve solving or avoiding a problem of some kind: addressing a particular need. There will be negative emotions like fear or anxiety associated with the category need, and the brand as the solution will 'solve' the problem. In doing so, using the brand changes the negative feelings associated with the problem to a positive emotion like relief. For years, Michelin tyres has run television commercials that begin with a situation fraught with fear and anxiety, such as a woman with a baby in a car driving at night in a storm. Having built this fearful situation, it is then resolved by reminding that with Michelin tyres they will be safe (relief).

It is a sequence of emotions that parallel the emotional experience that should be reflected in marketing communication. The same thing applies to transformational brand attitude strategies. Moving from a neutral, or dull state, advertising for expensive chocolate should excite a feeling of joy or happiness at the prospect of eating some (sensory gratification); or with social approval, beginning from a feeling of perhaps shame or apprehension, being motivated to buy jewellery for a wife or girlfriend, or a sports car for yourself, in order to excite within yourself feelings of pride or being flattered.

In terms of creative execution, for informational brand attitude strategies the emotional response will follow *indirectly* from an evaluation of the benefit claim. The negative emotion associated with the category need should be initiated first in the sequence, underscoring the feelings associated with the problem to be solved or avoided. Then, move the target audience to a positive emotional response linked to the brand's benefit as the solution.

With transformational brand attitude strategies, as we have seen, emotional response will follow *directly* from executional elements within the advertising. In print, the emotional association with the need are necessarily assumed in most cases, with a strong feeling elicited by the emotional authenticity of the imagery used providing a sense of the positive emotional consequences of using the brand. With television, especially when social approval is the underlying motive, it will be possible to establish the prior neutral or negative feelings that are resolved by the brand and replaced with positive emotions.

Summary

In this chapter we have explored a number of creative tactics that may be used in marketing communication in order to facilitate message processing. These tactics are based on work by psychologists in psycholinguistics and visual imaging that has revealed ways in which the written word and pictures should be used in communication in order to increase the likelihood of it being positively processed. Specific tactics to help attract and hold attention include using unexpected elements in print and visual, colour rather than black-and-white illustrations, larger pictures where possible, attention to placement in media, and format.

Perhaps the most important creative tactic for facilitating learning is to keep everything simple. This is at the heart of all learning. Use familiar words and simple sentences, avoiding compound sentences and inverted clauses, passive constructions, puns, and negatives. Headlines should be held to less than six to seven words so they may be fully processed at a glance without the need to 'read' them. In television commercials, the pacing is important, minimizing the number of visual cuts, especially for informationally driven strategies.

One of the most important creative considerations for IMC is the need for consistency across messages and over time. This consistency does not require a 'cookie-cutter' approach where everything looks exactly like everything else, but rather a look and feel that is clearly associated with the brand. The key to this consistent look is the visual feel, and this requires a unique visual look.

It was pointed out that different brand awareness and brand attitude strategies require different creative tactics. Recognition brand awareness requires a clear visual of the package as it will appear at the point-of-purchase. Recall brand awareness requires establishing a link between the need and the brand, in that order, and repeated within the execution. This is necessary so that when the need occurs, it will be linked in memory with the brand, and the brand will come to mind as satisfying that need.

Brand attitude creative tactics are dependent upon the brand attitude strategy as indicated by the Rossiter–Percy Grid. Each quadrant demands very particular creative tactics in order to accommodate the processing requirements associated with the involvement and motivation driving brand choice. With low-involvement informational messages, the key is to use one simple benefit, presented in the extreme. For low-involvement transformational messages, the critical creative consideration is the emotional authenticity of the execution, because this in effect becomes the benefit. Because of the risk involved, high-involvement informational messages must be believed and accepted. This means the message must present an initial benefit claim in the headline and visual that is consistent with the target audience's existing beliefs about the brand in relation to the benefit, and presented at the upper level of acceptance, careful not to overclaim. High-involvement transformational messages, like low-involvement transformational, must also be seen as emotionally authentic, but additionally the target audience must personally identify with that feeling.

■ Review questions

1 What are the key creative tactics for gaining attention?
2 Find examples of advertising that is likely to hold attention and discuss why.
3 What is the key to facilitating learning in marketing communication?
4 Identify adverts that do a good job of facilitating learning and ones that do not, and discuss why.
5 Why is consistency in IMC executions so important?
6 What is the fundamental difference in the creative tactics needed for recognition versus recall brand awareness?
7 Find examples of adverts that you feel do a good job establishing the category need – brand awareness links needed for recall brand awareness.
8 What is the key difference in the way the benefit is presented in informational versus transformational executions?
9 Find good examples of adverts for each of the four quadrants of the Rossiter-Percy Grid and discuss why you feel they are good executions.
10 Why would it be inappropriate to use the head of a company as a spokesperson for a high-involvement product?
11 Discuss the importance of eliciting the correct emotional sequence in marketing communication.
12 Identify adverts that you feel do a good job in presenting the correct emotional sequence for the motivation involved and discuss why.

References

Ahn, E. and Edwards, S.M. (2002) Does size really matter? Brand attitude versus click-through in response to banner ads. *Proceedings of the 2002 Conference of the American Academy of Advertising*, 8–9.

Brainerd, C.J., Desruchers, A., and Howe, M.L. (1987) Stages of learning analysis of picture–word effects in associative memory. *Journal of Experimental Psychology: Human Learning and Memory*, 7, 1–14.

Bryce, W.J. and Yalch, R.F. (1993) Hearing versus seeing: A comparison of learning of spoken and pictorial information in television advertising. *Journal of Current Issues and Research in Advertising*, 15(1), 1–20.

Eyesenk, M.W. (1977) *Human Memory: Theory, Research, and Individual Difference*. Oxford: Pergamon.

Franke, G.R., Huhmann, B.A., and Mothersbaugh, D.L. (2004) Information content and consumer readership of print ads: A comparison of search and experience products. *Journal of the Academy of Marketing Science*, 32(1), 20–31.

Freeman, L. (1989) Wisk rings in a new ad generation. *Advertising Age*, 18 September, 1, 81.

Hammond, L.J. (1970) Conditioned emotional states. In P. Black (ed.), *Physiological Correlates of Emotion*. New York: Academic Press, Chapter 12.

Henderson, P.W. and Cote, J.A. (1998) Guidelines for selecting or modifying logos. *Journal of Marketing*, 62(2), 14–30.

Holman, R.H. and Hecker, S. (1983) Advertising impact: Creative elements affecting brand recall. *Current Issues and Research in Advertising*, 157–172

Kosslyn, S.M. and Thompson, W.L. (2003) When is early visual cortex activated during visual mental imagery? *Psychological Bulletin*, 129(5), 723–746.

MacLachlan, J. and Logan, M. (1993) Commercial shot length in TV commercials and their memorability and persuasiveness. *Journal of Advertising Research*, 33/2, 7–16.

Maloney, J.C. (1962) Curiosity versus disbelief in advertising. *Journal of Advertising Research*, 2/2, 2–8.

Mower, U.H. (1960) *Learning Theory and Behaviour*. New York: Wiley.

Myers, G. (1994) *Words in Ads*. London: Arnold.

Nelson, D.L., McEvoy, C.L., and Pointer, L. (2003) Spreading activation or spooky action at a distance? *Journal of Experimental Psychology: Learning, Memory, and Cognition*, 29(1), 42–52.

Paivio, A. (1971) *Image and Verbal Processing*. New York: Holt, Rinehart, & Winston.

Rossiter, J.R. (1988) The increase in magazine ad readership. *Journal of Advertising Research*, 28/5, 35–39.

Rossiter, J.R. and Bellman, S. (2005) *Marketing Communication: Theory and Application*. Frenchs Forest, NSW, Australia: Pearson Education Australia.

Rossiter, J.R. and Percy, L. (1997) *Advertising Communication and Promotion Management*. New York: McGraw-Hill.

Rossiter, J.R. and Percy, L. (1987) *Advertising and Promotion Management*. New York: McGraw-Hill.

Ritson, M. (2003) *What do people really do during TV commercials?*, working paper. London: London Business School.

Sherif, M. and Hovland, C.I. (1961) *Social Judgement*. New Haven: Yale University Press.

Wearing, A.J. (1973) The recall of sentences of varying length. *Australian Journal of Psychology*, 25, 155–161.

Young, C.E. and Robinson, M. (1989) Video rhythms and recall. *Journal of Advertising Research*, 29/3, 22–25.

Young, C.E. and Robinson, M. (1992) Visual connectedness and persuasion. *Journal of Advertising Research*, 32/2, 51–59.

SECTION IV

The IMC plan

Up to this point we have dealt with various aspects of IMC. The role of IMC in building brands and its contribution to corporate communication goals has been considered. The distinction between traditional advertising and promotion has been discussed, along with various ways of delivering IMC messages. How messages are process was introduced to gain a better idea of what is required of an IMC message if it is to be successful, and how to execute the message in order to increase the likelihood it will be processed and lead to a positive decision for the brand. Now, it is time to put it all together.

In this section we address the IMC plan and its implementation. There are a number of key considerations a manager must take into account as the planning process begins, and these are dealt with in Chapter 10. To develop an effective IMC plan, the manager must have a good appreciation of the strengths and weaknesses of advertising-like messages versus promotion-like messages, and how they may be best used together in meeting the overall marketing communication objectives for a brand. Each has particular strengths in terms of specific communication objectives, and these must be considered. Additionally, various conditions in the market will inform the mix of advertising and promotion in the plan.

The specific steps involved in the planning process are addressed in Chapter 11. This process begins with a review of the marketing plan because that will provide an overview of the brand and its marketing objectives. This is an essential foundation, because IMC must support the marketing plan. With the review completed, the manager's first tasks is to identify the target audience and gain an understanding of how they go about making purchase decisions in the category. This is often overlooked, but is critical because it will identify where in that process marketing communication is likely to have a positive effect upon brand choice.

With this established, is time to consider the message itself. The key consideration here is how the brand should be positioned within the message, and selection of the benefit to be used as the basis for the benefit claim in the message. Additionally, the communication objectives must be set. While brand awareness and brand attitude are always objectives, the manager must decide if category need should also be addressed, and if short-term brand purchase intention may also be needed. With the communication objectives set, one can then put together a set of media options that are compatible with those objectives.

Once the planning process is complete, the manager has all of the information needed to finalize and implement an IMC plan. Chapter 12 deals with how this information is used to make the decisions required in finalizing the IMC plan, and the steps necessary to implement it. Finalizing a plan requires coordinating marketing communication efforts aimed at identifying a number of touch points in the decision process. By its very nature, this almost always means there are a number of communication tasks involved. The planning process will have identified many potential opportunities for positively affecting the brand purchase decision. Because budgets rarely are large enough to afford addressing all of the opportunities, deciding what will be essential to accomplish, and then how to make the best use of the remaining budget, is the most important aspect of finalizing the IMC plan. The finalized plan will include various media options that are appropriate for the communication tasks that are to be addressed.

To implement the plan, the manager must decide how to allocate the available budget in terms of media selection. Specifically, decisions must be made about what should be the primary versus secondary media used for each communication task, and a media plan developed. And of course, the marketing communication itself, the creative executions, must be produced. This follows directly from a creative brief that distills the essence of the IMC plan, and serves as a guide to those creating the executions. This is what ensures that the actual executions reflect the IMC plan.

CHAPTER 10

Planning considerations

In this chapter we shall be looking at some of the considerations a manager must take into account before beginning to develop an integrated marketing communication (IMC) plan. Key to this is an understanding of the role of advertising-like messages and promotion-like messages in the mix. Communication objectives are important here (beyond the obvious reason) because the appropriateness of using advertising or promotion in the IMC plan will be a function of the communication objectives selected; and the role advertising versus promotion will play in the mix will be a function of not only the communication objectives involved, but also various market conditions.

■ Communication objectives

Much goes into creating a successful IMC plan, as we shall see in the next chapter. But, perhaps the most important consideration is the communication objective. Communication objectives follow from the specific communication *effects* the manager is looking for as a result of the brand's marketing communication. All aspects of IMC work on the same basic communication effects: category need, brand awareness, brand attitude, and brand purchase intention (see Figure 10.1).

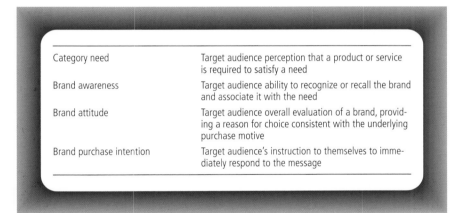

Category need	Target audience perception that a product or service is required to satisfy a need
Brand awareness	Target audience ability to recognize or recall the brand and associate it with the need
Brand attitude	Target audience overall evaluation of a brand, providing a reason for choice consistent with the underlying purchase motive
Brand purchase intention	Target audience's instruction to themselves to immediately respond to the message

Figure 10.1
The four basic communication effects

It should be noted that while we use the term 'brand' in describing some of these communication effects, we are using the word in its broadest possible sense to include products, services, corporate identity – in short, whatever might be the beneficiary of marketing communication. Each of the four basic communication effects are briefly outlined below. This review will provide a foundation for the discussion that follows of where and how advertising and promotion should be used in IMC.

Category need is the target audience's perception that they require a product or service to satisfy a need, and associating that need with a brand. In other words, they must 'be in the market' for the brand.

Brand awareness is the target audience's ability to recognize or recall the brand. As we saw in Chapter 4, in the case of recognition brand awareness, the potential consumer need only recognize the brand at the point-of-purchase; with recall brand awareness, they must recall or remember the brand name when the need for the product or service occurs.

Brand attitude refers to the target audience's overall evaluation of the product or service being offered in relation to its perceived ability to satisfy the reason they want it (the relevant motivation). It is important to remember that reasons for purchase or usage can differ at various times, even for the same individual. That is why it is important to always think about brand attitude in terms of the motivations that are likely to be driving behaviour when the target audience is 'in the market'.

Brand purchase intention is the target audience's instruction to themselves to purchase or use the brand. In other words, it is a commitment to take action, but it does *not* necessarily insure actual purchase or use of the brand.

As one might gather, even from these brief descriptions, there is a lot involved with communication effects that must be considered in IMC planning. It is not enough to simply say you want people to like the brand; or want people to use it more often. The manager must look carefully at what it will take to accomplish those ends, and what type of marketing communication will best do the job.

It will be from this set of four marketing communication effects that the manager will select the appropriate communication objectives. But often in marketing, there are particular problems that must be addressed that lie outside the main thrust of its marketing communication. For example, a company may introduce a new product and find it so successful that sales outstripped production. This is a problem any company might like to have, but if one is not careful, it could become a serious problem. Potential customers, disappointed at not being able to find the product, might form negative attitudes, or almost certainly look for an alternative. With a seldom-purchased product this could take a lot of people out of the market.

A brand may occasionally need to go outside of the basic set of communication effects in choosing a specific communication objective in order to deal with a particular circumstance unique to the market at that time. This is something Rossiter and Percy (1997) talked about as purchase facilitation. In the above example, the manager may feel that a message is needed to alert the target market that because of demand for the new product they are having a hard time meeting it, but that the problem has been solved and more product will be available within a few weeks. Nevertheless, even in a case like this where a special circumstance must be addressed, brand awareness and brand attitude will be communication objectives because they are *always* communication objectives.

■ Relative advertising versus promotion strengths

Generally speaking, traditional advertising makes its strongest contribution to brand awareness and brand attitude. Traditional promotion makes its strongest contribution to brand purchase intention. Nevertheless, promotion-like messages must still contribute to both brand awareness and brand attitude. Even though brand attitude is not a particular strength of promotion, the best promotion offers will be those that have a positive effect upon brand attitude. This was recognized many years ago by Prentice (1977), a marketing practitioner, who called them *consumer franchise building* promotion offers. In other words, the promotion works well beyond its short-term tactical goal of immediate purchase, also helping contribute to positive brand attitude and building strong brand equity.

One should also bear in mind that promotion alone, as well as advertising, can actually create all of the communication effects. Store brands and so-called 'price brands' are marketed successfully without advertising by using point-of-purchase promotion. Although there is now a trend toward advertising private label and store brands, even when store brands are only promoted at the point-of-purchase, promotion must stimulate awareness and build at least a tentatively positive attitude for the product.

Promotion-like messages, just like advertising-like messages, work through successful message processing and either can satisfy all the communication objectives. But as we have seen, the whole idea of IMC is to approach one's marketing communication tasks with an open mind, and to explore all marketing communication options in order to maximize the brand message to the target audience. The relative strengths of advertising and promotion (Figure 10.2) are discussed next for each of the four communication effects.

Communication objective	Relative strength	
	Weak	**Strong**
Category need		
Advertising		
Promotion		
Brand awareness		
Advertising		
Promotion		
Brand attitude		
Advertising		
Promotion[1]		
Brand Purchase Intention		
Advertising		
Promotion		

[1] This assumes a 'consumer franchise building' promotion addressing brand attitude and consistent with the advertising message. Otherwise, it would be weak.

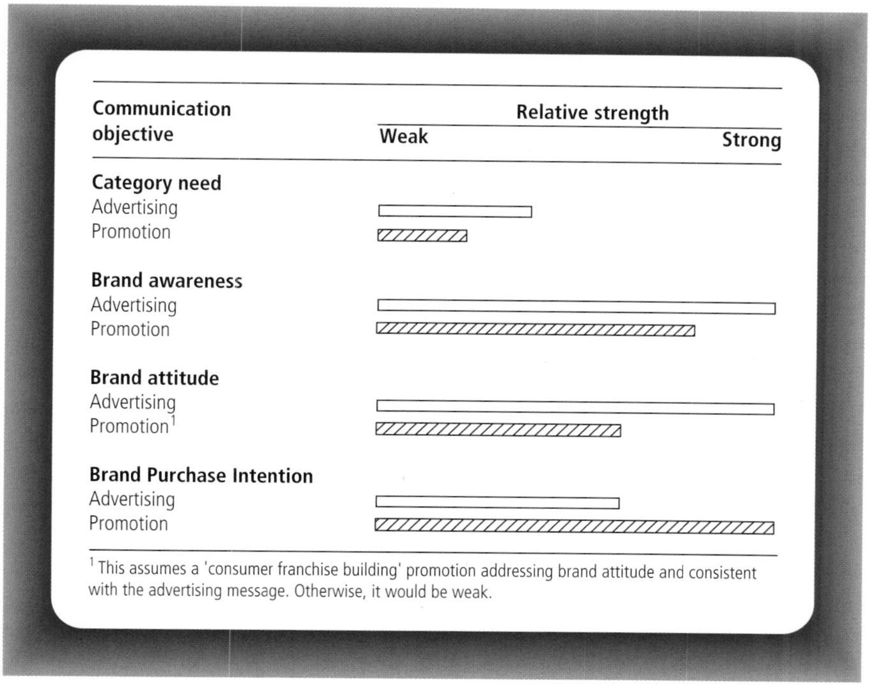

Figure 10.2
Relative strengths of advertising and promotion

Category need

Category need, for most product categories, originates mainly from market changes (for new categories) and arises from a person's overall or temporary circumstances (for new and existing categories). Traditional advertising can have some effect on category need by stimulating a perceived need. However, this is more a matter of suggesting the category need. If there is not an underlying motive to be tapped, 'selling' this need will be all but impossible. For example, the successful introduction of passenger mini-vans by Chrysler (now Daimler-Chrysler) would not have been possible if there was not an already reasonably strong motivation for such a practical vehicle. Only rarely can advertising create a motivation as such. Rather, it positions the category as a better way of meeting an existing motivation. In the case of mini-vans, it was the motivation of incomplete satisfaction with alternatives for family transportation.

Various forms of promotion can help accelerate category need, making it occur earlier, although usually only to a fairly minor degree. This is one of the reasons couponing and other price promotions are almost always a part of new consumer product introductions, and why direct marketing as a means of delivering a very targeted promotion can play such an important role in the introduction of an innovative service or product for a business. *Accelerate* is the key term here. None of this really sells the category need so much as it attempts to speed it up.

Overall, both the advertising and promotion components of IMC have, in general, only a relatively minor influence on category need (as we see in Figure 10.2). Again, this is only a general effect, for one may certainly find specific instances of successfully selling or accelerating category need with either advertising-like or promotional-like messages.

Brand awareness

Brand awareness is one of the strengths of traditional advertising. However, almost any form of marketing communication can and should contribute to brand awareness, at least to some extent. New product introductions, for example when brand awareness is a major objective, typically utilizes several marketing communication options.

Promotion offers help prospective buyers to consider new brands and to reconsider existing brands. Promotion offers can achieve this by drawing reflexive attention to the brand (e.g. a point-of-purchase display or a sample pack) and also by producing selective attention (e.g. price-off or coupons promising extra value). Various promotions and most messages (whether promotion-like or advertising-like) delivered through direct marketing are primarily useful for increasing brand recognition (or initial cognition for previously unfamiliar brands) at the point-of-purchase or at the point-of-decision rather than stimulating brand recall prior to purchase (although this is possible). As a result, promotion and direct marketing are less often an option when brand recall is involved.

Brand attitude

Building brand attitude has historically been the province of advertising. However, as already pointed out, all marketing communication should help build positive brand attitude. In the case of promotion, because it is aimed primarily at causing a short-term increase in sales, for competitive or inventory moving reasons, without regard to brand attitude, their execution is often weak in this regard. But the ideal communication should always help create longer-term communications effects, and this is especially true for promotion where it is important to seat this long-term effect in order to maximize full value purchases when the promotion is withdrawn.

Consumer Franchise Building promotions as described by Prentice (1977), or as we shall consider them, any promotion that pays attention to consistently reinforcing a brand's equity, will contribute to inducing full price purchases by working, like advertising, on brand attitude (e.g. free samples). Promotion too often does not help build brand attitude, concentrating only on brand purchase intention. This is a mistake. There should always be some reinforcement of brand attitude, consistent with the overall brand attitude communication strategy.

Chuck Mittelstadt (1993), a long time consultant to the Interpublic Group of Companies (the group that owns McCann and other major advertising agencies and media companies), has offered an interesting observation on this subject. He points out that years ago image-building promotions were the norm. Among others, there were such classic promotions as the Pillsbury bake-off and the launch of White Rain hair-care products, which date back to well over 50 years ago. The Pillsbury bake-off he sees as a classic example of IMC. Advertising in many media linked to the promotion, in-store merchandising, events, and sponsorship were all involved. Women were encouraged to contribute recipes and baked goods, all made with Pillsbury flour. The bake-off created an image of well-crafted quality products and constant innovation. As a result, this promotion was a major contributor to the Pillsbury brand image.

For the introduction of White Rain, a young lady (consistent with the demographics of the target audience) dressed in a white raincoat and white boots and holding a white umbrella was used as the most prominent element on the package. Models dressed in the same fashion were used to dispense free samples. They used white raincoats and umbrellas as premiums and as point-of-purchase displays. The advertising spokeswoman was dressed the same, and the copy stressed the widely accepted folklore on the softness of rainwater. Here we have a very good example of a consistent IMC program.

The launch of Elizabeth Arden's Curious brand perfume in Sweden offers an excellent recent example of a consistent message using both advertising and promotion together in an effective IMC program. The benefit claim for the new perfume was: 'Curious – do you dare?' This is an emotionally charged line, exactly what is needed for transformational marketing communication. This was enhanced by linking the brand with

Britney Spears, providing a strong source with whom the young women making up the target audience could identify. Note too that she reflects the appropriate source characteristics needed for transformational executions: both the likability and similarity components of attractiveness.

Complementing the introductory advertising, 'do you dare' promotions were run in *Elle* and *Cosmopolitan*, live competitions on radio to 'sing like Britney' were conducted, and samples of the product were offered at outdoor sites (see Figure 10.3). Here we have an IMC campaign where the promotions are directly linked to the overall benefit, and consistent with the advertising in look and feel. The results of the launch significantly exceeded sales targets.

Unfortunately, too often today many package goods brand managers lean too heavily upon short-term price promotions to help reach sales objectives without attention to brand attitude, and are injuring long-term brand equity. The proof of this may be seen in the overwhelming allotment of promotion dollars given to the trade, where half the money is kept by the trade and the rest usually passed along to consumers by way of price-off 'specials'. As Mittelstadt (1993) put it, somewhere along the line marketers took a short-cut into price promotions as a way of life, and a lot of brands are now paying dearly for it.

Brand purchase intention

Brand purchase intention has historically been the communication strength of the promotion component of IMC. With the exception of retail advertising and other direct response advertising, most traditional advertising does not deal directly with brand purchase intention. However, all promotion, and most messages delivered through direct marketing and channels marketing, are aimed at moving sales forward immediately (too often, as noted above, regardless of their longer-term consequences), and they achieve this by stimulating immediate brand purchase intentions. More particularly, promotions stimulate intentions to buy now, or to buy more than usual. Additionally, there are the many purchase related intentions for consumer durables and industrial products such as intention to visit showrooms, call for a sales demonstration, and so forth.

■ Market characteristics that influence IMC effectiveness

In a very interesting study, senior marketing executives from large companies that manufacture nondurable consumer goods were interviewed (Strang, 1980) . Among other things, they were asked whether they felt different market scenarios would be likely to increase the importance of either advertising over promotion, promotion over advertising, or have no effect. While we must bear in mind that these are basically packaged

Figure 10.3
An excellent example of using advertising and promotion together to deliver a consistent message. *Courtesy*: OMD and Elizabeth Arden

goods marketers, the results nevertheless provide valuable insight into how marketers actually allocate their marketing budget in communication planning.

The product lifecycle is an idea introduced many years ago by Dean (1950). One of the points made by the Strang study is that marketers feel advertising and promotion have different strengths relative to a brand's position in the product lifecycle: introduction, growth, maturity, or decline. For example, advertising is more important than promotion earlier in a product's life cycle (especially in the 'growth' stage), and that promotion is more important late in the product's life (especially in the decline stage). While this reflects a relative use of advertising-like and promotion-like messages in IMC during the product lifecycle, there are absolute cost considerations here as well (Farris and Buzzell, 1979).

This, of course, fits nicely with our understanding of the overall strength of advertising versus promotion just discussed. It is essential to build and nurture brand equity as a product grows, and this is what brand attitude, advertising's strength, is all about. A product in decline is often being phased out, and while managers want product to move through the pipeline, they are not interested in any real investment in the brand. The tactical strength of promotion to stimulate brand purchase intention fits this need well.

There are a number of other market characteristics that seem to call for different advertising versus promotion strategies, and four key areas are discussed next.

Product differentiation

If a product or service is truly different from competition in the mind of the target audience, and (importantly) that difference is seen as meaningful, there is a strong reason to advertise that difference. On the other hand, if the target audience perceives all brands in the category as more or less the same, then at least in the short-term promotion will make more sense than advertising. Why do we emphasize the short-term? Because in the long-term one would hope to create at least a meaningful perceptual if not actual difference for the brand with advertising. In fact, it must be remembered that when we talk about differentiated brands, we are talking about *perceived* differences. Whether or not the difference is 'real' is beside the point if the target audience believes it is real.

Two general characteristics that should be considered are price and quality. In both cases, when consumers perceive a difference, it calls for attention to how one uses advertising and promotion. If a brand is seen as significantly higher in price than other major competitors, advertising is *more* important than promotion. At first this may seem counter-intuitive, but upon reflection you will see that it really isn't. Yes, a price promotion will make a higher-priced brand *temporarily* more price-competitive, but it does nothing to justify its regular price in the long-term. Advertising, via brand attitude, can build brand equity and provide a reason why a higher price is justified.

Once again one must be alert to perceptions. For example, consumers say they 'know' some brands of frozen prepared foods are *much* more expensive than others. But how much, and is the difference really that significant? Interestingly, the actual price of more expensive brands is often not that much higher (no more than a few pence more), but the *perception* is that 'quality' brands are much higher priced. Under such circumstances if you are the manager of one of the 'quality' brands seen as more expensive it makes no sense to decry this misconception of a significantly higher price, and to try and convince people that for only a little more you get a much better product. Consumers already believe it is better. Advertising must reinforce this perception, along the lines of 'naturally it costs more – good quality is expensive'. If a brand is seen as being of higher quality than its major competitor, it makes sense to advertise and reinforce the perception. If a brand is in fact of lower quality than its major competitors (not too low, of course), promotion will often help overcome a reluctance on the part of the target audience to 'trade down'.

In general, one can say that when a brand is perceived to be positioned differently from major competitors, advertising is more important than promotion in IMC planning.

Market position

If a product or service is frequently purchased or used, advertising is more important in the IMC mix than promotion. There are many reasons for this, but again they centre around the need to continually reinforce a positive brand attitude under circumstances where the opportunity for brand switching is high. Promotions of course may be used tactically, but without a strong brand equity all promotions really do is 'steal' usage. This is a problem underscored by the on-going 'cola wars'. Both Coke and Pepsi seem to have turned more and more to price promotion. As a result, it is not unusual for the leading brand in a market at any one time to be the one with the best price promotion. If taken to an extreme, this can lead to brand suicide because in effect it is telling consumers not to pay attention to the brand's advertising, but to make their brand choice based only upon price.

It also makes more sense to advertise than use extensive promotion when a brand has a clear market share advantage. Once again, it is the brand attitude strength of advertising that nurtures the brand equity sustaining market share advantage.

Overall then, with a strong market position through either frequent purchase or high market share advantage, advertising will be more important than promotion in IMC planning.

Poor performance

When a brand finds itself struggling, promotion becomes more important than advertising. When what is needed is help *now*, the more immediate sales results from promotion make sense. This flows naturally from promotion's strength, brand purchase intention. While this is unlikely to provide a long-term solution to the problem, it is definitely a way to accelerate sales in the short run. This in turn should help increase cash flow and enable a return to the marketing plan. A corollary to this is when a brand is in danger of losing distribution (which can be a natural consequence of disappointing sales performance) or having trouble building distribution. This is a perfect time to use trade promotion.

When brand performance, either at the store or trade level, is faltering or not up to expectation, promotion will assume more importance than advertising in IMC planning.

Competitive activity

Not surprisingly, when competitors cut advertising and increase promotion, most brands will follow suit for fear of losing sales. And if competitors increase spending on advertising while cutting back on promotion, again most brands will do the same. While this may make sense as a short-term tactical move, the actions of competitors should not necessarily guide one's own marketing communication strategy. Each brand must take a careful look at its own situation, and respond in its own best interest.

As noted above, a high priced brand may indeed increase its advertising expenditures (correctly) to help nurture a strong positive attitude toward the brand in the face of aggressive pricing strategies by competitors. But a 'price' brand should probably not increase its advertising expenditure, and may wish to counter with even deeper short-run price promotions. The point here is that each situation must be looked at within the context of a brand's marketing objectives and its position in relationship to major competitors.

In recent years, at least for consumer packaged goods, there has been a strong increase in market share for private label product. Private label remains a small proportion of any market, but its share can certainly rival the share of many individual brands in a category. Where private label is a significant factor, it makes sense to increase *advertising* activity, *not* try to compete on price with promotion. More often than not this will take the form of stressing 'quality' or some other aspect of brand equity. Unfortunately, as scanning data continue to show, as shares increase for private label brands too often companies turn to price promotion rather than attempting to reinforce the equity value in their brand.

What we are talking about here are traditional private label brands. We do not mean 'branded' private label products. These better quality private label products (in fact often of comparable quality with national brands) must be considered like any other lower priced competitor. The actual price differences are generally not that great, and they are being marketed much like any other widely distributed brand, including the use of advertising.

How should competitive activity be treated in IMC planning? Managers must look at each situation and respond with increased advertising or promotion in the best interest of their brand regardless of what major competitors may be doing. This usually means a short-term tactical response, increasing advertising or promotion when competitors increase theirs, but this need not be a blind response. Also, when private label is a serious competitor, increased emphasis on advertising is usually called for.

Overall, we have seen that various market conditions will direct the strategic and tactical use of advertising and promotion. Managers cannot afford to think of advertising or promotion as independent means of marketing communication. Each has particular strengths, and within each there are particular types of advertising or promotion that may be used singly or in combination to address various situations in the market. It is not a question of 'should we use advertising or promotion,' but rather 'should we *emphasize* advertising or promotion' in IMC planning. The market considerations discussed and their impact upon IMC planning are summarized in Figure 10.4.

Market characteristic	IMC planning emphasis
Product differentiation	Advertising
Market position	
High brand share	Advertising
Frequently purchased product	Advertising
Poor brand performance	
Slow sales	Promotion
Distribution problems	Promotion to trade
Competitive activity	
Increase in spending by competition	Analyze situation carefully and respond accordingly
Strong private lable	Advertising

Figure 10.4
Market characteristic impact upon advertising versus promotion emphasis in IMC

■ Advantages of using advertising and promotion together

We have noted that more and more money is spent today in marketing communication areas outside of traditional advertising. In fact, about three to one. However, for most marketing communication problems, advertising-like messages will almost always be central to a brand's marketing communications planning, even if not in the form of traditional advertising (i.e. delivered via traditional media).

What is it about using advertising and promotion together that offers advantages relative to using only advertising or promotion alone? We have already discussed the fact that advertising and promotion have different strengths in relation to communication objectives. But the critical communication objective with regard to the joint effectiveness of advertising and promotion is advertising's *prior* establishment of a strong brand attitude, which is the main link to brand equity.

Schultz (1995), while perhaps not going quite so far as this, has talked about the role traditional advertising has to play in IMC, stating that 'image advertising is a critical ingredient in any marketing and communications program.' He goes on to talk about the need to 'protect or build the perceptual value of the brand.' To our way of thinking, this is just another way of talking about brand equity, and the communication strength of advertising, brand attitude. People may approach the matter somewhat differently, and use different words, but there is no doubt that advertising-like messages must almost always play a crucial role in IMC planning.

The key to this importance lies in the fact that when advertising has been effective in generating a strong brand attitude that has led to a strong brand equity, all of a brand's promotional efforts will be that much more effective. There are two fundamental reasons for this:

- First of all, when the target audience holds strong favourable attitudes toward a brand, it means that when the brand does use promotions the target audience will see them as a much better value, and
- When the target audience holds strong favourable attitudes toward a brand, when competitors offer promotions the target audience will be less likely to respond to them.

If one thinks about it, this makes sense. The more someone likes a product or service, the less likely they will be to switch because of a promotion; and when the brand offers its own promotion, they will think that much better of it, *and* it will tend to reinforce their already positive brand attitude.

Before leaving the impression that advertising, in creating a favourable brand attitude, may be all that is really needed, there is something else to consider. No matter how favourable brand attitude may be, it is unlikely that everyone in the market buys or uses that brand exclusively. It is unlikely that any core market is ever dominated by totally brand loyal customers. What brand attitude is working on is maintaining a dominant share of favourable brand switchers. Of course, it also holds brand loyal customers, but in today's markets consumers switch among various competitive alternatives. Unfortunately, this phenomenon of declining loyalty is being accelerated by an over-reliance upon promotion, especially price promotion, to attract switchers. We have already referred to the cola wars. In fact, in one major supermarket chain, over 80% of all Coke and Pepsi sales were price-off deals. The leading brand was simply the brand on special that day.

This does not change anything we have just discussed about the critical importance of advertising. It only underscores the fact that it is advertising and promotion working together that will create the most effective IMC programs. Without effective advertising, it is unlikely that a brand will maintain its equity over time. But, this must be coupled with appropriate tactical use of promotion. One of the best ways to understand how this strategy of combining advertising and promotion optimizes IMC planning is by looking at something Moran (1978) has called the 'ratchet effect'.

The advertising and promotion 'ratchet effect'

The notion of a 'ratchet effect' rests upon the idea that when advertising is used in combination with promotion, it increases the value of a brand's promotion while minimizing the effect of competitor promotions. As mentioned earlier, promotions tend to 'steal' sales, especially from existing customers. The promotion more often than not will merely accelerate an already planned purchase by customers, or attract a switcher to the brand for this purchase only. The hope, of course, is that the promotion will increase the number of purchases of the brand by switchers. In other words, encourage them to 'switch-to-us' more often. If someone is using (for example) coupons as the key to switching, *without* a coupon or other price promotion, it is unlikely they will 'switch' to a brand. The price promotion will attract a switcher, but without advertising support, what reason would there be to continue buying at the regular price? There would be nothing to nurture a positive brand attitude.

When running a promotion, it should generate higher than normal levels of sales. But with promotion alone, without adequate prior and on-going advertising, once the promotion is over sales levels will dip below average levels until the product purchased on promotion has been exhausted, and customers are 'back' in the market. Switchers are back on their normal switching pattern and loyal customers have used up the product they stocked-up on while it was on promotion. This effect is illustrated in Figure 10.5.

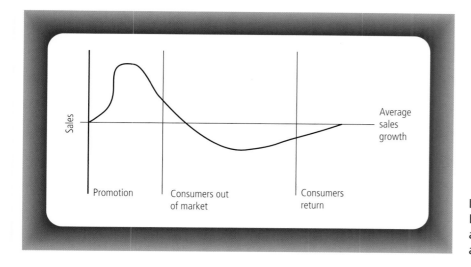

Figure 10.5
Effect of promotion alone without advertising

However, when advertising and promotion are used effectively together, the effect of promotion on top of prior advertising is to *increase* the rate of growth stimulated by advertising alone. Remember, of course, that this rate of growth may be flat or even declining. There is no guarantee that advertising alone will stimulate sales growth. The point is that the *combination* of advertising and promotion should improve overall market performance when it is part of a good IMC program.

This is what Moran (1978) has described as the *ratchet effect*. Because of prior advertising, there is a positive brand attitude. When the brand is promoted, loyal customers' favourable brand attitude is reinforced. Switchers, attracted by the promotion will be more likely to continue purchasing or using the brand on a more regular basis after the promotion is withdrawn *because* of the advertising's positive brand attitude effect. This means the regular customer base grows, and the average sales level 'ratchets' up. This 'ratchet effect' is illustrated in Figure 10.6.

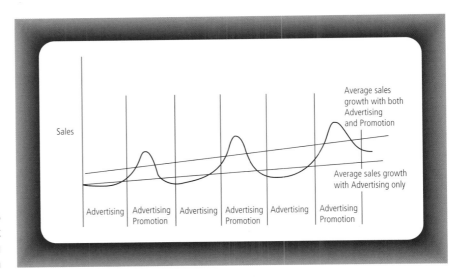

Figure 10.6
Moran's ratchet
effect: advertising
with promotion

All of this assumes, of course, that the combination of advertising and promotion is cost effective and the IMC campaign has been well conceived and truly *integrated*. One must be alert to the fact that price promotion has the potential of actually increasing prices at the consumer level. There are major costs tied to promotions, beyond the obvious. Uneven production runs and distribution adds cost. Carrying extra inventory costs the trade money. Tracking promotions can absorb a great deal of brand marketing overhead. In-store pricing and re-pricing adds costs. Without careful planning, all of this could lead eventually to significant price differentials.

The impact of demand elasticity

At the heart of consumer response to the interaction between advertising and promotion is the economist's notion of demand elasticity. Again, this is a point made by Moran (1978). Understanding the relationship between a brand's and its competitor brand's demand elasticities is an important part of IMC planning. Specifically, in Moran's terms, one needs to be concerned with 'upside' and 'downside' elasticities. We especially like his ideas here because they focus the manager's thinking on the relationship between advertising and promotion in effecting sales, not simply the overall price elasticity of a brand.

Upside elasticity refers to the sales increases resulting from a price cut or promotion; downside elasticity to the sales decline resulting from a price increase. While these definitions reflect a brand's action with regard to pricing strategy, it is important to understand that a brand's *competitors'* pricing strategy will directly effect the demand elasticity of the brand – both upside and downside. Competitors' price increases in effect cut the price of those brands that do not raise their price. Aggressive price-cutting or promotion by competitors in effect raises the price of brands that do not.

The on-going market dynamic, especially in a time of heavy price oriented promotion, underscores the need for effective advertising in most IMC programs. Our discussion of positive brand attitude and brand equity illustrates how effective prior advertising creates a more fertile ground for long-term sales benefit from promotion. We also discussed how effective prior advertising helps lessen the impact of competitor promotion. In other words, relative to competitors, effective advertising will generate *high* upside elasticity and *low* downside elasticity.

A brand's upside and downside elasticities will depend to a great deal on its current brand equity (unfortunately, an elusive concept to measure). As a result, to the extent that a brand's promotional activities contribute to brand attitude, and reinforce brand equity, they will make advertising's job easier. Brand equity oriented promotions act just like advertising, increasing upside demand elasticity and reducing downside demand elasticity. As a result, with the exception of short-term tactical promotion, all IMC should aim for positive demand elasticity.

We are not suggesting that a firmly calibrated calculation of demand elasticities must be a part of IMC planning, only that it is important to *think* about it. We know, for example, that frequent or heavy price promotion on its own can negatively affect brand attitude. Managers must think about where their brands stand in terms of target audience brand attitude versus attitude toward major competitors, the brand's pricing strategy versus competition, and how one is allocating marketing monies versus competitors. This, along with what we have been discussing, should greatly help understanding of the interdependence of advertising and promotion in successful IMC planning.

Summary

There are two fundamental areas the manager must consider at the beginning of the IMC planning process. The first is potential communication objectives. Communication objectives are at the heart of the process, reflecting what will be needed to positively influence the target audience's brand choice, and to inform the basic roles of advertising and promotion within the IMC campaign. Reviewing, category need becomes an objective when the target audience must be reminded of the need for the product itself; brand awareness is always an objective in order to enable the target audience to identify the brand and associate it with the need for the product; brand attitude, also always an objective, provides the target audience with a motivating reason to purchase; and brand purchase intention becomes an objective when immediate action on the part of the target audience is desired.

While both advertising and promotion may be used for any communication objective, owing to the nature of their particular strengths and weaknesses, depending upon the communication objective one or the other will be more appropriate. Marketing communication can only contribute partially to category need. Advertising can help stimulate the need, and promotion can help accelerate the need, but more will be needed through such things as public relations and word-of-mouth. Brand awareness is a traditional strength of advertising, but promotion should also make a contribution. Brand attitude is the primary job of advertising, although all promotion should help reinforce the benefit claim. The real strength of promotion is brand purchase intention.

In addition to consideration of the communication objectives, certain characteristics of the market at any particular time will inform whether advertising or promotion should be emphasized. If the brand is really different from competitors in terms of a meaningful benefit, advertising should be emphasized. Frequently purchase brands and brands with a high market share calls for an advertising emphasis, while poor performance calls for promotion as a tactic in the short-term. When competitors increase their marketing communication, the manager should carefully access the situation and respond with advertising or promotion accordingly. If there is a strong private label presence in the market, use advertising and do not try to compete on price with promotion.

The manager should look at both advertising and promotion, and how they can be used together to optimize the overall effectiveness of the IMC plan. As Moran (1978) described it, the optimum use of advertising and promotion together will create a 'ratchet effect' where the short-term gain from promotion is more likely to be held and built upon by the long-term effects of advertising. This means that a good IMC plan optimally utilizing advertising and promotion together where appropriate will be more effective than using only advertising; and certainly more effective than only using promotion.

■ Review questions

1 Discuss why communication effects are the source for communication objectives.
2 Why are brand awareness and brand attitude always communication objectives for all marketing communication?

3 When does a manager need to consider a communication objective outside of the set of four communication effects?

4 What are the traditional strengths of advertising versus promotion, and why?

5 What is meant by a 'consumer franchise building' promotion, and why is this important?

6 Find examples of promotions that are well integrated with the brand's advertising.

7 How can certain characteristics of a brand's market influence how advertising and promotion should be used in an IMC program?

8 Why should an advertised brand not try to compete with price brands or store brands?

9 What is the advantage of using advertising and promotion together in IMC?

10 Discuss demand elasticity and what it means to IMC planning.

References

Dean, J. (1950) Pricing policies for new products. *Harvard Business Review*, 28(6), 45–53.

Farris, P.W. and Buzzell, R.D. (1979) Why advertising and promotion costs vary: Some cross-sectional analyses. *Journal of Marketing*, 43(4), 112–122.

Mittelstadt, C.A. (1993). The coming era of image-building brand promotions, lecture given at Yale University, 3 March.

Moran, W.T. (1978) Insights from pricing research. In E.B. Bailey (ed.), *Pricing Practices and Strategies* New York: The Conference Board, 7–13.

Prentice, R.M. (1977) How to split your marketing funds between advertising and promotion, *Advertising Age*, 10 January, 41.

Rossiter, J.R. and Percy, L. (1997) *Advertising Communication and Promotion Management*. New York: McGraw-Hill.

Schultz, D.E. (1995) Traditional advertising has role to play in IMC, *MarketingNews*, 28 August, 18.

Strang, R.A. (1980) *The Promotion Planning Process*. New York: Praeger.

CHAPTER 11

The IMC
planning
process

In this chapter we shall be looking at the specific steps involved in the strategic planning process for integrated marketing communications (IMC). Before a manager can begin to think of specific marketing communications issue, it is very important to carefully analyze what is known about the market. This means that the first step in the IMC strategic planning process is to outline the relevant market issues that are likely to effect a brand's communications. The best source of information will be the marketing plan, since all marketing communication efforts should be in support of the marketing plan. (If for some reason a marketing plan is not available, answers to the questions posed below will need to be based upon the best available management judgment.)

After a review of the marketing plan, it is time to begin the five-step strategic planning process introduced in Chapter 1. First, target audience action objectives will need to be carefully considered. Most markets have multiple target groups, and as a result, there may be a number of communication objectives required to reach them. In fact, it is for this very reason that a brand generally needs more than one level of communication, occasioning the necessity of IMC. After identifying the appropriate target audience, it will be time to think about overall marketing communication strategy. This begins at the second step in the strategic planning process by considering how purchase decisions are made in the category. Then the manager must optimize message development to facilitate that process, which involves steps three and four, establishing the positioning and setting communication objectives. Finally, in step five, the manager must decide how to best deliver the message. We shall now look into each of these three areas in some detail.

■ Reviewing the marketing plan

The first step in strategic planning for IMC is to review the marketing plan in order to understand the market in general and where a brand fits relative to its competition. What is it about the brand, company, or service that might bear upon what is said to the target audience? There are at least six broad questions that a manager should answer before beginning to think specifically about the IMC plan. (See Figure 11.1)

What is being marketed? The manager should write out a description of the brand so that anyone will immediately understand what it is and what specific need it satisfies. Taking time to focus one's attention like this on the details of a brand often enables the manager to see it in a clearer light. This is also very important, because it is just this information that will serve as a background for the people who will be creating and executing the brands' marketing communication.

What is known about the market where the brand will compete? This is information that must be current. If it comes from a marketing plan, one must be sure nothing has occurred since it was written that could possibly be outdated. What one is looking for here is knowledge about the market

Key consideration	Question
Product description	What is being marketed?
Market assessment	What is known about the market where the brand competes?
Competitive evaluation	What is known about major competitors?
Source of business	Where will sales and usage come from?
Marketing objective	What are the brand's marketing objectives
Marketing communication	How is marketing communication expected to contribute to the marketing objective

Figure 11.1 Marketing background questions

that is going to influence how successful the brand is likely to be. Is the market growing, are there new entries, have there been recent innovations, bad publicity? While enough information must be provided for a good understanding of the market, the description should be simple and highlight only the most relevant points.

What is known about major competitors? What are the key claims made in the category? What are the creative strategies being used, what types of executional approaches and themes? Here it is helpful to collect actual examples. Something else to consider here is an evaluation of the media tactics being used by competitors. What seems to be their mix of marketing communication options, and how do they use them? All of this provides a picture of the communications environment within which the IMC program will operate.

Where will sales and usage come from? The manager needs to look at this question both in terms of competitive brands and the consumer. Again, this reflects the increasing complexity of markets. To what extent is the brand looking to make inroads against key competitors? Will the brand compete outside the category? Where specifically will customers or users of the brand come from? What, if anything, will they be giving up? Will they be changing their behaviour patterns? This is really the first step toward defining a target audience (which is dealt with in detail in the next section), and begins to hint at how a better understanding of the target will lead to the most suitable IMC options to reach them.

What are the brand's marketing objectives? This should include not only a general overview of the marketing objective, but specific share or financial goals as well. When available, the marketing plan should provide these figures. Otherwise, it is important to estimate the financial expectations for the brand. If the IMC program is successful, what will happen? This is critical because it will provide a realistic idea of how much marketing money can reasonably be made available for the marketing communication program.

How is marketing communication expected to contribute to the marketing objective? As we now know from the previous chapters, the answer is much more than 'increase sales.' It is likely that marketing communication will be expected to make a number of contributions toward meeting the marketing objectives. This is where the manager begins to get an idea of just how much will be expected from the IMC program, and the extent to which multiple messages and different types of marketing communication might be required.

■ Selecting a target audience

Once the manager has thought through the market generally, it is time to take the first step in the strategic planning process and focus more particularly upon whom it is that should be addressed with marketing communications. When thinking about the target audience one must look well beyond traditional demographic considerations. It is also important to 'think ahead'. What type of person will be important to the future of the business? In this stage of the planning process there are three questions that should be addressed. (See Figure 11.2)

- What are the relevant target buyer groups?
- What are the target group's demographic, lifestyle ,and psychographic profile?
- How is the trade involved?

Figure 11.2
Key questions in target audience selection

What are the relevant target buyer groups? While one always hopes business will be broadly based, realistically one must set a primary objective concentrating on either existing customers or non-customers, what are known as trial versus repeat purchase action objectives.

Following a useful designation of buyer groups introduced by Rossiter and Percy (1987), one may think about customers in terms of being either brand loyals (BL) or favourable brand switchers (FBS). Some customers buy a brand almost exclusively, others buy the brand along with others in the category. Non-customers too may be loyal to one brand (OBL, other brand loyals) or switch among other brands (OBS, other brand switchers); or, they may not buy any brands in the category now, offering potential for the future (NCU, non-category users).

It is useful to consider the potential target audience in these terms because it *reflects* brand attitude. Ideally, one would select a target audience in terms of their attitudes. Unfortunately, it is not possible to find people profiled in terms of their attitudes in media buying databases.

However, brand purchase behaviour is available. Although not a perfect substitute, these buyer groups do reflect a certain degree of brand attitude. BL and OBL should have strong positive attitudes toward the brands they buy. FBS and OBS too will hold generally positive attitudes toward the brands they buy. Interestingly, in fact, most consumers actually prefer two or three brands in a category, primarily for variety or because of slightly different end uses (vanTripp et al., 1996). Brand attitudes, however, cannot be inferred for NCU. They may indeed have rejected the brands in the category, or they may simply see such products as inappropriate for them at the time (for example, baby products if you do not have a baby).

Communication strategies will differ significantly, depending upon which of these target groups is selected; and could differ within groups of customers or non-customers. If the target is primarily BL or FBS who use the brand along with competitors, promotional tactics would clearly differ between these two groups. The brand is looking to retain BL, but to increase the frequency with which the brand is purchased by FBS. Among non-customers OBL would be very difficult to attract. On the other hand, those who switch among several brands (but not the company's) are at least behaviourally susceptible to trying the brand because they already buy several brands, and should be open to trial promotions. It is very important to think about various alternative buyer groups, and where it makes the most sense to place the primary communications effort.

What are the target groups' profile? Traditionally, target audiences have been described in demographic terms: women, 18–34 years, with some university training. Sometimes efforts have been made to include so-called 'psychographic' or life-style descriptions (Antonides and vanRaaij, 1998). All of this is important, but it is not enough when considering IMC programs. As already suggested one must understand the target audience(s) in terms of behaviour and attitude, but also in terms of patterns that are relevant to communication and media strategies. This means how they now behave or are likely to behave in relationship to the brand and competition, what their differing information needs or motivations might be, and how they 'use' various media. This is important information for IMC strategy, and should be gained through research, and regularly updated.

How is the trade involved? It is important to think about the trade in the broadest possible terms, including all those who are involved in the distribution and sale of the brand without necessarily buying, stocking, or using it themselves. What one needs to think about here is whether or not people not directly concerned with the purchase and use of the brand might nevertheless be an important part of the target audience. For example, one may need to pre-sell a new product to distribution channels or inform possible sources of recommendations about the brand (e.g. doctors or consultants). Where the trade might fit should be considered when thinking about how purchase and brand decisions are made, which we cover next.

In selecting the target audience, at this point the manager is identifying the primary target for the brand. As we shall see in the next section, in determining how decisions are made in the category this selection will be refined, looking at the roles played by the primary target group at different points in the decision process, as well a secondary targets that may be involved.

■ Determining how decisions are made

If IMC is to positively affect brand purchase, it is essential to understand just how purchases in the category are made by the target audience, and this is what is involved at step two in the strategic planning process. In consumer behaviour, decisions are often described in terms of need arousal leading to consideration, then action. While this does provide a general idea of how decisions are made, for IMC planning purposes, it is not specific enough. A very good way to look at how brand purchase decisions are made has been offered by Rossiter and Percy (1997) with something they call a behavioural sequence model (BSM). A generic BSM is illustrated in Figure 11.3.

Consideration at each stage	Decision stages			
	Need arousal	**Brand consideration**	**Purchase**	**Usage**
Whom all is involved and what role(s) do they play?				
Where does the stage occur?				
What is the timing?				
How is it likely to occur?				

Figure 11.3
Generic BSM

It asks six fundamental questions: What are the stages consumers go through in making a decision; Whom all is involved in the decision and what roles do they play; Where do the stages occur; What is the timing; and How is it likely to occur? This results in a flow chart that identifies where members of the target audience are taking action or making decisions that will ultimately affect purchases. Each of these questions are addressed next.

What stages do consumers go through? A BSM first asks the manager to think about the major decision stages a brand's target audience goes through prior, during, and following actual purchase or use of a product or service. A generic decision model may be built upon the general consumer behaviour model mentioned above: need arousal, brand consideration, purchase, and usage. Notice that *usage* is included as part of the purchase decision here because it provides an opportunity to communicate with the consumer in anticipation of future purchase or use. Also, it helps reinforce the purchase decision. It has been found, for example, that people continue to pay attention to advertising for brands that have been purchase (Ehrlich et al., 1957). Additionally, especially for high-involvement decisions, attending to advertising for the brand purchased reduces dissonance as Festinger (1957) pointed out in his theory of cognitive dissonance.

While the generic model of decision stages can be very useful, and can generally be adapted to almost any situation, always remember that the *best* model is the one that comes closet to how decisions are actually made in the brand's specific category. For example, in many business situations, distribution or trade hurdles must be surmounted before there is any thought of need arousal in the target audience. Other decisions may be even more complicated; or quite simple. The idea is to capture the essence of the decision process, and use this as the basis for planning. Qualitative research can be helpful here in providing specific details unique to particular categories.

Two examples will help illustrate this. First, consider a retailer that has a chain of lamp stores. A hypothetical model of the decision stages involved in a lamp purchase, might be as follows. The first stage in the decision to buy a new lamp probably involves a decision to redecorate. One of the most popular ways to redecorate is to buy a new lamp. These two stages would constitute *need arousal*. Next, one must decide *where* to shop for the lamp, shop the store (or stores) and make a choice. These three steps would be a modification of *brand consideration*. Once the lamp has been chosen, the *purchase* is made and the lamp is taken home and *used*. The decisions stages would then be: decide to redecorate→consider new lamp→look for places to buy lamp→shop→select lamp→purchase→replace old lamp with new. (Figure 11.4)

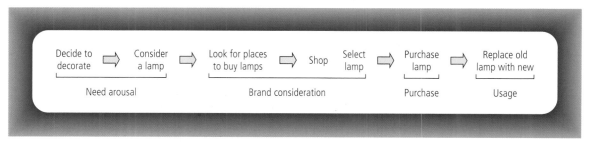

Figure 11.4
Decision stages involved in a lamp purchase

It should be apparent just how helpful this discipline can be for IMC planning. Even with a simple example such as this, you can see how thinking about the decision process suggests a number of possible ways to communicate with potential lamp purchasers. The most obvious insight here is that a lamp purchase is unlikely to take place outside the context of 'redecorating' (and research has indeed suggested this). This means to interest people in lamps one must first awaken an interest in redecorating or changing the look of a room.

As a second example, consider a manufacturer of commercial kitchen equipment that is distributed through restaurant supply companies. How does a restaurant supply company go about deciding what items and brands they will distribute? A probable decision model might begin with keeping an eye out for better items to stock in order to maintain a competitive edge. This could lead to an awareness of a potential new line or item to stock. These two stages would correspond to *need arousal* in the generic model. Once interest is aroused, the new item will then be compared with what is now carried; the *brand consideration* stage. If the evaluation is positive, it will be ordered and added to inventory; *purchase*. Once stocked, sales will be monitored, and if positive, the item or line will be reordered. These last two stages would correspond to the generic model's *usage* stage. The decision stages for a restaurant supply company then might be: monitor new items→identify potential items to carry→compare with current items stocked→if positive, add to stock→ monitor sales→if good, reorder.

Here is a good example of where the decision process suggests it might make sense to pay a lot of attention to the *usage* stages. An important question for a manufacturer of a new kitchen product would be: how much end-user 'pull' would be necessary to insure sufficient sales for their customer, the restaurant supply company, to reorder? If initial sales are anticipated to be slow, it might make sense to offer a reorder incentive. These are the kinds of questions a good understanding of the stages in a decision process stimulates.

Who is involved and what roles do they play? Once the specific stages of the decision process have been established, one must assign the roles individual members of the potential target audience are likely to play at each stage. Those who study consumer behaviour generally identify five potential roles involved in making a decision: initiator, influencer, decider, purchaser, and user (Figure 11.5). Let us consider as an example the roles that might be involved in a simplified illustration of a cruise vacation decision, using the four generic decision stages.

What role or roles are most likely to be involved during the *need arousal* stage? Since those who play the role of an initiator in the decision get the whole process started, it is the initiators that will be included under *need arousal* in the BSM model. This could include family members, friends who have been on a cruise, potential cruisers, travel agents, and cruise fairs. Notice that the trade is considered here in terms of travel agents and cruise fairs. Since influencers recommend and deciders choose what to do, both roles will be influential during the *brand consideration* stage

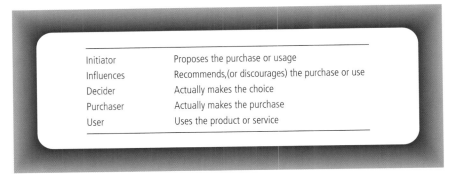

Initiator	Proposes the purchase or usage
Influences	Recommends,(or discourages) the purchase or use
Decider	Actually makes the choice
Purchaser	Actually makes the purchase
User	Uses the product or service

Figure 11.5
Decision roles

of the decision process. The influencers may include family members, friends who have been on a cruise, and travel agents. The decider is either an individual adult potential cruiser or a couple. The actual *purchase* is made by the purchaser, whom is likely to be an individual adult potential cruiser, while the *usage* stage is experienced by all those who go on the cruise.

Understanding the roles people play in the decision process can lead to messages in an IMC campaign addressed to very specific target segments. McDonald's understood the importance of mothers as both influencers and deciders when it comes to what fast food restaurants the family visits. Recognizing the concern over child obesity, to help overcome potential negative associations with fat content in much fast food, McDonald's in Sweden ran a series of inserts in magazines oriented to mothers specifically addressing their role as influencers and deciders in matters of family health and eating habits, positioned to build more positive brand attitude through increasing trust in McDonald's food (see Figure 11.6).

This may be a good point to deal with the issue of individual versus group decisions. It is certainly true that many family decisions are made through a husband/wife or family consensus, and many business purchase decision are the result of a group effort. However, when it comes to IMC, we are interested in the *individual* and the role they are playing in the overall decision process. Communication efforts must first persuade the individual *prior* to their participation in any group decision. So, while many actual decisions are the result of group action, specific advertising or promotion must address individuals in the roles they are playing in the decision process.

Where do the stages occur? Locating opportunities for marketing communication is vital to successful IMC, and a BSM can help pinpoint likely places. In fact, as one considers a BSM, the first thing one notices is that different stages in the decision process occur at different times, and as a result where individuals may be reached as they play their role at each stage can certainly vary. There are exceptions of course. For example, someone could be shopping and given a sample of a new cookie to taste along with a coupon. They like it, and decide to buy some. They see the special end-aisle display, pick up a box, open it, and enjoy a few

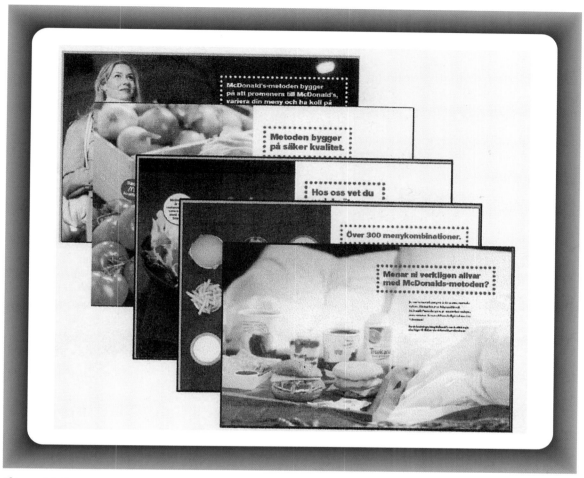

Figure 11.6
An excellent example of advertising specifically addressing the target audience in the role they play, here mothers in their role as influencer and decider in matters of family health and eating habits. *Courtesy*: OMD and McDonald's

while they finish shopping. In this case all of the stages occur at one location – the store. However, this is not likely to be the case very often. And because potential locations can vary widely under different circumstances, unusual media might be appropriate.

Building upon situation theory (Belk, 1975) in buyer behaviour and Foxall's (1992) work on selling and consumption situations in marketing, Rossiter and Percy (1997) offer four points for marketing communications managers to consider for each location identified:

1 *How accessible is the location to marketing communication?* This could range from no accessibility to too much, in the sense of a lot of clutter from other marketing communication or competition from other things.

2　*How many role-players are present?* Is the message directed to an individual or are several people participating at this stage of the decision at that location.

3　*How much time pressure exists?* This could range from none to a great deal and the greater the time pressure the less opportunity there will be to process the message. The difference between relaxing at home and dashing in and out of a store will seriously effect the likelihood of a message being processed.

4　*What is the physical and emotional state of the individual?* Certain personality states can seriously effect message processing. For example, is someone in a doctor's waiting room there for a routine check-up and generally relaxed (assuming they haven't been kept waiting too long) or because of symptoms of a serious illness and therefore upset and anxious.

As you can see, it is important to think about what is going on at each location where part of the decisions is made. Some locations are going to be better than others as potential place to reach the target audience.

What is the timing? The timing of decision stages should reflect the general purchase cycle or pattern for the category. Understanding when each stage of the decision process occurs, and the relationship between the stages, is important for media scheduling. Obvious examples would be seasonal decision such as back-to-school shopping or holiday purchases. But understanding the timing of even such routine behaviour as meal planning is important.

A good example of this is the decision process for choosing a dessert. Obviously, for the average day, what to buy and serve for dessert is a low-involvement decision. In fact, most dessert decisions are made *after the meal*. This means that whatever is to be served must be in inventory, and even more importantly, *must be ready to serve*. This is no problem for such things as cookies, ice cream, and fruit. But what if you are selling cake mix or something like Jell-O brand gelatin? If all you do is 'sell' the end product, all you will do is move the product from the store shelf to the pantry shelf. This will *not* move it from the pantry to the table. For a cake or Jell-O to be served for dessert it must have been made some time *before dinner*. This suggests advertising to homemakers in the morning to make the dessert so it will be ready *after* dinner.

This example underscores the fact that even the simplest seeming decision process can have hidden traps if it is not fully understood. This is also why we talk about both purchase *and* usage in the decision stages.

How is each stage likely to occur? The last thing to consider in the BSM is *how* each of the stages is likely to occur. What is it that arouses need? How is the target audience likely to go about getting information? What are they likely to be doing at the point-of-purchase? In what way will the product or service be used? These are questions managers will want to have answers to prior to thinking about message development and delivery.

The usefulness of the BSM for IMC planning is that it forces the manager to think about what is likely to be going on when various stages of a decision occur, and this will provide a perspective on marketing communication options that are likely to be effective under those circumstances. Figure 11.7 illustrates a BSM for a cruise vacation using the generic decision stages. An actual BSM for a cruise vacation would require many more specific stages, but this will provide an example of how everything fits together.

Considerations at each stage	Decision stages			
	Need arousal	**Brand consideration**	**Purchase**	**Usage**
Decision roles involved	Family members, friends who have been on a cruise, potential cruiser as *Initiator* Travel agents and cruise 'fairs' as *Initiator*	Family members, friends who have been on cruise, and potential cruiser as *Influencer* Individual adult potential cruiser or couple as *Decider* Travel agents as *Influencer*	Individual adult potential cruiser as *Purchaser*	All adults traveling on cruise as *Users*
Where stage is likely to occur	At home, travel agent's office or cruise 'fair' for consumers At office for travel agent or cruise 'fair' operator	At home, talking with friends, travel agent's office or cruise 'fair' for consumers At office, trade shows or actual cruises for travel agents or cruise fair operators	At home or travel agent's office	On cruise
Timing of stage	Special trip or vacation holiday planning, or word-of-mouth	3–6 months following need arousal	Shortly after completing information search and evaluation	1–3 months after purchase
How it is likely to occur	Looking for something special	Ask, call, write for brochure, visit cruise 'fair,' talk with experienced cruiser of travel agent	Call or visit travel agent	Enjoy cruise

Figure 11.7
BSM for cruise holiday

■ Message development

Up to this point in the strategic planning process we have been dealing with broader issues linked to the market where the brand competes, and the target audience. This helps the manager understand the marketing objectives for the brand, and where the brand is looking for business. Now it is time to address how specific marketing communication messages can best contribute to the brand's overall marketing objectives. It must be remembered that IMC is *always* in aid of the marketing plan.

In this section we will be looking at message development from a strategic standpoint. This involves steps three and four of the strategic planning process where the manager must make decisions in order to ensure that IMC messages will positively affect brand choice. First, how should the brand be positioned within its marketing communication? This provides the foundation for the development of effective benefit claims to be used in the messages. Then, the manager must set specific communication objectives.

Establishing brand positioning

It is important to remember that what is involved here is how the brand is positioned *within* its marketing communication. The brand will already have been generally positioned as a part of the overall marketing strategy. It may be a niche brand, a 'price' brand, broadly based, etc. How it is positioned within marketing communication addresses the best way to link the brand to category need and a benefit. In Chapter 2 the importance of positioning in IMC was introduced and discussed. Now, it shall be considered within the context of the planning process and its role in message development. In the strategic planning process for IMC, the manager must first establish whether the brand assumes a central versus differentiated position. To be centrally positioned, the brand must be seen by the target audience as being able to deliver all of the benefits associated with its *product category*. Otherwise, a differentiated position must be used, which is almost always the case.

Once this initial decision is made, the manager must then determine if the benefit claim for the brand should be about specific benefits associated with the brand, or about the brand's users. Again in almost every case, the positioning will reflect a product-oriented rather than user-oriented benefit. There are only two situations where a user-oriented positioning could be considered. These are when the target audience represents a specific market segment or niche, or when the underlying motivation driving purchase behaviour is social approval. But even in these cases, one could still adapt a product-oriented positioning. All of this was dealt with in some detail in Chapter 2.

Having addressed these two issues, the manager must then deal specifically with developing the benefit claims; that is, how the benefit will be dealt with in the creative executions. This means addressing the links between the brand and category need in order to optimize brand awareness, and the links between the brand and benefit in order to maximize positive brand attitude. In terms of the planning process, this must be determined before considering the more creative issues involved in message development.

For effective IMC, awareness for a brand must be quickly and easily linked in memory with the category need, reflecting the way in which the brand choice decision is made. This requires a positioning where the need for the product reflects how the target audience perceives that need. This is not always so straightforward as it may seem. The manager must know how the consumer refers to the need that products in the category satisfy, which is a function of how they define the market. For example, is a household cleaner brand seen as a general cleaner, or as a heavy-duty cleaner? Is a television made by B & O simply a television or is it seen as part of a home entertainment system? These differences are critical, because they inform how the brand is stored in memory. Long ago in his classic article 'Marketing Myopia', Levitt (1960) pointed out the need to understand a brand's market in terms of how the *consumer* sees it. This is what establishes the true competitive set.

If a brand is seen as a heavy-duty cleaner, its marketing communication should position it as such, linking the brand to heavy-duty cleaning needs and *not* general household cleaning. If the brand talked about itself in terms of a household cleaner, it would be inconsistent with how the target audience sees the brand, and unlikely to tap into the relevant associations in memory. This assumes, of course, the brand is not trying to *re-position* itself as a more general household cleaner. The question the manager must answer here is: How does the target audience think about the brand?

Ramlösa offers an excellent example of this. They wanted to introduce a line of tastevaried waters to challenge LOKA, who dominated the market, especially among young women. Unfortunately, consumers perceived the brand as something for older, more serious people. Clearly, the brand needed to be re-positioned in the consumer's mind. They did this by running a saturation campaign emulating a movie launch or rock concert announcement, using outdoor media in a very unique way (see Figure 11.8). After only 3 weeks Ramlösa had passed LOKA in the scented waters category.

If a brand is centrally positioned, the benefit to the category are assumed, and must be reinforced. If a user-oriented positioning is adopted, the benefit is subsumed by an identification with brand usage. In all other cases, which again is most of the time, the manager must select the benefit most likely to maximize positive brand attitude in differentiating the brand from competitors in the eyes of the target audience, and to determine the best way in which to focus upon that benefit with the executions. The benefit selection will provide the basis for the benefit claim made about the brand in its marketing communication. In effect, it will let the consumer know what the brand offers and why they should want it.

Benefit selection and focus

Most people who study consumer behaviour feel that attitudes result from a summary judgement of everything one knows about something, weighted by how important those things are to them. This is usually expressed in terms of something known as the expectancy-value model of attitude (Fishbein and Ajzen, 1975), as discussed in Chapter 2. For brands, this means a person's attitude toward a brand will be made up of the summation of those things they know about it, weighted by how important those things are to them. In selecting a benefit for positioning, the manager should look for a potential benefit that is *important* to

Figure 11.8
An example of creatively using an IMC campaign to emulate a movie launch or rock concert promotion to reposition a brand toward young women. *Courtesy*: OMD and Ramlöso

the target audience; that the target audience feel the brand either *delivers* now or could believably deliver; and ideally, do it *better* than competing brands. What one is looking for here is the perception of *uniqueness* for the brand, and this must come from the way in which the benefit claim is made in the creative execution (Boulding et al., 1994).

A brand benefit may be expressed in terms of either an objective *attribute*, a subjective *characteristic*, or an *emotion*. As an example, a benefit associated with a sports car might be related to the engine. One could create a message where the benefit claim talked about a 5.8-litre engine (an attribute), a 'powerful' engine (a subjective characteristic), or about it being 'exhilarating' (an emotion). However, the way in which a benefit is expressed in a message must be informed by the underlying motivation driving behaviour in the category.

When the underlying motive is positive (transformational brand attitude strategies), the benefit claim should be built upon a positive emotion. For products such as food, beverages, or fashion that are driven by a positive motive, the benefit should be a positive feeling associated with the brand. For example, this means creating a sense of sensual pleasure for food or sexual allure with fashion. The focus in the execution can be on the emotion alone, or perhaps associated with a subjective characteristic along the lines of 'our decadent flavors will leave you in ecstasy'. The emotion 'ecstasy' in this case is stimulated by the brand's 'decadent flavors'.

If the underlying motive is negative (informational brand attitude strategies), positive emotions are not appropriate as *benefits*. This does not mean that one should not create a positive emotional response to the message, only that the benefit claim should be built upon either a subjective characteristic of the brand, an attribute supporting the subjective characteristic, or the subjective characteristic resolving a problem. Such a focus is more in line with the need for the benefit to provide information that will help mediate the underlying negative motivation. For a cold remedy, for example, the benefit claim might be built around a subjective characteristic such as 'long-lasting relief', an attribute in support of the subjective characteristic such as 'our time-released capsules ensure long-lasting relief', or resolving a problem with the subjective characteristic, 'why take four capsules a day when one of ours gives you long-lasting relief?'

Of course, these illustrations are not meant to be an example of what the actual *creative* content of the message would be, but rather to provide a sense of the strategic possibilities associated with benefit focus in positioning. The point is that benefit selection must not only be based upon an important, uniquely delivered benefit, but also the appropriate motivation. The benefit focus for informational brand attitude strategies will be different from transformational brand attitude strategies, and these must be considered by the manager as part of positioning before moving on to setting communication objectives and specific brand attitude strategies. This means that the final question the manager must consider in terms of positioning is: What is the appropriate benefit focus?

Setting communication objectives

In earlier chapters we talked about the four basic communication effects of category need, brand awareness, brand attitude, and brand purchase intention, and saw in the last chapter how communication objectives follow directly from them. Since these are the possible effects of marketing communication, the manager must establish the importance of each to the overall communications strategy. As already emphasized, an important point to remember is that communication effects result from all forms of marketing communication. In other words, regardless of which type of marketing communication is considered, it will have the ability to stimulate any of the major communication effects. However, as we have seen, all types of marketing communication are not necessarily equally effective in creating particular effects.

Communication objectives are quite simply the communication *effects* one is looking for. Next, we will summarize how the four communication effects are likely to translate into communication objectives in the IMC plan.

Category need

If there is little demand for a category, or people seem less aware of it, establishing or reminding people of it becomes a communication objective. For example, one could not really do much of a job advertising or promoting a specific brand of a new product such as when Blackberries were introduced until people learned just what they were. Market share leaders can sometimes benefit from category need advertising when category demands slackens. A not too long ago example of reminding people of a category need was when in the US Campbell Soup ran a 'soup is good food' campaign. By stimulating category need for soup they generated differentially high sales for Campbell's because of their overwhelming share in the category.

Brand awareness

Brand (including trade) awareness is *always* an objective of any marketing communication program, whether advertising or promotion. We know that based upon how people make purchase decisions this awareness will occur via recognition or recall. As we have seen, recognition brand awareness is when the brand is seen in the store and remembered from advertising or promotion. Recall brand awareness is when one must remember the brand or store name first, prior to buying or using a product (e.g. when deciding to have lunch at a fast food restaurant, or when an industrial buyer decides to call several suppliers for a quotation). A principal communication objective of all advertising is to create or maintain brand awareness.

While brand awareness is usually seen as a traditional strength of advertising, as pointed out in the last chapter promotion can make a significant contribution. Generally, promotion is best utilized for increasing brand recognition. Merchandising promotions do this by drawing more attention to a brand at the point-of-purchase (e.g., with coupons or special displays).

An excellent and innovative use of advertising and promotion together to raise awareness won for OMD a Medallion Award at Cannes in 2003 for their work for a small bank, SBAB. In a direct challenge to larger banks, an IMC campaign was launched to raise awareness of SBAB and increase loan applications. Under the umbrella positioning of 'loans in a jar' a variety of media were used to deliver both advertising-like and promotion-like messages.

The key to the program was an innovative use of outdoor and the Internet for the promotion-like messages encouraging loan applications, supported by awareness-building messages in print and television. Messages were tailored to specific apartment buildings pointing out how much owners of flats in the building could save by switching to SBAB (see Figure 11.9). Promotion-like messages on the Internet provided an opportunity for individuals to calculate how much they would personally save if they switched. (This is a promotion because its objective was to stimulate an immediate intention to switch.) The results were an immediate increase in brand awareness and a 46% increase in loan applications during the campaign period.

Brand attitude

Brand attitude too is *always* a communication objective, again as we have discussed. What is meant by brand attitude is the information or feeling the brand wishes to impart through its marketing communication. Information about a brand or emotional associations with it that are transmitted by consistent advertising over time build's brand equity.

We have dealt with brand attitude a great deal in this book because it is really at the heart of marketing communication. Strategies for implementing the brand attitude objective are derived from one of the four quadrants of the Rossiter–Percy Grid. Reviewing, the manager must consider whether the target audience sees the purchase of a brand as low or high risk (involvement), and whether the underlying motivation to buy or use the brand is positive or negative. Where the brand falls in relation to this will determine the appropriate brand attitude strategy:

- Low Involvement informational is the strategy for products or services that involve little or no risk, and where the underlying motivation for behaviour in the category is one of the three negative motives. (You may want to look back at Figure 4.10 to refresh your memory of these motives.) Typical examples would include pain relievers, detergents, and routinely purchased industrial products.
- Low Involvement transformational is the strategy for products or services that involve little or no risk, but when the underlying motivation in the category is positive. Typical examples would include most food products, soft drinks, and beer.

Figure 11.9
A unique and effective use of outdoor, tailored to residents of specific apartment buildings.
Courtesy: OMD and SBAB

- High Involvement informational is the strategy for products or services where the decision involves risk (either in terms of price or for psychosocial reasons), and where the underlying behaviour is negatively motivated. Typical examples would include financial investments, insurance, heavy-duty household goods, and new industrial products.
- High Involvement transformational is the strategy for products or services where the decision involves risk, and where the underlying behaviour is positively motivated. Typical examples would include high-fashion clothing or cosmetics, automobiles, and corporate image.

Whereas traditionally one thinks of advertising for building brand attitude, as suggested in the last chapter the best promotions will also work on building brand attitude. While the immediate aim of a promotion is a short-term increase in sales, they can also create more long-term communication effects, maximizing full-value purchase once the promotion is withdrawn. For example, free trail periods or free samples help create a positive feeling for a brand, as do coupons seen as a small gift from the manufacturer. Promotions can also provide useful information to ensure a continued favourable attitude after trial as well, for example with such things as regional training programs for businesses, cookbooks, on-package usage suggestions, and the like.

Brand purchase intention

Brand (or trade) purchase intention is a communication objective when the primary thrust of the message is to *commit now* to buying the brand or using a service. Note that purchase-related behavioural intentions are also included in this communication objective, things like dealer visits, direct mail inquiries, and referrals.

Along with brand awareness, stimulation of brand purchase intention is the real strength of promotion. All promotions are aimed at 'moving sales forward' immediately, and they do this by stimulating immediate brand purchase intentions, or other purchase-related intentions such as a visit to a showroom or a call for a sales demonstration. For consumer target audiences, the potential power of promotion is underscored by research that has shown that purchase intention can be influenced at the point-of-purchase in about two out of every three supermarket decisions (Haven, 1995).

■ Matching media options

The fifth step in the strategic planning process involves identifying appropriate media options for delivering the brand's message. IMC media strategy is not a simple matter of finding media that reach the target audience, or satisfying particular reach and frequency objectives. While this is important to media planning, it is *not* the first step. In considering the wide range of media options available for delivering IMC messages, the critical concern is to first identify those media that will facilitate the type of processing necessary to satisfy the communication objectives.

There are three areas in which media differ that will have a direct bearing on this: the ability to effectively deliver visual content, the time available to process the message, and the ability to deliver high frequency (the number of times the target audience will be exposed to a message through a particular media). Each of these media characteristics has particular significance for both brand awareness and brand attitude strategy, as we shall see below. Additionally, managers must also consider media options in terms of the size and type of their business. This too will inform what IMC media options will make the most sense given the markets within which they operate.

In this section we will be addressing three questions the manager should consider in developing an IMC media strategy. First, what media options are appropriate for recognition versus recall brand awareness strategies? Then, what media options help facilitate the brand attitude strategy? Finally, from this set of media options, what media make the most sense, given the size and type of business?

Appropriate media for brand awareness

Visual content and frequency are issues for brand awareness processing. When the brand awareness strategy is *recognition*, one must be able to see the package. This means that almost any visual media should do, but not radio. Newspaper, while able to show a package, should be considered with caution because of potential limitations in colour reproduction. If correct colour is essential for brand package recognition (e.g. because of similarity of package colour among brands in the category), newspaper may not be a good option. An exception to these restrictions for recognition awareness would be where brand recognition is verbal, not visual. This could be the case for companies that rely upon telemarketing, when the target audience must recognize the brand name when they hear it.

When a recall brand awareness strategy is used, frequency is a concern. Media selected must be able to deliver a high frequency in order to seed the category need-brand name link in memory. Certain media like monthly magazines and direct mail have obvious frequency limitations. Posters have potential frequency limitations, unless they are positioned in an area of high target audience traffic.

A very good example of using IMC to build the link between category need and the brand for recall brand awareness is a campaign run in Sweden for Apoteket. Integrating advertising and public relations, a bus tour was carried out across Sweden to educate people about pain (the category need), providing booklets about pain and how to avoid it. The bus tour was supported with advertising and public relations in local newspapers and radio announcing when the bus would be stopping in various towns and cities. As a result of the tour, when people experienced pain, Apoteket was firmly linked in memory as the solution; someone caring and in position to determine the best medical care. Figure 11.10 illustrates the tour bus and some of the support collateral.

Appropriate media for brand attitude

The four brand attitude strategies that follow from the Rossiter–Percy Grid are a function of the level of involvement in the decision and the underlying motivation driving behaviour, as we have seen. If the brand attitude is *low involvement informational,* almost any media will work. This is because these are the easiest messages to process, needing only to communicate a single, simply presented benefit that is easily grasped, not requiring repeated exposure. There may, however, be creative constraints

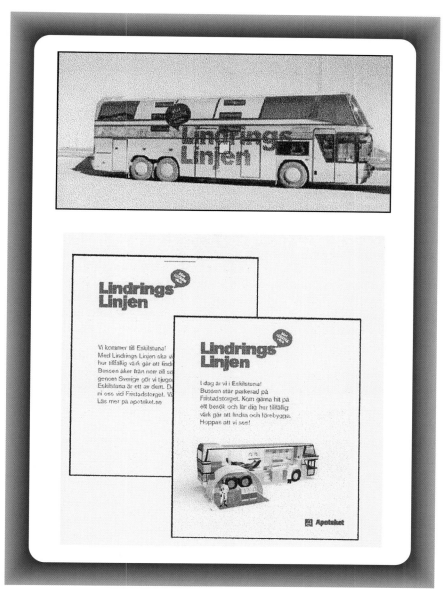

Figure 11.10
A good example of using IMC to build a link in memory between category need and a brand, integrating traditional advertising and public relations. *Courtesy*: OMD and Apoteket

that might limit media choice. This would be the case, for example, if the product must be demonstrated in order to effectively communicate its benefit. For *low-involvement transformational* strategies, good visual content capability is critical, and high frequency is needed to build the positive effect associated with the benefit.

When the brand attitude strategy is *high involvement informational*, the key requirement is enough time to process and consider the message since it must be accepted. This means that broadcast media (radio and television) should not be considered because the target audience is not able to control the pace at which they process the message. For *high-involvement transformational* strategies, it is important to ensure the ability to provide strong visual content. For some products falling in this category, especially high-priced luxury goods, a strong visual image will immediately stimulate a strong emotional response and positive attitude (if the target audience identifies with the image), and higher frequency may not be necessary. But this is something the manager must carefully consider, based upon research.

A number of IMC media options appropriate for brand attitude strategies are summarized in Figure 11.11. An important consideration in putting together the media strategy is to remember that while one medium may be appropriate for brand awareness, it may not be for the brand attitude strategy. This does *not* mean that it should not be used, but it does mean that the manager must keep firmly in mind that the message may be building brand awareness but not doing much for brand attitude. In such a case, make sure to also use appropriate brand attitude media. A good example here would be high-involvement informational strategies. Broadcast is inappropriate for this brand attitude strategy, but could be perfect for brand awareness. The brand might use television to build awareness and introduce the key benefit, while delivering a more detailed message in print where there is more time to process.

Mass media options	Brand attitude strategy			
	Low-involvement informational	Low-involvement transformational	High-involvement informational	High-involvement transformational
Television	Yes	Yes	No	Yes
Cable television	Yes	Yes	Yes	Yes
Radio	Yes	No	No	No
Newspaper	Yes	Colour limitation	Yes	Colour limitation
Magazines	Yes	Frequency limitation	Yes	Yes
Posters	Yes	Frequency limitation	Processing time limitation	Yes
Internet	Yes	Yes	Yes	Yes
Direct mail	Yes	Frequency limitation	Yes	Yes

Figure 11.11
Appropriate media for brand attitude strategies

Appropriate media for the size and type of business

Depending upon the size of a business and its market, the primary media used will be different. Rossiter and Bellman (2005) have made this important point, and define four groups to consider: large-audience advertisers, including both business-to-business and consumer; small-audience local retail advertisers; small-audience business-to-business advertisers; and direct-response advertisers.

Most marketers with large audiences will select from among appropriate major mass media for the brand awareness and brand attitude strategies. This will generally include television, radio, newspapers, magazines, posters, and the Internet. Notice that we are talking about large *audiences* or markets, not necessarily large businesses. Airbus is a very big company, but with very few potential buyers. Small-audience local retailers will not usually use mass media because of the expense and wasted coverage. Unless there are enough stores in an area covered by local mass media, it makes no sense. Rather, they are more likely to use local print and direct mail, as well as event marketing and sponsorships. Whatever media is used, however, it must be appropriate for the communication objective. Small-audience business-to-business marketers will be likely to use print almost exclusively as their primary media, especially trade publications and direct mail.

Direct-response businesses tend to use direct marketing, and as discussed in Chapter 7, this primarily means direct mail and telemarketing. But some direct-response is not database driven, and as such not direct marketing. These businesses will be likely to use telemarketing and print, or even television. But direct-response advertising is different from traditional advertising in that its primary communication objective is brand purchase intention, and *immediate* response. This means there is no time to build brand awareness, and very little time to build positive brand attitude for all but low-involvement informational strategies. In using television, say to demonstrate a product (especially a high-involvement product), the message will require more than 30 or 60 seconds. In fact, it is not unusual for direct-response marketers to use a *30-minute* television 'program', so-called infomercials. The rules for effective processing still hold, but the media is used differently.

Summary

The first step in the IMC planning process is a careful review of the marketing plan. This is what provides the necessary background for understanding a brand's overall marketing objectives, which the IMC program will support. Beyond these marketing objectives and how marketing communication is expected to support them, key issues to address in this review are the specifics of the brand itself and the market within which it will compete, with special emphasis on its competition. Finally, the marketing plan will outline where sales are expected to come from.

Once the marketing plan has been reviewed, the actual IMC planning begins with target audience selection. This will have been informed by what the marketing plan has to say about where the brand is looking for business. If trial is the objective, brand switchers who switch among other brands (OBS) are the key buyer group because they already exhibit switching behaviour and will be the easiest group to attract. Those loyal to other brands (OBL) or non-categories users (NCU) offer potential for trial, but are much more difficult to attract. If increased repeat purchase is the objective, brand switchers who include the brand in their set (FBS) will be encouraged to select the brand more often; BL will be encouraged to buy more, or more often.

Having identified the target audience it is important to gain an understanding of how they go about making purchase decisions in the category. The BSM is a good way of looking at this, identifying the stages involved in the decision, and for each stage whom all is involved and the roles they play, where it is likely to occur, the timing, and how it happens. With the target audience selected and an understanding of how they make purchase decisions in the category, is time to begin planning message development.

The first step in message development is to determine the appropriate positioning for the brand within its marketing communication. For most brands, this will mean a differentiated positioning rather than a central positioning, which is only appropriate if the brand is seen as delivering on all of the benefits associated with the category. It will also almost always mean a benefit-oriented rather than user-oriented positioning, which is only appropriate for very specific market niches or when social approval is the motivation involved. Once these two basic issues are addressed, a benefit must be selected around which to base the message. This could be a specific attribute of the product, a subjective characteristic of the brand, or an emotional response, alone or in some combination depending upon the underlying motivation. This benefit must be seen by the target audience as important, something the brand delivers (or could deliver), and ideally delivers it better than other brands.

Having positioned the brand, the next step is to set the communication objectives. These objectives are selected from the set of four communication effects: category need, brand awareness, brand attitude, and brand purchase intention. Brand awareness and brand attitude will always be objectives, and must reflect the type of awareness needed (recognition or recall) and the appropriate strategic brand attitude quadrant of the Rossiter–Percy Grid.

After the message development section of the plan is complete, the final step in the IMC planning process is to identify an appropriate set of media options that are consistent with the communication objectives.

■ Review questions

1 Why is it important to review the marketing plan at the start of the IMC planning process?

2 What are the important considerations in target audience selection?

3 Why is it important to IMC planning to understand how the target audience goes about making brand decisions?

4 What are the decision stages likely to be in choosing a mobile phone?

5 Why is it important to IMC planning to understand the roles people play in the purchase decision process?

6 Discuss the importance of positioning in IMC planning.

7 Find examples of advertising where the brand is well positioned and examples where it is not and discuss why.

8 How is brand attitude related to positioning and benefit selection?

9 Find an example of advertising that has category need as a communication objective.

10 What is the key to selecting media for the IMC plan?

11 Discuss the criteria for making media selection decisions for the different brand attitude communication objectives associated with the Rossiter–Percy Grid.

12 Why is it important to look at the size and type of business in selecting the primary media for an IMC plan?

References

Antonides, G. and van Raaij, W.I. (1998) *Consumer Behaviour: A European Perspective*. Chichester: John Wiley and Sons.

Belk, R.W. (1975) Situational variables and consumer behaviour. *Journal of Consumer Research,* 2(3), 157–164.

Boulding, W., Lee, E., and Staelin, R. (1994) Mastering the mix: Do advertising, promotion and salesforce activities lead to differentiation? *Journal of Marketing Research*, 31(2), 159–172.

Ehrlich, D., Guttman, F., Schonbach, P., and Mills, J. (1957) Post decision exposure to relevant information. *Journal of Abnormal and Social Psychology*, 54, 90–102.

Festinger, L. (1957) *A Theory of Cognitive Dissonance*. Stanford: Stanford University Press.

Fishbein, M. and Ajzen, I. (1975) *Belief, Attitude, Intention, and Behaviour: An Introduction to Theory and Research*. Reading, MA: Addison-Wesley.

Foxall, G.R. (1992) The consumer situation: An integrative model for research in marketing. *Journal of Marketing Management*, 8(4), 383–404.

Haven, L. (1995) Point of purchase, marketers getting with program. *Advertising Age*, 23 October.

Levitt, T. (1960) Marketing myopia. *Harvard Business Review*, 38 (July–August), 45–56.

Rossiter, J.R. and Bellman, S. (2005) *Marketing Communication, Theory and Applications*. Frenchs Forest NSW, Australia: Pearson Prentice-Hall.

Rossiter, J.R. and Percy, L. (1987) *Advertising and Promotion Management*. New York: McGraw-Hill.

Rossiter, J.R. and Percy, L. (1997) *Advertising Communication and Promotion Management*. New York: McGraw-Hill.

vanTripp, H.C.M., Hogen, W.D., and Inman, J.J. (1996) Product category-level explanations for true variety seeking behaviour. *Journal of Marketing Research*, 33(3), 281–292.

CHAPTER 12

Finalizing and implementing the IMC plan

The planning process discussed in the last chapter yields all of the information needed to put together the integrated marketing communication (IMC) plan. The overall context for the plan is provided by the brand's marketing plan, the target audience is identified, and an understanding of how they make brand decisions established. The creative positioning and objectives are determined, and a set of media options appropriate for delivering the message selected. Now it is time to put it all together.

In this chapter we shall look at how the knowledge gained through the IMC strategic planning process is used in finalizing a plan for the actual IMC campaign, and how to implement it. Finalizing a plan requires identifying the touch points in the decision process where marketing communication is likely to have the most significant effect on a brand decision, the communication tasks required at each of these touch points, and media appropriate for accomplishing these tasks. Once this is determined and the plan detailed, it is time to implement the plan. A creative brief is prepared to establish the parameters for message execution, and the appropriate media selected to optimize the delivery of the message. The manager is then in position to deliver an effective IMC campaign for the brand.

■ Finalizing the plan

Once the strategic planning process is complete, the manager is in a position to begin finalizing a plan for implementing an IMC campaign. Based on the understanding of how purchase decisions are made in the category, in conjunction with target audience objectives and the communication strategy, the manager must decide whether or not the brand's marketing communication goals:

1 Can be satisfied with a *single* message directed at one primary target audience, using one primary type of marketing communication (e.g. advertising, direct-mail, brochures, etc.) or
2 If a number of communication tasks should be considered, directed at one primary target, but to different roles in the decision process; different messages to different targets; and/or utilizing various types of marketing communication directed to different times or places in the decision process.

If the brand's communication objective can be satisfied by a single message and one primary medium based on what was learned from the strategic planning process, the manager can proceed directly to selecting the most appropriate medium and to finalizing a creative brief for the development of the message (creative briefs are discussed later on in this chapter).

It is important to understand that even if all that is necessary is a single message delivered through one primary medium, this is still IMC. If a brand has gone through a strategic planning process such as the one described in Chapter 11, and all potential options were considered, but in the end one message delivered to the target audience through one primary medium satisfies the brand's communication objective, we would argue this is still an IMC program. It only means that at this particular point in time, this is all that is needed. Of course, this is rarely the case, but it underscores the importance of seeing IMC as a *planning process*. IMC is an ongoing process. Market dynamics could change, and different messages in other media might become necessary. The brand will be ready to respond to these changes because the manager has been through an IMC planning process.

When a more detailed plan is required, which again is almost all of the time, it will be necessary to first determine the important touch points in the decision process where marketing communication can be most effective, second establish the communication tasks needed at each of these touch points, and finally select the appropriate media to deliver the message.

Identifying touch points

In the last chapter a behavioural sequence model was introduced, underscoring the need to understand consumer brand decisions as a *process* involving multiple stages with potentially several people involved, playing different roles in that process. Finalizing a consumer decision model like the behavioural sequence model (BSM) makes it possible to organize all of the available knowledge about how brand choices are made in a category into a usable form for strategically integrated communication planning. An effective IMC plan can only be achieved if it is based on the decision process for a brand.

This understanding is extremely valuable because the manager must be able to identify those places in the decision process where marketing communication can have a positive impact upon brand choice. One might think about these places where marketing communication may influence the brand decision as touch points. It will be these *touch points* that provide the framework for the IMC plan.

Many of those who are interested in IMC have pointed out the importance of a solid understanding of the consumer in the effective implementation of IMC programs. In fact, it is important to look carefully at how consumers behave and see the world *before* it is possible to develop an effective IMC plan. The BSM is an ideal way of gaining this insight. It is indeed this insight into the consumer, more than anything else, which will help identify the touch points for effectively implementing an IMC program.

In order to help pull this together and demonstrate how one goes about identifying the important touch points in a decision process, consider the hypothesized BSM shown in Figure 12.1 for a word-processing system. Suppose a company is marketing an innovative new word-processing system, and has developed this BSM of how companies go about deciding upon introducing new systems into their operations. Given this understanding of the decision process, what does it suggest about how

Decision stages			
Need arousal	**Brand consideration**	**Purchase**	**Usage**
Users of current system/managers as **initiator** Dealers or outside consultants as **initiator**	Users/managers as **influencers** Dealers or outside consultants as **influencers** Manager as **decider** Senior management as **decider**	Manager or purchasing agent as **purchaser**	Users/manager as **user**

Figure 12.1
Decision roles for an hypothesized BSM for a word processing system

best to positively effect the decision with marketing communication? Let us think through this process, which is in effect what a manager would be doing in finalizing an IMC plan. It is obvious that in the real world this would be a complex decision process, with multiple potential target audiences, but for this example we shall utilize only the generic decision stages. As we look at the BSM, there is no doubt that more than a single message in one medium will be needed. Can one really imagine that a single advertising campaign, let alone a single promotion of some kind, would be able to do the job? Of course not.

Looking at the *need arousal* stage we see that a number of people might be involved. At the simplest level, the users of the current system in an initiator role might be complaining to their manager that they can't get the increasing workload out on time. On the other hand, the manager in charge may be dissatisfied with the quality of the work, as the result of seeing or hearing about better alternatives. The need of the users or managers may be aroused without marketing communication if the work is falling behind, but if a brand wishes to help stimulate need, some form of marketing communication will be required. Since it is a *new* system being marketed, it will be necessary to communicate with both those involved as initiators within a company and those in the trade, which will be asked to carry and sell the new system. At the very least there will be two target audiences participating at the need arousal stage who must be aware of the new system, and begin to form a positive attitude towards it.

Once initial interest has been aroused, at the brand evaluation stage the potential user and the trade will begin to form attitudes about the various alternative systems available. The same individuals who were involved as initiators will also probably fill the role of influencer as well. But, others could also play a part. Consultants may be called in, and at some point during the evaluation senior management will become involved. At this stage, managers and senior management will assume the role of decider.

Does it make sense to use the same message for everyone involved? While the message to the trade (both consultants and distributors), users, and managers should be basically the same (and certainly reflect the same look and feel), the medium of delivery will likely vary. Messages to senior management will certainly be different. Management is not interested in the technical aspects of the system, but they are interested in 'value' issues. There would appear to be a number of different marketing communication opportunities as this stage in the decision process. Additionally, if the brand does not already have a database in place, it would be a good time to begin. If there is one, it should be updated during this stage.

At the *purchase* stage, the manager or perhaps a purchasing agent, will be involved in the actual purchase. What message, if any, might we wish to deliver at this stage that differs from earlier material? The trade may wish to follow-up with an incentive promotion; the brand may wish to send direct mail to those the trade has indicated have shown interest in the new system.

Finally, what should be done during the *usage* stage? At the very least, it would make sense to do something to reinforce the manager's choice of the new system. Some form of direct mail would be appropriate, but so too would general advertising that reinforces overall brand image. This positioning affects not only the manager, but also those who are actually using the new system.

Even using only the four generic decision stages in this example, one can see that there are a number of potential touch points where marketing communication can help inform brand choice. The task of the manager is to now identify the communication tasks that will be necessary to address these touch points, and then to set priorities in terms of what is essential for brand success, and what else might be helpful. Then, from this set of communication tasks the manager determines what will be affordable given the budget. In other words, the foundation has been late for an effective IMC plan.

Identifying communication tasks and media options

The important touch points in the decision process reflect where marketing communication will have the best opportunity of positively influencing the decision in favour of a brand. The manager must next consider the communication tasks necessary for each touch point. This means identifying the relevant target audience at each stage in the decision process and what marketing communication is expected to accomplish at each stage.

Finally, in the development of the IMC plan, the manager must identify what appropriate media options are available to deliver the message.

Communication tasks

At each touch point in the decision process there may be a number of potential target audience roles involved. These must be carefully considered, and those most likely to be responsive to marketing communication at that point identified. At the same time, the manager must decide exactly what is required of marketing communication at each touch point in order to positively influence the decision process. Together, these decisions identify the communications tasks required.

Target audience What specific members of the target audience should be addressed at each stage, and what roles are they playing? It would be rare indeed for all of the potential target audience members in all of their roles to be included. This is where the manager must begin making choices. Which target audience members in what roles are critical? These become the primary target audiences at that stage. One may also identify secondary or even tertiary audiences, in the event that there is enough in the budget to consider them after all the primary target audiences for each stage is addressed.

Communication objectives Next, the manager needs to translate the appropriate communication effects into specific communication objectives for each stage. For example, brand awareness is always an objective, but what kind (recall versus recognition); and is it necessary to raise or simply maintain the awareness? With brand attitude, is it necessary to educate the target audience? Does the message at that point need to interest the target audience in the brand, stimulate enquiry, give them a good feeling, or underscore a unique feature? Should brand purchase intention be a commitment to call and make a reservation or place an order; or to ask for more information? Should the target audience request the brand specifically, say from an investment broker or health care provider; or pick the brand on their next visit to the store?

What is needed here is a clear, concise interpretation of the proper communication effects required to meet the overall communication objectives for the IMC campaign. This can be a very involved process, drawing together all of the knowledge and understanding that came out of the strategic planning process. To illustrate, let us look at just some of the possible communication tasks associated with each stage of the generic decision model.

What communication effects are likely to be relevant to need arousal? Since this is the stage when someone begins to think about possible purchase or usage of a brand, raising brand awareness will be a primary objective. An initial favourable brand attitude will also be needed, especially for low-involvement decisions. It is clearly not enough for people to simply be aware of a brand at this initial stage. Some tentatively positive attitude will also be required if the brand is to remain a contender in the decision process. But the manager must also consider category need here. It may not be necessary, but one should always ask if the target audience is both experienced *and* active in the category.

At the brand evaluation stage one must be concerned with both brand attitude and brand purchase intention effects. For low-involvement decisions, the tentatively favourable brand attitude built during need arousal must be reinforced, providing again what Maloney (1962) called 'curious disbelief', leading to a positive intention to try. For high-involvement decisions, it is essential that enough appropriate information is provided at this stage because the target audience must be both informed *and* convinced. At the same time, if dealing with positive motives, one must be concerned with nurturing the appropriate feelings as well. Authentically reflecting the emotion involved in decision processes involving positive motives implies more than just a favourable attitude. A positive intention to buy or use the brand is needed, and this will follow from a favourable evaluation owing to the correct emotional associations.

But deciding to choose a brand does not guarantee it will actually be purchased or used. So at the actual purchase stage it will be necessary to ensure that the positive brand attitude is reinforced, and that the brand purchase intention is actually carried out. During usage, messages should help continue reinforcing brand attitude and encourage re-purchase or continued use of the brand. All of these decision stage–communication effects relationships are summarized in Figure 12.2.

Decision stage	Communication effect
Need arousal	• Consideration of category need • Raise brand awareness • Tentative brand attitude
Brand consideration	• Build positive brand attitude • Convincing benefit claim for high-involvement strategies • Establish authentic emotional link for transformational strategies
Purchase	• Reinforce positive brand attitude • Ensure positive brand purchase intention
Usage	• Reinforce positive brand attitude • Encourage repeat brand purchase intention

Figure 12.2
Decision stage–
communication
effect relationship

Media options
Once the manager has determined the communication tasks, it is necessary to identify appropriate media options for delivering the message at each

touch point in order to accomplish the task. This is where the manager specifies exactly what media options are available to reach the target audience, consistent with the primary communication objective for the task. How can recognition awareness be sustained? Should print advertising, billboards, or coupons be used? Will broadcast advertising or direct mail be appropriate? To facilitate purchase, should the brand use in-store banners or special displays? What about incentive promotions? This may be a good place to point out that if multiple media are used in an IMC campaign, it is done because of the specific appropriateness of the various media to the communication tasks, *not* from any sense of 'synergy' (Dijkstra, 2002).

IMC planning worksheet

The touch points identify those stages in the decision process where IMC can positively effect the brand decision, communication tasks establish what marketing communication must accomplish at each of those points, and media options are selected that are appropriate for those tasks. A good way of summarizing this is with an IMC planning worksheet along the lines of the one shown in Figure 12.3.

Touch points for decision stages	Communication tasks		Media options
	Target audience	Communication objectives	

Figure 12.3
IMC planning worksheet

The first column lists is the touch points that were identified from a BSM or some other model of the consumer decision process for the category. In the next two columns the specific target audiences and their role, and the communication objectives making up the communication tasks, are listed for each touch points. The last column provides those media options appropriate for the corresponding communication tasks. Summarized in this way, the manager may objectively review the various communication tasks likely to positively influence the brand decision along with appropriate media options for each, and consider what would best fit the brand's overall objective and budget.

To illustrate what we have been discussing, let us consider the case of Acuvue, and look at what was involved in the development of the IMC plan for the introduction of disposable contact lenses. This is a particularly good case to consider because it involves a somewhat complex decision process where both the patient as consumer and their doctor or eye care professional are involved. Figure 12.4 offers an overview of the eyeglass lens decision process, and illustrates the interrelationship between patient and doctor considerations. This model reflects what was learned from a BSM, and from it comes the significant touch points. You can see that both the patient and doctor are involved together in making the decision to use disposable contact lenses, and this will clearly require a carefully IMC program.

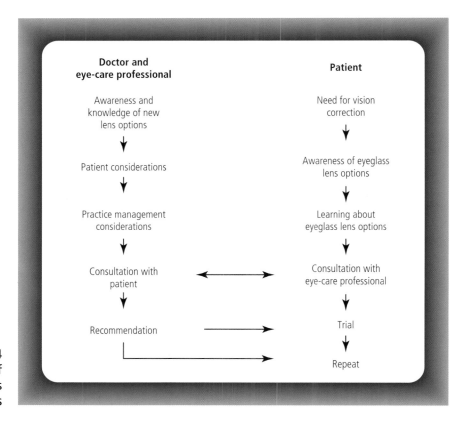

Figure 12.4
Overview of
prescription lens
decision process

Using the IMC planning worksheet just described, the manager can summarize the communication tasks and media options available for each touch point, as we see in Figure 12.5 for patients and Figure 12.6 for doctors. What these worksheets suggest for the IMC plan are discussed below.

Looking at the first touch point for patients, *Awareness Need and Options*, although family members and friends could play an important role as initiators and influencers, the primary target audience will be those who currently wear prescription eyeglasses or contact lenses. At

Touch points	Communication tasks		Media options
	Target audience	**Communication objective**	
Awareness of need and options	Current prescription eyeglass and contact lens users as initiators and influencers Doctor and eye-care professional as initiator and influencer	Create awareness of disposable contact lenses Build brand awareness and initial brand attitude	Broadcast and print advertising Direct mail to doctors, advertising in professional journals, professional conferences
Learning about options	Current prescription eyeglass and contact lens users as influencers and deciders	Strengthen brand awareness Build brand attitude by providing information to convince	Print advertising Point-of-purchase (for doctor's office) Direct mail Internet
Consultation and decision	Current prescription eyeglass and contact lens users as influencers and deciders Doctors and eye-care professionals as influencers	Strengthen positive brand attitude Stimulate brand purchase intention	Point-of-purchase (for doctor's office) Incentive promotions via direct mail, point-of-purchase or Internet
Usage and reinforcement	Current prescription eyeglass and contact lens users as users and influencers	Brand purchase intention Maintain brand attitude	Broadcast and print advertising Direct mail

Figure 12.5
Patient IMC planning worksheet

this first touch point in the decision process, category need must be initiated. But because only one brand is available (Acuvue), creating awareness and initial interest in disposable contact lenses will correspond to brand awareness and initial brand attitude. The best way of accomplishing these communication objectives will be with traditional advertising in broadcast and print. At the same time, for the doctor's role in the *patient's* decision, it will be necessary to build brand awareness along with a clinical understanding of its performance in order to stimulate interest in looking more deeply into them. Obviously, the doctor must feel comfortable in bringing disposable contact lenses to the attention of their patients or recommending them. Much of this initial awareness and attitude will follow from the patient advertising, but must be reinforced by more targeted communication through advertising in professional journals, direct mail, and at professional conferences.

At the *Learning about Options* touch point, the most logical point for the patient to seek information about disposable contact lenses is from their doctor or eye-care professional. This will require providing them with brochures or other merchandising material not only for point-of-purchase

Touch points	Communication tasks		Media options
	Target audience	**Communication objectives**	
Awareness of needs and options	Doctor and eye-care professional as initiator and influencer Sales force as initiator and influencer	Create awareness of disposable contact lenses Build brand awareness and initial brand attitude	Broadcast and print advertising (to patients) Professional journals, direct mail, professional conferences Sales force collateral and merchandising kits
Learning about options	Doctor and eye-care professional as influencer and decider	Build positive attitude for both disposable contact lenses and brand	Professional journals Professional conferences Direct mail
Practice management considerations	Doctor and eye-care professional as influencer and decider Sales force as influencer	Build positive brand attitude Link brand to practice	Point-of-purchase merchandising program Joint program through channels marketing
Acquisition and review	Doctor and eye-care professional as purchaser, user and influencer	Build positive brand purchase intention Reinforce positive brand attitude	Incentive promotions Direct mail Professional journals Patient advertising in television and print

Figure 12.6
Doctor and eye-care professional IMN planning workshop

(the doctor's or eye-care professional's office), but also for possible inclusion as statement stuffers or self-contained mailers for the doctor to send to patients. Additionally, on-going advertising, especially print where there is more time to process, will continue to build brand awareness and attitude. Also, toll-free numbers and the Internet offer opportunities to provide more information.

To facilitate the actual purchase at the *Consultation and Decision* touch point, the patient must consult with the doctor and try the product. Again, this will require good point-of-purchase material and possibly a promotion to reinforce positive brand attitude and purchase intention. At the final patient touch point, *Usage and Reinforcement*, it will be necessary to reinforce confidence in the decision, building and sustaining positive category and brand attitude. Here traditional advertising with television and print can reassure the patient, and give them the comfort of feeling part of a much wider group of users than may actually be the case. Direct mail can also help reinforce the decision, perhaps also including an incentive to continue using.

Now that we have considered the patient along with the doctor's participation in their decision, let us briefly look at the two touch points dealing specifically with the doctor and eye-care professional, where it is important to reinforce for them the positive business side of the decision. At the *Practice Management Consideration* touch point, independent of satisfying the patient's needs, doctors must be attentive to the impact of what they dispense in their practice. A key concern, of course, is patient demand. A program to acquaint them with the patient IMC support can address this issue. Additionally, educating them regarding the brand's potential contribution to their business practice can be accomplished via merchandising programs, direct mail, sales calls, and professional seminars. Also, positive brand attitude can be built by using some form of channels or tactical marketing to specifically associate the practice with the brand. At the last touch point, *Acquisition and Review*, promotion incentives can be offered to stimulate brand purchase intention, along with continued reinforcement of brand attitude via patient and trade advertising in television and print.

This example not only underscores the often complex nature of the decision process, but also how many communication tasks can be involved in putting together an effective IMC plan. The IMC planning worksheet offers the manager a good way of looking at all of the options available. It suggests what will be needed to meet communication objectives, and the media options that can be used. In effect, it provides an outline for completing the IMC plan.

This does *not* mean that the manager now has the 'answer'. What is provided is a summary of the best reading of everything known coming out of the strategic planning process, and what the brand hopes to accomplish with its marketing communication program. If the budget was large enough, it would be possible to proceed directly to implementing everything outlined in the worksheet. Unfortunately, that is rarely the case. Realistic budget constraints will no doubt limit what may be accomplished. But using the worksheet as a guide, it will be possible to make more efficient *and* effective decisions on which communication tasks to implement in order to most effectively drive brand success. It will be these decisions that inform the final IMC plan.

■ Implementing the plan

Once the communication tasks required have been identified and the IMC plan completed, it must be implemented. This means creating the advertising and promotion called for, and determining how best to deliver it. In previous chapters we have considered what is necessary to create effective marketing communication. But before *any* marketing communication can be created, a creative brief is required. This is what ensures the executions created reflect the IMC plan. We shall deal with this next, and then look at how media is selected to address the communication tasks identified in the plan.

The creative brief

It is the creative brief that ensures that the results of the strategic planning process inform message execution, and that everyone is on the same page. In fact, all of the key people involved in the planning and execution of an IMC campaign should ideally be part of the development of a creative brief. This would include account executives, planners, and creative from the agency, as well as brand management from the company; or, whatever individuals in comparable positions are involved if the brand is not using a traditional advertising agency. The reason it is so important to include all of those playing a key role in the process is that once completed, the creative brief provides the consensus of how the message will be executed, and the benchmark against which the resulting advertising and promotion will be evaluated.

The creative brief format outlined in this section includes all of the points that are essential to an effective creative execution. Many companies and advertising agencies have their own way of writing a creative brief, but most will in some fashion or other cover the 10 key areas discussed here. Overall, one might think of a creative brief in three sections: one that helps define the task at hand, one that is principally concerned with the creative objectives, and one that is concerned with executional elements.

Task definition

The first four points of the creative brief deal with task definition: Key market observation, source of business, customer barrier/insight, and target audience. The purpose of these points is to help answer why the IMC program is being put together. What is the brand hoping to accomplish, who in the market are being addressed with this creative, what do they already know, think, or feel about the brand, what is the message trying to effect? All of this information should be available from the marketing plan and strategic planning process. The four points that help define the specific task are:

1 *Key market observation* – What one point can the brand make about the market that will help the creatives understand and believe in the rest of the brief? There is no need to be exhaustive, just provide the basics.
2 *Source of business* – Where, specifically, is the business expected to come from? One is not looking for general descriptions here, but specific sources (e.g., current holders of long-term bonds, people unhappy with the restrictions on their current brand, etc.).
3 *Consumer barrier/insight* – What one thing is known about the potential target audience that may need to be overcome, or that may help reach them? What do they know, or think they know about the brand or product category; how do they feel about it; how interested are they in it; how do they distinguish between different brands?
4 *Target market* – What is the most vivid description that can be offered of the types of individuals to whom this communication will be directed? This description must go further than a simple listing of

demographics or even lifestyle characteristics. It is important to provide enough information for the creatives to be able to picture in their mind's eye whom they are addressing. Copywriters like to imagine they are talking directly to an individual, and specifically in their decision role (Kover, 1995).

Objectives and strategy

The next four points deal with communication objectives and strategy. What one is seeking to do here is help provide creatives with the best orientation possible, including the *one point* that, if communicated, will achieve the desired objective. Also, provide the evidence available to convince the target audience.

1 *Communication objectives and tasks* – What is the specific communications objective for this creative, and where does it fit within the total IMC program? Here is where to designate the primary objective (category need, brand awareness, brand attitude, brand purchase intention), and what communication tasks are to be accomplished.
2 *Brand attitude strategy* – What is known about the way consumers make decisions? Is the decision high or low involvement, and is the behaviour positively or negatively motivated? This positions the strategy into one of the four strategic quadrants of the Rossiter-Percy Grid.
3 *Benefit claim and support* – What is the *primary* consumer benefit and why? Identify the benefit claim that is most strongly associated with the relevant motivation, and provide the evidence that supports this choice. Anything that could be used in the communications to demonstrate or communicate the correctness of the benefit claim should be included. For example, if it is understood that consumer motivation is likely to centre upon incomplete satisfaction, pointing out comparative advantages and how they should be presented might be appropriate.
4 *Desired consumer response* – What is it that the target audience should know, think, feel, or do as a result of the communication? This should be a brief summary of what is expected to happen.

Executional elements

The last two points in the creative brief deal with the actual execution, providing guidance on what sort of communication this should be and what information must be included. These last two points are:

1 *Creative guidelines* – What tactics are appropriate for the type of brand awareness involved, and for the strategic quadrant chosen?
2 *Requirements/mandatory content* – What are the requirements, either creatively, legally, or corporately, that must be included? Here, for example, is where the logo treatment is spelled out.

Now that we have detailed each of these points, there is one thing to always keep in mind when putting together a creative brief. It is important to create a balance between there being enough information for clear guidance and providing so much information that the creative people working on the assignment are placed in the position of working out their own communication priorities from the information provided. Generally speaking, there are two areas where it is hard to give too much information – target market and support for the benefit claim. But for the rest, keep it to the bare essentials. There is a reason it is called a creative *brief*. It should be *complete* on one page (an example is shown in Figure 12.7). If more detail is desired, creatives should be referred to the marketing plan and results of the strategic planning process.

Product	Job	Date

Key market observations
Consumer research identifies dissatisfaction with maintenance of contact lenses

Source of business
Current contact lens and prescription eyeglass wearers

Consumer insight
Residual concern over the idea of disposable lenses

Target market
Adult contact lens and prescription eyeglass wearer; doctors and eye-care professionals

Communication objectives and tasks
Seed category need and build awareness and brand attitude that communicates to the target the advantages of disposable lenses

Brand attitude strategy
High involvement informational brand strategy driven by problem-solution and incomplete satisfaction motives

Benefit claim and support
Acuvue disposable lenses are available. Support: no more solvents and cleaning

Desired consumer response
Accept the viability of disposable contact lenses and interest in looking into Acuvue lenses

Creative guidelines
Address potential concern over the idea of disposable lenses

Requirements/mandatory content
See your doctor or eye-care professional

Figure 12.7
Patient creative brief for disposable contact lenses

Selecting the best media options

In developing the plan, the manager includes all the media options appropriate for each communication task. To implement the plan, it is now necessary to select the *best* media options from that set, and develop a media plan. This will require the manager to identify a primary medium for each task, along with potential secondary media that might be appropriate. Once this has been done, the difficult task of allocating the available budget to the various communication tasks must be dealt with. While it is beyond the scope of this book to go into the details of media planning, we would like to offer one last planning worksheet to help visualize what is required in allocating the IMC media budget.

But before dealing specifically with these issues, we should look more broadly at media allocation for advertising-like versus promotion-like messages. The IMC planning worksheet helped identify whom the brand wanted to reach, and with what type of marketing communication, in order to satisfy the communication objective. This all bears significantly on IMC media strategy. Depending upon the communication tasks, either an advertising-like message, promotion-like message, or both, could be appropriate.

While mass media for advertising-like messages is often the best way to satisfy many communication tasks, when it is *not* the best solution, it is unlikely to figure in the media strategy at all. Of course, this is not a hard-and-fast rule, but it is a good rule of thumb. The reason for this lies in the general reach objectives of advertising and promotion. As we have seen, most of the time promotions are aimed at a more highly targeted audience or a narrow reach. Given the broad-based reach of mass media, it is unlikely to be efficient in support of a more narrowly based target audience.

Yet as we have seen, many promotions simply are not very efficient *without* corresponding or prior advertising support. This can be a real problem. But the key here is that with things like specialized print media, local radio, and cable television, traditional mass media can be adapted to more targeted audiences and narrower reach. When broad-based, mass markets are not the target, for effective IMC media planning the manager must begin to think of traditional advertising media in a more narrow way.

Media for advertising-like messages

While almost any medium can serve as a means of delivering an advertising message, those traditionally considered are mass media such as television, radio, newspapers and magazines, outdoor, and increasingly the Internet. As noted in the last chapter, when looking at the effectiveness of individual media in meeting brand awareness and brand attitude communication objectives, as a group, these traditional mass media tend to be more effective in satisfying brand awareness objectives than the more narrowly targeted media typically used for promotion.

In fact, the *best* overall media, period, is television (Barlow and Papaziou, 1980). It is the best way for achieving any of the communication objectives. It has also been shown in study after study that when television is compared with other mass media such as radio or magazines, messages delivered by television do a better job driving sales. There are several reasons for this. To begin with, television employees words and pictures, movement, and sounds. Radio offers words and sound, but no pictures or movement. Magazines offer words and pictures, but no movement or sound. Television offers high reach, and can combine it with high-effective frequency. This is very difficult for either radio or magazines. Newspapers generally have the same problems as magazines.

Does this mean one should always consider television when selecting media for advertising? The general answer is yes. However, for many reasons television may not be a viable choice. Nevertheless, when possible, television should be the medium of choice for mass advertising, *except* for high-involvement, informational strategies.

Media for promotion-like messages

Are there such things as promotion media? Of course, only they are not usually thought about in terms of media. But in IMC planning it is important to think of any way in which an advertising or promotion message can be delivered as a medium within the overall media strategy. Promotion media would of course include mass media (as a group), but also such things as direct mail, FSIs (free standing inserts) and point-of-purchase. Again, each of these vehicles could be (and often all are) used to deliver an advertising-like message, but with the exception of mass media, the others are primary means of delivering a promotion. New media is not yet considered truly a 'mass' media, nor necessarily a 'promotion' media. Nevertheless, it can be appropriate depending upon the communication task. The best media for delivering the six consumer promotions introduced in Chapter 5 are discussed below (Figure 12.8).

Promotion	Media options
Trial promotions	
Coupons	Direct mail
	FSIs
	Internet
Sampling	Point-of-purchase
	Direct mail
Refunds and rebates	Mass media
	Point-of-purchase
	FSIs
Repeat purchase promotions	
Loyalty and loading devices	Direct mail
	Point-of-purchase
Premiums	Mass media
	Direct mail
	Point-of-purchase
Sweepstakes, games, and contests	Mass media
	Point-of-purchase

Figure 12.8
Media for basic consumer incentive promotions

Coupons: There are many ways of delivering coupons, but the most effective are direct mail and FSIs; and increasingly, through the Internet. Direct mail and the Internet offer greater flexibility in targeting, but FSIs are about half the cost. Coupons may also be offered at the point-of-purchase.

Sampling: The two best ways of delivering samples are at the point-of-purchase or with direct mail. Sampling in-store or at a central location is perhaps the least expensive way of sampling, and for many products it is the only effective way. Direct mail is somewhat limited by the type of sample one can mail, but with a good mailing list it has the advantage of being able to better target delivery.

Refunds and rebates: The primary medium for a refund or rebate promotion is mass media. The reason for this is that refunds and rebates must be 'announced' and explained. This is ideally accommodated with an advertising-like message. The next most likely means of handling a refund or rebate would be at the point-of-purchase or through an FSI.

Loyalty and loading devices: Depending upon the specific promotion, direct mail or point-of-purchase are the most likely media for a loyalty or loading promotion. Loyalty programs are perhaps best suited to direct mail, while most loading promotions are best delivered at the point-of-purchase. While loyalty and loading devices do not necessarily require advertising, it is often useful to include mass media announcements or explanations of the program, especially if they are aimed at a broad-based target audience.

Premiums: Much like refunds or rebates, to be successful a premium promotion will generally require mass media advertising to generate awareness and interest. This is especially true if the premium is aimed at a broad-based target audience. More narrowly targeted premium promotions utilize direct mail or point-of-purchase. Point-of-purchase can provide a good recognition cue for a brand's advertising, if well done, by including specific elements from the advertising (Keller, 1987). Regardless of the primary medium, any premium promotion will also want to utilize in-store merchandising.

Sweepstakes, games, and contests: Again, here is a situation where mass media is going to be required to announce and explain the promotion, unless it is aimed at a more targeted audience where direct mail will work. Also, as with premiums, point-of-purchase display will generally be needed.

Selecting primary and secondary media

In the last chapter we saw that the media selected for an IMC program must be able to facilitate the processing requirements of the communication objectives (visual content, time to process, and frequency). The principal difference between primary and secondary media in an IMC campaign is that primary media must be able to satisfy *all* of a brand's communication objectives while secondary media are selected to reinforce specific tactical concerns.

In effect, the primary medium selected should be the single most effective option, and capable of doing at least an adequate job on its own without using other media (always assuming that the budget is sufficient). The key consideration in selecting primary media is that it addresses the combined requirements of both the brand awareness and the brand attitude objective.

Secondary media are used in IMC programs for three reasons (Rossiter and Percy, 1997). There may be important segments or niches that are not effectively reached by the primary medium. Secondly, it may be that one or more of the communication objectives would be more effectively satisfied with another medium. For example, while print should be the primary medium for a high-involvement informational product because of the need for sufficient time to process the message, television would do a better job of driving up awareness. This would be especially true with a new product introduction. Third, there could be specific tactical reasons for including other media at certain times during a campaign. Promotion, for example, as we have just seen, will likely use a secondary medium other than the primary medium carrying the advertising.

Next, we shall briefly review the primary and secondary media likely to be selected for the four basic types of advertising addressed in Chapter 4: consumer-oriented brand advertising (COBA), retail advertising, business-to-business (B2B) advertising, and corporate image advertising. While these are not hard-and-fast rules, they do reflect the general nature of the media appropriate for meeting overall IMC objectives.

COBA: For most widely distributed consumer products, the primary medium will be television. This is because television is generally the overall best medium for generating exposure and facilitating the processing of the message (except, of course, for high-involvement informational messages). A wide variety of secondary media are used to boost reach and provide support for specific communication objectives. For example, in a classic study Grass and Wallace (1974) showed that print, when used as a secondary media, can increase image transfer for a brand by using key visual elements from television.

Retail advertising: Most retail advertising has two jobs. It must advertise the store itself (image advertising) as well as the products it sells (brand advertising). The primary medium is likely to differ, depending upon the job. Retail store image advertising requires brand *recall* as well, and short-term brand purchase intention (visiting the store). This means that any local high-frequency media could be considered for the primary medium (e.g. broadcast or newspaper), which may then be supplemented by an appropriate secondary media.

Retail product advertising takes two forms: advertising for the store's own products, or re-advertising other brands the store carries. The primary medium used will vary, depending upon the specific characteristics of the retailer and its market. Because of the wide range of brands a retailer is likely to carry, newspapers are a good primary medium for re-advertising. In advertising or promoting its own products, local television and newspapers are effective.

B2B advertising: The key factors in selecting a primary medium for B2B advertisers are the size of the target audience and the decision-makers involved (the target audience itself). With a small target audience, under 100 decision-makers, it is unlikely that any mass-media–based advertising would make sense. Personal selling should be all that is necessary, backed up with collateral material (brochures or pamphlets) for the sales call. As the target audience size increases, the reach of particular IMC options will help determine what is appropriate. Generally speaking, this will mean specialized print media. Trade publications will serve as the primary medium for lower-level decision-makers in the target audience, with direct mail or relevant business magazines for upper-level decision-makers. To the extent that any secondary media are needed, it is likely to simply be more targeted uses of other specialized print media.

Corporate image advertising: With corporate image advertising, the primary medium will vary with the size of the company. For smaller companies, or those with very localized target audiences, beyond the carry-over from the company's product-oriented marketing communication (primarily stimulated through logo or slogan associations), local public relations and sponsorships can be effective. Larger companies should be looking to drive *recognition* of the company name, and to build positive attitudes towards the firm. This means the primary medium should be television or print, with secondary media as appropriate.

Recall from Chapter 3 that in addition to corporate image, corporate *identity* is an important part of IMC. All companies must address their identity through IMC options appropriate for relevant internal and external communication; and public relations should be used whenever there is a positive story worth relating. As Rossiter and Percy (1997) have pointed out, it is incredible how many companies use corporate image advertising while ignoring the image-transmitting aspects of direct-contact media. As they put it, this is like a large-packaged goods brand running a great advertising campaign that is offset at the point-of-purchase by a terrible package.

Allocating the media budget

Once the primary and secondary media are selected the final step in finalizing a media plan to implement an IMC campaign is to determine how to allocate the media budget. Just as the IMC planning worksheet provides the manager an opportunity to summarize the critical considerations necessary for developing the IMC plan, we can also use a worksheet to help organize the information needed to help optimize the allocation of the media budget. Figure 12.9 illustrates what this might look like for the patient part of the disposable contact lens case discussed earlier. What it does is bring together from the touch points the various communication tasks that are to be accomplished and the various media options that will be needed to get the job done. This information comes directly from the IMC planning worksheet, and it looks at those media options in terms of primary versus secondary options. Across the top we have filled in the communication tasks that were identified, and down

	Communication tasks					
	Build category and brand awareness	Create category need and initial brand attitude	Provide incentive to consider	Seek positive brand purchase intention	Act as intention	Reinforce decision
Primary medium television						
Secondary media Magazines						
Newspapers Internet						
Point-of-purchase						
Direct mail						

Figure 12.9
Media allocation worksheet for implementary patient IMC plan

the side are the various media options that were selected as appropriate for each task. Actually, *specific* media should be included here (e.g. cable TV, newspaper, brochures, etc.), but for our example we are using general types of media. In this example, broadcast advertising has been chosen as the primary media, reinforced by various secondary media. Because the communication tasks reflect what needs to be done at the various stages of the decision process, it also serves as a timeline. The shaded areas indicate times when a particular option is not needed.

What the worksheet shows is that Acuvue should be using television advertising ongoing as the primary medium to stimulate category and brand awareness, and attitude for disposable contact lenses. Additionally, a number of secondary media have more specific roles for particular communications tasks. While television would do a generally good job in satisfying all of the communications tasks, because this is a high-involvement informational decision we know additional information will be needed to convince the patient, and time to process it. Here is where newspapers and magazines can play a role, along with point-of-purchase merchandising material such as brochures and posters, direct mail, and the Internet. All of the secondary media provide an opportunity for delivering both advertising and incentive promotions (where and if needed).

Not shown here because this is the patient worksheet, but advertising to the doctor or eye-care professional will also find its way to the patient during consultation. For example, it will inform the doctor's recommendation, and it may include such things as flip-charts for the doctor to use in explaining disposable contact lenses. This, of course, underscores the importance of consistency for everything in the IMC campaign.

Looking at the summary worksheet, the manager now knows what is needed in order to accomplish the communication tasks in terms of primary and secondary media, and it only remains to set priorities and allocate the budget. The boxes in the worksheet would, of course, contain media costs for each task. One of the real advantages of using a worksheet like this is that it permits the manager to see at a glance where, and importantly *why*, the budget is being spent. If adjustments must be made, for example because there is simply not enough money to deal with all of the communication tasks, or if budget cuts are needed over the course of the campaign, any adjustments can easily be considered within the context of the overall IMC program.

Summary

The IMC plan is created out of the planning process. The target audience has been identified and an understanding of how they go about making decisions establish. This understanding helps the manager identify those touch points in the process where marketing communication is most likely to have a positive effect on the decision. The overall communication objectives that were established in the planning phase inform specific communication tasks that must be accomplished at each touch points in order to achieve that positive effect on the decision. Media options must then be selected that are compatible with the communication objectives in order to deliver the message.

In putting the plan together, it is helpful to look at the component parts in a way in which an assessment of all the options available may be considered. An IMC planning worksheet is one way of getting at this, where for each touch point identified the specific target audience and communication objectives associated with the communication tasks needed, along with the media options appropriate to deliver the message, are summarized. The ability to consider all of the opportunities to positively affect the brand purchase decision with a worksheet like this simplifies the manager's task in putting together the final plan. It enables the manager to optimize the IMC program for selecting those communication tasks that are essential, and then to decide what trade-offs must be made among the remaining opportunities because it is rare that the budget will be large enough to accommodate everything.

All of the ingredients are then in place to implement the plan. Based on the plan, the creative brief will be developed. It is important that when building the creative brief that everyone involved with the brand's marketing communication be involved. The creative brief distills the plan to its essence, providing the direction for creative development. Everyone must be in agreement on that direction because the brief becomes the basis against which the final creative executions are evaluated.

The final step in implementing the plan is to select the best media for delivering the message. The IMC plan identifies the set of media options appropriate for each communication task, and now the manager must select the primary and secondary media that will best accomplish the job. But just as the manager must in almost all cases make trade-offs among the communication tasks, in the same way it is unlikely that every appropriate medium can be used. Trade-offs will be necessary because of budget constraints. Again, a worksheet can provide a useful way of summarizing the options a manager has to consider in order to more easily evaluate those options and make the best media budget allocation decision.

■ Review questions

1 How does the manager go about identifying touch points for the IMC plan?
2 How does an IMC planning worksheet help the manager in finalizing the IMC plan?
3 In Figure 11.4 (from the last chapter) the decision stages for a lamp purchase was illustrated. What are the important touch points likely to be?
4 Complete an IMC planning worksheet for these touch points.
5 What is necessary to implement the IMC plan?
6 What are the most important points to make in a creative brief?
7 Develop a creative brief for the introduction of a new 'healthier' soft drink.
8 What are the important criteria in media selection for the final IMC plan?
9 How do secondary media contribute to the effectiveness of the IMC plan?
10 How can a media budget allocation worksheet help the manager implement the IMC plan?

References

Barlow, W.E. and Papaziou, E. (1980) *The Media Book*. New York: The Media Book, Inc.

Dijkstra, M. (2002). *An Experimental Investigation of Energy Effects in Multiple-Media Advertising Campaigns*. Tilburg University, The Netherlands, Published Ph.D. Thesis.

Grass, R.C. and Wallace, W.H. (1974) Advertising communication: Print vs. TV. *Journal of Advertising Research*, 14(5), 19–23.

Keller, K.L. (1987) Memory factors in advertising: The effect of advertising retrieval cues on brand evaluation. *Journal of Consumer Research*, 14(3), 316–333.

Kover, A.J. (1995) Copywriters' implicit theories of communication: An exploration. *Journal of Consumer Research*, 21(4), 596–611.

Maloney, J.C. (1962) Curiosity versus disbelief in advertising. *Journal of Advertising Research*, 2(2), 2–8.

Rossiter, J.R. and Percy, L. (1997) *Advertising Communication and Promotion Management*. New York: McGraw-Hill.

Glossary

Acceptance: A response in processing a message where the receiver believes the benefit claim to be true, and necessary for high-involvement brand attitude strategies.

Advertere: The Latin root of the word advertising, roughly translated as 'to turn toward'.

Allowance promotion: Any incentive promotion for the trade where a monetary allowance is given in return for stocking or promoting a brand and achieving specific performance or purchase requirements.

Assimilation-contrast theory: Sherif and Hovland's idea that someone's current attitudes provide a point of reference in any attempt to persuade, where a person assimilates positions close to their own and rejects position significantly different from their own.

Attention: Necessary first step in processing a message, central to perception and consciousness.

Attitude: A relative concept that reflects those things people believe weighted by how important they are to them.

Attribute: The objective characteristics of something, for example 25% fewer calories.

Awareness-trial-reinforcement (ATR): A low-involvement model of purchase behaviour introduced by Ehrenberg where awareness is followed by a tentatively favourable attitude leading to trial, after which a final attitude is formed.

Behavioural sequence model (BSM): A model of buyer behaviour built upon the stages involved in brand choice, identifying touch points where marketing communication is likely to positively affect the decision.

Benefit: What a brand offers in terms of attributes, subjective characteristics, and emotional stimulation.

Benefit focus: How the benefit is used in an execution, consistent with the underlying motive driving behaviour in the category.

Bottom-up processing: The direct response to a stimulus without integration with one's knowledge and assumptions about it.

Brand attitude: A communication effect that is always a communication objective, reflecting a link between a brand and its benefit.

Brand awareness: A communication effect that is always a communication objective, reflecting the link in memory between the brand and the need it fulfils (category need).

Brand portfolio: A company's brands and those linked through alliance that are considered together in the formation of business strategy.

Brand purchase intention: A communication effect that is the primary communication objective for promotion.

Branding strategy: The management of brand-product relationships, especially in terms of the indication of its origin (e.g. a stand-alone brand or linked in some way to a parent brand).

Buzz marketing: A formalized attempt to create favourable word of mouth for a brand.

Central position: Usually the positioning strategy for market leaders, when the brand is seen as delivering all the main benefits associated with the product category.

Channel marketing: The term used to describe all levels of marketing communication to the retail trade, combining co-op advertising and tactical marketing.

Cognitive response: A term used in psychology to describe a response based on conscious knowledge or assumptions.

Communication effect: One of the four possible responses to marketing communication from which communication objectives are selected: Category need, brand awareness, brand attitude, and brand purchase intention.

Communication objective: The communication effects that are targeted by the message execution, and must always include brand awareness and brand attitude.

Communication response sequence: The sequence of steps necessary for marketing communication to be effective: exposure to the message, processing of the message, achieving the desired communication effect, and the desired target audience action.

Communication strategy: Setting the overall communication objectives and selecting the appropriate brand awareness and brand attitude strategy consistent with how the target audience makes decisions.

Communication tasks: What marketing communication is expected to accomplish at each important touch point in the decision process.

Conscious processing: Utilization of declarative or explicit memory in the processing of a message.

Consumer franchise-building promotion (CFB): An idea first introduced by Prentice recognizing the need for effective promotion to not only stimulate immediate target audience action, but also to contribute to long-term positive brand attitude.

Co-op advertising: Retail advertising where both the marketer and retailer cooperate in a part of the marketing communication.

Corporate advertising: Advertising for the company as a corporate brand rather than a specific brand from its portfolio.

Corporate brand: A term used by companies to describe the organization itself as a brand.

Corporate identity: The visual and verbal symbols used by a company to set itself apart from other companies so that the consumer can readily identify it.

Corporate image: The set of emotions and beliefs held about a company.

Corporate reputation: Those values such as honesty and integrity associated with a company, and evoked by its image.

Corporate story: A comprehensive narrative about a company including such things as its mission statement and history.

Coupon: A certificate redeemable at retail for a specific price reduction on a brand.

Creative brief: A one-page document summarizing the strategic direction for a brand's marketing communication, used to guide the development of creative executions.

Database: A collection of information about a target market available for use (usually on computer), interactive, and necessary for direct marketing.

Decision roles: The part(s) a person plays in the decision process, as initiator, influencer, decider, purchaser, and/or user.

Decision stages: The important steps involved in making a brand choice, forming the foundation of the behavioural sequence model.

Declarative memory: Conscious or explicit memory, for information that can be consciously recalled as words or visual images.

Differentiated positioning: The positioning strategy for most brands, based on a benefit that is seen by the consumer as giving the brand an advantage over competitors.

Direct mail: A medium for delivering messages via the post (or private letter distributors), often used for promotions.

Direct marketing: Marketing technique targeted towards specific target audiences based on a database, bypassing traditional distribution channels.

Downside elasticity: When sales decline as a result of a price increase.

Duchenne smile: Named for the 19th century French anatomist Duchenne de Boulogue, it is a form of smile believed to occur spontaneously and only during the experience of true enjoyment.

Embodiment: The bodily state, such as facial expression, posture, or tone of voice, that occurs in response to an emotional stimulus, and the later use of that emotional response.

Emotion: A coordinated change in the body at several levels in response to a stimulus, for example in processing marketing communication, especially the subjective feelings linked to it in conscious memory.

Emotional sequence: The desired portrayal of emotion in marketing communication, reflecting the motivation involved: negative to mildly positive for informational brand attitude strategies and neutral to strongly positive for transformational brand attitude strategies.

Encoding specificity: Tulving's notion that in order to successfully retrieve something from memory there must be a match between how information is originally encoded and how it is available when being retrieved from memory.

Endorser branding strategy: A sub-branding strategy where the parent brand serves as the guarantor for a brand, but less directly linked then with a source branding strategy.

Episodic memory: Memories for a specific event, and part of declarative memory.

Event marketing: Brand or company sponsorship of a single event such as a concert or sporting event.

Expectancy value model: Generally considered the best model of attitude, it considers a person's attitude towards something to be the summation of everything believed about it weighted by how important each of those beliefs are to them.

Explicit memory: Information that is consciously understood to have been recalled from memory.

Feeling: Often considered a synonym for emotion, it is not, but does reflect the subjective feeling component of emotion, which is that part of an emotion that can be felt with the aid of consciousness.

fmcg: A term standing for 'fast moving consumer goods'.

fMRI: The abbreviation for functional magnetic resonance imaging, a neuroimaging procedure.

FSI: The abbreviation typically used for 'free standing inserts', marketing communication inserted in a print medium, but not bound into it.

Hierarchical partitioning: Looking at a market in terms of the order in which consumers use characteristics of the product or market in making decisions.

Hierarchy-of-effects: The general high-involvement decision model where awareness is followed by learning *and* acceptance that leads to a positive attitude before action is taken.

High involvement: Where there is a perceived risk in making a brand or product choice, either economic or psychological, and full acceptance of the message is required before action is taken.

Implicit memory: Defined by Schacter as that part of memory that facilitates the performance of a task without conscious or intentional recollections (e.g. typing).

Information processing paradigm: McGuire's model of the steps required in processing a message in order to achieve attitude change: The message must be presented, attended to, comprehended, yielded to, that intension retained, and then acted upon.

Informational brand attitude strategy: Those strategies from the Rossiter–Percy Grid dealing with negatively motivated brand decisions.

Involvement: Perceived risk attached to making a brand or product decision, and a determinate of brand attitude strategy.

Latitude of acceptance: Following Sherif and Hovland's assimilation-contrast theory, one's area of agreement with a message, an understanding of which is required for high-involvement brand attitude strategies.

Latitude of indifference: Following Sherif and Hovland's assimilation-contrast theory, information in a message that one neither agrees with nor disagrees, and a potential level to pitch high-involvement messages in order to initiate attitude change.

Latitude of rejection: Following Sherif and Hovland's assimilation-contrast theory, message content not consistent with one's existing beliefs, and therefore not likely to be believed.

Learning: An essential step in the processing of all marketing communication, it is the acquisition of information from a message with or without conscious effort, the result of long-term potentiation.

Loading device: An incentive promotional technique for encouraging larger than normal purchase quantities to effectively remove the target from the market in the short term, for example with bonus packs.

Long-term potentiation (LTP): The neural basis of learning following repeated stimulation of a neuron's dendritic spine leaving it more responsive to additional input of the same type.

Low involvement: Where there is no perceived risk in making a brand or product choice, and where only a tentatively favourable attitude is necessary for action to be taken.

Loyalty devices: An incentive promotion technique designed to reward and retain loyal customers, perhaps the most familiar example being frequent-flier programs.

Marketing plan: An outline of the goals and objectives set for a brand, and how to reach them, which must form the foundation for the IMC strategic planning process.

Marketing public relations: The term introduced by Harris to describe public relations activities in support of marketing objectives.

Media vehicles: The specific publications, programs, events, etc. through which marketing communication messages (both advertising and promotion) are delivered.

Memory: Representations in the brain of learning, in a sense physical records of our experiences encoded within our neural system.

Mere exposure: A term associated with Zajonc and his colleagues that reflect an unconscious affective memory, independent of declarative memory, a result of priming.

Message processing: The steps necessary for effective communication, involving attention, learning, acceptance (in high-involvement cases), and emotion.

Mobile marketing: Using mobile communication sources such as cell phones for delivery of marketing communication, with the potential for interactive response.

Motivation: The innate or acquired drive that underlies behaviour, negatively originated (to solve or avoid a problem) or positively originated (for sensory gratification or social approval), and a determinate of brand attitude strategy.

Neural network: A collection of neurons that learn and organize themselves via a synaptic learning rule advanced by Hebb leading to long-term potentiation (LTP) in the brain.

Neuroimaging: A way of identifying those areas of the brain active under particular circumstances (such as making a choice between brands of soft drinks), measured by such procedures as PET scans (positron emission tomography) and fMRI (functional magnetic resonance imaging).

New media: The general term given to such non-traditional ways of delivering a message as the Internet and mobile phones.

Nondeclaritive memory: Unconscious memory that results from experience and leads to a change of behaviour (learning to ride a bicycle) but not as recollection.

Partitioning: Looking at markets according to how consumers group products in relationship to various category characteristics or benefits.

Permission marketing: Where prior permission is granted a marketer to send text messages on mobile phones, e-mails, or messages via other personal media.

Personal selling: Any direct contact with consumers in an effort to communicate a brand's message, either face-to-face or via telephone.

PET scan: Positron emission tomography, one of the first methods used for neuroimaging studies.

Point-of-purchase (p-o-p): Retailer promotion often provided by the marketer as part of a co-op or tactical marketing program, it gives visual prominence for a brand and may or may not include an incentive.

Positioning: Locating a brand in a consumer's mind via marketing communication in terms of the need it is seen as satisfying (what it is) and its benefit (what it offers).

Premium: An incentive promotion that is offered free or at reduced price with purchase of a brand, and which should have a logical link to the product.

Primary media: The medium that does the best job of delivering all the communication objectives in an IMC campaign.

Product placement: More appropriately brand placement, it is the inclusion of a brand in entertainment vehicles such as television shows, movies, and video games, in a conspicuous fashion in the expectation of raising brand awareness and brand attitude through association with a celebrity or situation; a practice raising ethical concern.

Product portfolio: The range of products offered by a company.

Promovere: The Latin root of the word promotion which roughly translates to 'move forward or advance'.

Publicity: Often used as a synonym for public relations, it is more than public relations, including sources outside of the company.

Public relations (PR): Activities paid for by a company to generate positive publicity about the company or a brand.

Ratchet effect: Moran's idea that using advertising and promotion together, as appropriate, produces stronger results than either alone by 'ratcheting up' the effects of advertising with occasional promotion coupled by retaining more customers attracted by the promotion through the effects of the advertising.

Recall brand awareness: The brand awareness strategy needed when the purchase decision relies upon the category need bringing to mind brands to satisfy that need.

Recognition brand awareness: The brand awareness strategy needed when the purchase decision relies upon recognizing the brand at the point-of-purchase stimulating or reminding of category need.

Refunds and rebates: An incentive promotion technique where a set amount of money is refunded to buyers upon submitting proof of purchase.

Refutational strategy: A creative strategy used when there is a well-known objection to a product, where the objection is acknowledged first and then countered.

Repeat-purchase action objective: When the marketing focus is on existing customers, communication is aimed at increasing the rate of repeat purchase.

Retail promotion: Promotions initiated by the retailer for the store itself or specific brands, or promotions provided by marketers and delivered through the retailer.

Rossiter–Percy Grid: A four-cell grid that highlights the need for different creative tactics for the four types of brand attitude strategy, based on the different processing requirements associated with the level of involvement in the purchase decision (high versus low) and whether the motivation driving behaviour in the category is positive or negative (transformational versus informational strategies).

Sales promotion: The traditional way of referring to promotion, generally associated with an incentive.

Sample: An incentive promotion technique designed to provide the consumer with an opportunity to try the product prior to a purchase.

Secondary media: Media used to reinforce a specific communication effect that is an objective of the IMC campaign.

Semantic memory: That part of declarative (i.e. conscious) memory containing knowledge and assumptions unconnected with specific experiences (episodic memory).

Source branding strategy: A sub-branding strategy where the parent brand is directly linked to the sub-brand in its branding and marketing communication, associating its identity with the brand.

Sponsorships: An arrangement where a brand provides financial support for an athlete, team, charity, or such in return for publicity associated with that support.

Stakeholders: A term describing all those groups with an interest in a company, both inside and outside of an organization, including consumers, investors, trade, and employees.

Stand-alone brand: Brands that do not include a parent source or endorser as part of their branding strategy.

Strategic planning process: The five step process involved in developing the communication strategy for IMC: target audience identification, determining how they make brand decisions, positioning, establishing the communication objectives, and identifying appropriate media to deliver the message.

Sub-brand: A brand name linked with a parent brand either directly through a source branding strategy or secondarily through an endorser strategy.

Sweepstakes: Along with contests and games, an incentive promotion technique designed to create excitement for a brand.

Tactical marketing: Grew out of a desire for more control over co-op monies, providing programs tailored to specific retailer's needs but maintaining control over content and timing.

Target audience: The specific segment of a brand's target market identified in the strategic planning process is to receive advertising and/or promotion.

Telemarketing: Personal selling using the telephone.

Top-down processing: The use of knowledge and assumptions in the processing of a stimulus, for example of marketing communications.

Touch points: Those places in the decision process where marketing communication is likely to have a positive effect.

Trade promotion: Incentives offered to retailers and distributors to encourage them to stock or promote a brand.

Trade show: An event where products from a particular industry or related industries are exhibited and demonstrated.

Transformational brand attitude strategy: Those strategies from the Rossiter–Percy Grid dealing with positively motivated brand decisions.

Trial action objective: When the marketing focus is on attracting new customers, and communication is aimed at stimulating trial.

Unconscious processing: Processing of information at a subconscious level as part of implicit or nondeclaritive memory.

Up-side elasticity: When prices are cut and sales go up.

User-oriented positioning: Where the focus is on the user of the brand, not the product, and the target audience represents a specific segment or the underlying motivation is social approval (although a benefit positioning is also appropriate in these cases).

Index